Also from Westphalia Press
westphaliapress.org

The Idea of the Digital University

Dialogue in the Roman-Greco World

The Politics of Impeachment

International or Local Ownership?:
Security Sector Development in
Post-Independent Kosovo

Policy Perspectives from Promising
New Scholars in Complexity

The Role of Theory in Policy Analysis

ABC of Criminology

Non-Profit Organizations and Disaster

The Idea of Neoliberalism: The
Emperor Has Threadbare
Contemporary Clothes

Donald J. Trump's Presidency:
International Perspectives

Ukraine vs. Russia: Revolution,
Democracy and War: Selected Articles
and Blogs, 2010-2016

Iran: Who Is Really In Charge?

Stamped: An Anti-Travel Novel

A Strategy for Implementing the
Reconciliation Process

Issues in Maritime Cyber Security

A Different Dimension: Reflections on
the History of Transpersonal Thought

Contracting, Logistics, Reverse
Logistics: The Project, Program and
Portfolio Approach

Unworkable Conservatism: Small
Government, Freemarkets, and
Impracticality

Springfield: The Novel

Lariats and Lassos

Ongoing Issues in Georgian Policy
and Public Administration

Growing Inequality: Bridging
Complex Systems, Population Health
and Health Disparities

Designing, Adapting, Strategizing in
Online Education

Secrets & Lies in the United Kingdom:
Analysis of Political Corruption

Pacific Hurtgen: The American Army
in Northern Luzon, 1945

Natural Gas as an Instrument of
Russian State Power

New Frontiers in Criminology

Feeding the Global South

Beijing Express: How to Understand
New China

Demand the Impossible: Essays in
History as Activism

A History of All Religions

Containing a Statement of
the Origin, Development,
Doctrines, Forms of Worship
and Government of
All the Religious
Denominations in the
United States and Europe

by Samuel M. Smucker, LL.D.

WESTPHALIA PRESS
An Imprint of Policy Studies Organization

A History of All Religions: Containing a Statement of the Origin,
Development, Doctrines, Forms of Worship and Government of
All the Religious Denominations in the United States and Europe
All Rights Reserved © 2019 by Policy Studies Organization

Westphalia Press
An imprint of Policy Studies Organization
1527 New Hampshire Ave. NW
Washington, D.C. 20036
info@ipsonet.org

ISBN-13: 978-1-63391-832-0
ISBN-10: 1-63391-832-7

Cover design by Jeffrey Barnes:
jbarnesbook.design

Daniel Gutierrez-Sandoval, Executive Director
PSO and Westphalia Press

Updated material and comments on this edition
can be found at the Westphalia Press website:
www.westphaliapress.org

A

HISTORY OF ALL RELIGIONS,

CONTAINING

A STATEMENT OF THE ORIGIN, DEVELOPMENT, DOCTRINES,
AND GOVERNMENT OF THE

RELIGIOUS DENOMINATIONS

IN THE UNITED STATES AND EUROPE,

WITH BIOGRAPHICAL

NOTICES OF EMINENT DIVINES.

EDITED AND COMPLETED BY

SAMUEL M. SMUCKER, LL. D.,

AUTHOR OF "COURT AND REIGN OF CATHERINE II.," "THE LIFE,
SPEECHES, AND MEMORIALS OF DANIEL WEBSTER," "MEMO-
RABLE SCENES IN FRENCH HISTORY," ETC.

PHILADELPHIA:
DUANE RULISON, QUAKER CITY PUBLISHING HOUSE,
NO. 33 SOUTH THIRD STREET.
1859.

PREFACE.

THE design of the following work is essentially different from that of other publications on the same subject, which already exist. The larger and more extensive of these are composed of articles on the Religious Sects in the United States, which were written by members of the several denominations described, and are often expanded into immense length by reïterated and familiar arguments intended to demonstrate the truthfulness and Scriptural authority of the Sects to which the respective writers belonged. This method of treatment is much better suited to works on Polemic Theology, than to those which profess merely to contain a statement of opinions and a narrative of events. On the other hand, the smaller works which have appeared on this subject are superficial and incomplete; being generally made up of very short articles, of clippings from Encyclopedias and Biographical Dictionaries; and are utterly unfit to convey even to the general reader a satisfactory idea of the various subjects which come under consideration.

How far the present writer has succeeded in avoiding the defects of cumbrous expansiveness on the one hand,

and of superficial condensation on the other; how far he has been able to present to the reader all that is most desirable and useful to know respecting existing and former religious sects, within a moderate and convenient compass; the reader himself must judge. A portion of the contents of the following pages was originally prepared for the columns of one of the leading journals of this city; but they are so altered and adapted as to suit the form in which they now appear. It may be proper also to add, that the present writer is responsible for nearly all the longer articles contained in the volume, together with the biographical notices included in the Appendix.

S. M. S.

PHILADELPHIA, *June 1st*, 1859.

CONTENTS.

(5)

6 CONTENTS.

A

HISTORY OF ALL RELIGIONS.

THE ROMAN CATHOLIC CHURCH.

The career of the Roman Catholic Church in the United States commenced in the winter of 1633, when Lord Baltimore landed with a number of immigrants near the mouth of the river Potomac in Maryland. He had obtained the charter of the colony of Maryland from Charles I., with the avowed intention of colonizing a new province, of which his brother, Lord Calvert, was to be the Governor. The great majority of the immigrants who accompanied these noblemen were Roman Catholics. The first act of the Governor after landing was to erect a cross upon the shore. He himself was a Catholic; the whole administration of the colony was in the hands of the Catholics; the laws which subsequently controlled the community were enacted and administered by Catholics; and, therefore, it is with great truth asserted that the State of Maryland was first established by members of the Catholic Church. Contemporary with the founding of the colony were also the introduction and establishment of the Catholic Church and religion.

The colony of Maryland was governed by laws of the most liberal description. Lord Calvert enacted that, in the civil government of the colony, there should be an absolute equality of rights extended to all religious per-

(7)

suasions, and that religious liberty and toleration should
be one of the fundamental principles upon which that community should ever afterward exist, and be conducted.
The Assembly of the Province, composed for the most part
of Roman Catholics, passed an "Act Concerning Religion," by which it was ordained that no person within the
limits of the colony should be compelled in any way to
the belief or observance of any particular form of religion; and that, provided they did not conspire against the
civil authority, no one should be interfered with in any
way, in the enjoyment of the most absolute religious liberty.   It cannot be denied that this enlightened and generous policy furnishes a singular contrast and a burning
reproof to the cruelty of the Puritans of New England,
who burned and hanged human beings on account of their
religious convictions; and to the Episcopalians of Virginia, who in their turn persecuted the Puritans with almost
equal ferocity.

The religious services of the Catholic Church in Maryland began on the 23d of March, 1634, when the first mass
was celebrated on the Island of St. Clement, in the river
Potomac.   The priests who accompanied the Maryland
colonists were Jesuits; and from that hour till the present
time, the Catholic community in Maryland has continued
to be numerous and influential; although in the progress
of time the influx of residents and settlers from various
other States and from Europe, who were Protestants,
gradually and without resistance withdrew from them the
authority of the State, constituted a majority of voters,
and divorced the administration of the colony from the
possession and supremacy of its original holders.   This
state of things existed at the commencement of the American Revolution.

While the Roman Catholic Church was thus taking firm
root in Maryland, her doctrines and worship were being
gradually introduced in various places throughout the original thirteen States, and elsewhere on the American continent.   From 1634 till 1687, Catholic missionary priests

chiefly Jesuits, were traversing the immense region which exists between Canada and the present site of New Orleans. A Jesuit, Claude Allouez, explored the then unknown southern shores of Lake Superior. Another Jesuit, Marquette, discovered the mouth of the Missouri River. A third, Menan, preached among the Mohawk Indians. Other members of the same order missionated among the Onondagas, the Oneidas, the Senecas, and the Miamis. During a hundred years this quiet and gradual process continued. Meanwhile, Catholics were emigrating into the various States from all the countries of Europe; and Catholic churches, generally small in the beginning, were erected, which were supplied and visited by missionary priests as often as they were able, who thus administered the rites, and kept up the celebration of the services of the Church. " Father Former" was one of the first and most celebrated Catholic missionaries in Pennsylvania. "Father Rasle" was equally distinguished for his apostolic zeal in Maine. Cardinal Cheverus was renowned for his sanctity and usefulness in Massachusetts. Bishop England, at a later day, was renowned throughout the Southern States, especially in South Carolina, for similar qualities and similar achievements. Archbishop Carrol was a worthy patron and advocate of the Church of Maryland. The first Episcopal See established in this country was that of Baltimore ; and the Rev. John Carrol was elected and consecrated as its first prelate. This event took place on August 15th, 1790, after the Catholic priests of the province, amounting at that period to twenty-four, had convened, and after due deliberation had chosen Dr. Carrol as the most suitable person to wear the Episcopal mitre, and therefore had commended him to the Pope for consecration. Dr. Carrol received twenty-two votes out of the whole number. Subsequent to this period the Sees of New York, Philadelphia, Boston, and Bardstown, were successively established, as the growth of the Church seemed to require. Several very eminent men have figured, and still flourish, in the more recent history of the Church. One of these

is Archbishop Hughes, of New York, who was formerly
pastor of St. John's Church, in this city, who is justly
esteemed as one of the most able, sagacious, and eloquent
churchmen of the present time; and whose rise from
poverty and obscurity to distinction and influence, by the
sheer force of his superior talents and personal merits,
constitutes one of the most interesting and remarkable
episodes in American history. Another very able Catholic prelate is Archbishop Kenrick, of Baltimore, formerly
Bishop of this diocese. He is a man of more profound
and extensive erudition than Dr. Hughes, and occupies an
equally elevated position in the Church; but he is his
inferior in popular eloquence, in dexterity and craft, and
in the efficiency with which he promotes the interests and
extension of the Church.

The Roman Catholic religion is pre-eminently a *ritual*
one. Forms and ceremonies occupy a prominent place
in her public worship and her private religious usages.
Earnest and enthusiastic Protestants call the Church of
Rome the *great drag-net of Christianity*, by which they
mean that, as that Church descended the stream of time
until the Reformation, she collected and preserved, as she
went along, all sorts of rites, observances, superstitious
conceits, doctrinal imaginings, and perversions, which the
peculiar circumstances of each successive age and country
may have originated and introduced; and that she has
preserved them all, by incorporating the whole of them,
without selection or rejection, into her present established
and now unalterable form of worship, belief, and government. We will leave our readers to judge for themselves
of the truth or the falsehood of this compliment. Since
the period of the Council of Trent, however, which commenced its sittings in the year 1545, no change whatever,
either in doctrine, or in government, or in ritual, has been
introduced. The *Decreta* of that memorable assemblage
fossilized the church, so that no change will ever again occur
in anything that concerns her, except it be in violation of
her wishes, and by persons hostile to her real genius. The

only alteration which has been made during three centuries in the doctrinal system, or *credenda* of the Church, has been the acknowledgment and proclamation of the dogma of the Immaculate Conception of the Virgin Mary, which has recently been promulgated at Rome as one of the established principles of the true faith.

What, then, are the chief doctrines which are taught by the Roman Catholic Church, and which are implicitly and universally believed by the "faithful" everywhere?

In every system of religious belief the doctrine concerning *God*, the Supreme Being, lies at the foundation of all the rest. The existence of God, then his attributes, then his works, and then his providence, are the first and fundamental points which are discussed, determined, and adopted. Thus it is in regard to the doctrinal system of the Romish Church. The first point is that concerning God, (*De Deo*,) and on this subject she teaches what Protestants term the Orthodox view of the Divine nature and being. She believes that God is self-existent, eternal, supreme, infinite in wisdom, goodness, justice, immutable, omnipresent, and omnipotent. At the same time she teaches that while there is but one true God, that single being is composed of three separate and divine persons— the Father, the Son, and the Holy Ghost—who exist together in a mysterious and inexplicable manner, constituting one single essence, yet composed of three divine and separate persons, who perform different and distinct functions. She teaches that the second person in the Trinity, the Son, proceeds by an eternal procession from the Father; and that the Holy Spirit, the third person in the Trinity, proceeds by an equally eternal procession from both Father and Son. She teaches that the Son descended from Heaven to earth, assumed human nature, in conjunction with the nature of the Infinite; that he taught, suffered on the cross, and died for human guilt in order to avert the vengeance of God incurred by the fall of Adam, by man's inherited and original sin, and by his actual and habitual rebellion against the Divine law. The Catholic

Church teaches that the Holy Spirit is the "Comforter" promised by Christ to his disciples; and that this Spirit is sent by the Father into the hearts of the faithful. This Spirit, thus sent by the Father, is coequal in every respect with the Father. It is, in truth, the Infinite, Omnipresent Jehovah, who, on one occasion, took the form of a dove, and descended visibly on Christ. At another time the Infinite Jehovah assumed the appearance of flames of fire, as at Pentecost, and thus sat visibly on the heads of the disciples.

Next in dignity to the Godhead, in the Catholic system, is the Virgin Mary. Innumerable prayers and petitions are offered to her, and she is invoked in all parts of the world at the same time. Hence we may infer that she is supposed to possess the attribute of Omnipresence; else it were vain to pray to her in more places than one at the same time. But Omnipresence is an attribute which belongs to God alone; and, therefore, the ascription of it to the Virgin Mary seems like the ascription to her of a portion of the Divinity. She is called, moreover, the " Mother of God ;" and those who make objection to this title are answered thus: " Mary was the mother of Christ, was she not ?" "Yes." " Christ was God, was he not ?" " Yes." "Then, surely Mary is the mother of God." But the obvious reply to this reasoning is, that Mary was the mother only of Christ's *human* nature ; and, therefore, even though Christ were God, the union of a human and divine nature in Christ did not extend the maternity of Mary to both natures. It would be utterly impossible, for many reasons, for Mary to have been the mother of Christ's divine nature ; because no finite human being can give existence to an infinite being, any more than a pint measure can possibly hold a quart. Moreover, the Catholic Church teaches that Christ, as God, created *all* things : hence he created Mary; and if Mary was the mother of his divine nature, she actually gave birth to the same Omnipotent Being who created her ;—and therefore Mary is not, and cannot be, the mother of God. She was simply the mother of the man, Christ Jesus.

Recently the Catholic Church, by her highest authorities, has decreed the Immaculate Conception of the Virgin Mary; and this doctrine is now, as we have said, a portion of the belief of the Church. A large portion of the ritual is devoted to prayers offered to her; and in one place the same expressions, addressed to her with slight variations, are repeated forty times. In truth, the invocation of saints occupies no insignificant position in the worship of Catholics; and doubtless many are encouraged and comforted by the idea, that their interests are promoted by the interposition and the prayers of the good and wise, who have gone before them to the land of spirits, and have already explored its solemn mysteries.

The inspired authority of the *Scriptures* is one of the leading tenets of the Catholic Church; yet she contends that, though inspired, the Scriptures are in themselves insufficient, incomplete, and defective; and that the aid of *Tradition* is necessary in order to constitute the whole sum of Christian truth and doctrine. By Tradition is meant the oral teachings and sayings of the Apostles, which, though not committed to writing by themselves or by their immediate successors, were repeated from one person to another, and by this means communicated to the whole Church. Thus Paul says to Timothy: "The things which thou hast *heard* from me, before many witnesses, the same commit to faithful men, who shall be fit to teach others also." 2 Tim. ii. 2. The chief argument used by Catholics in favor of Tradition is, that, by the use of Scripture, all the various sects may prove and establish their various and contradictory opinions; whereas, Tradition is uniform and harmonious in defending only those doctrines which are held and taught by the Catholic Church. Protestants, on the other hand, retort to this assertion, that Tradition is more variable, contradictory, and diversified in its teachings, than even the Scriptures; and if this argument has any weight against the authority and sufficiency of the Scriptures, it has much more weight against Tradition.

The doctrine of the Catholic Church, in reference to the *Church* herself, is peculiar. She believes greatly in the external organization, the visible form, the outward crust of religion, which is termed the Church; and holds that immense authority, prerogative, and sanctity, have been conferred upon her, as a separate and distinct entity, by Christ himself. Roman Catholics believe that the Church is entitled to absolute obedience from her members; and of course, in this connection, obedience to the Church means obedience to the priesthood—for who ever heard of the priesthood obeying the laity? And this doctrine is based on the words of Christ addressed to the Apostles: "Whosoever's sins ye remit, they are remitted." But the question naturally arises, whether this authority to forgive sins, like that of working miracles, was not confined to the Apostles only. The Catholic believes in the *Unity* and *Universality* of his Church. All theological writers, in treating of the attributes of the Christian Church, invariably enumerate these two qualities as being fundamentally essential to the existence of the true Church; whereas, every one who knows anything of the history of Christianity during all past ages, knows perfectly well that there never was a time when any church or denomination possessed either perfect Unity or Universality. Even previous to the Reformation, the Catholic Church could not boast of *Unity;* for in every age there were diversities of opinion and differences of doctrine. Even external Unity, the dryest, deadest, and most worthless of all, was never completely possessed; and sometimes the external divisions of the Catholic Church were carried even to the popedom, the supreme head of the Church, the infallible source of all authority; and as many as three rival and hostile Popes existed at one and the same time, who fulminated, fumed, and cursed away against each other. As to Universality, it would be difficult, we think, to prove that any religious sect possesses it at the present time, or ever possessed it.

The Roman Catholic Church teaches that she is infallible, and cannot err, in matters of faith. This opinion is defended by the following arguments: that Christ promised to his disciples that the Spirit of all truth should remain with them—she infers that this promise was intended to apply not only to the apostles, but also to their successors; that Christ appointed Peter as the foundation of the Church, and that therefore if the gates of hell are not to prevail against her, she must have some infallible protection against falling into error. This infallibility *centres* in the Pope as the head of the Church on earth; though unfortunately the Popes have at different times decreed directly contradictory decisions. To obviate this difficulty, a large proportion of eminent theologians in the Catholic Church have contended that this infallibility did *not* belong to the Pope *alone*, but to the Pope in conjunction with a general or œcumenical Council. But suppose the Pope and the Council differ, as has repeatedly been the case, how then? The Protestant answers, in fact, that the history of the Church proves that there has been as much disunion and difference of belief among Catholics as among other religionists; and that this results from the fundamental laws of the human mind, which lead to differences of opinion in spite of all authority.

The Roman Catholic Church has *seven* sacraments, while nearly all other sects have only two. The seven Roman Catholic sacraments are, . Baptism, the Lord's Supper, Confirmation, Penance, Extreme Unction, Holy Order, and Matrimony. The most important of these sacraments in the estimation of the laity, is the *Eucharist, or Lord's Supper*. Catholics believe that the bread or wafer, after being consecrated by the officiating priest, is the body, blood, and divinity of Christ, and that, as there are at one single period of time myriads of consecrated wafers distributed over various countries of the earth, the body of Christ is necessarily divided and subdivided into an infinite

number of portions, and received by the faithful everywhere, while at the same time that body remains unmuti-
lated in heaven.   In other words, the doctrine of transubstantiation, as held by Roman Catholics, is a mystery—
a thing, the *mode* of which cannot be explained and defended to the satisfaction of common sense ; which is
indeed revolting to every dictate of common sense ; but
which must be received, if received at all, by the exercise
of a submissive and obedient faith.   We must believe that
it is so, because the Church *teaches* that it is so ; and to
many sincere minds this is sufficient and satisfactory
authority.   The chief text of Scripture on which this doctrine is based, is that in Matthew xxvi. 26–28, where
Christ says : "Take, eat, this is my body," and giving the
cup, said : "This is my blood of the New Testament,
which is shed for the remission of sins."   A consecrated
wafer is constantly kept on the altars of the churches, and
hence it is that Catholics suppose that they are in the immediate presence of God while they are in church; and
therefore they kneel to the wafer on the altar frequently,
when entering and leaving the church, or when passing
from one side of the sanctuary to the other.   If indeed it
be true that the great Creator and Sovereign of the universe, or even a small fraction of him, is reposing on the
altar, it is certainly proper enough to kneel to him, when
in his direct presence.   And it cannot be denied that
this view of the thing leads to a much greater appearance
of devoutness and solemnity in Roman Catholic Churches,
than is to be seen in the churches of any other denomination of Christians.

The sacrament of *Penance* is connected with the duty
of Auricular Confession.   It is the popular notion that
Catholic priests claim the power absolutely to forgive sins ;
but though the laity may entertain this opinion, the
Church herself does not teach it.   Her doctrine really is,
that after a sin has been sincerely repented of and entirely
forsaken, and after it has been fully and freely confessed
to the priest, then the latter is empowered to forgive it,

and remit the penalty which might otherwise have followed it. St. James says: "Confess your sins to one another;" and on the authority of this passage the Confessional is based. But the Protestant here objects that these words plainly enjoin a mutual confession of each other's faults, whereas no priest ever confessed to a layman. Confession is always required in the Catholic Church before going to the Lord's Supper. A portion of Penance consists in satisfaction—satisfaction to God, and satisfaction to the Church, whom the penitent has offended. Sometimes the priest sees fit to relax the rigor of the Church, and remit a portion of the penance or satisfaction which would otherwise be enjoined. This is called an *indulgence*. Old Tetzel once did a thriving business in selling these indulgences for money, until Luther arrested his course, and "made a big hole in his drum," which silenced it forever. The abuses which existed in the sixteenth century, in reference to these indulgences, led to the first outbreak of the Reformation, and to the *down-break* of the Papal power throughout a large portion of Christendom.

Roman Catholics administer *Extreme Unction* to those about to die, as a sacrament—a rite which is based on the words of St. James: "Is any sick among you, let him call for the elders of the Church, and let them pray over him, anointing him with oil, in the name of the Lord." The Church also regards *Marriage* as a sacrament; meaning thereby that, when the ceremony is performed by a Catholic priest, a vow is thereby made to God, which cannot be dissolved. Hence the Church does not permit full divorces for any cause, even for those specified and allowed by the law of the land. Yet the Popes have frequently granted dispensations for divorces, whenever the interests of the Church were promoted by them, thus *apparently* making a fundamental law and principle subservient to interest. But the church permits limited divorces, or separations *a mensa et thoro*.

The *Invocation of Saints* occupies a very prominent place in the worship and religious exercises of the Catholic

Church; for the reason that, if pious friends and relations
when on earth pray for those whom they love, it is a reasonable inference that they would continue so to do, hereafter, in Heaven. Of the truth and propriety of this
view, there can be no doubt; yet whether this consideration justifies us in offering them our prayers, when in
another world, is a question on which men will be disposed
to differ.

Of *Purgatory*, or the intermediate state between death
and judgment, the Catholic Church teaches, that the justice of God will not punish those whose sins are of a
trivial nature, to the same severe extent as those who are
guilty of the most enormous crimes. Hence, as Hell is
believed to be composed entirely of the elements of brimstone and teeth-gnashing, without any grades of misery
or diversity of torment, another place named Purgatory
has very opportunely been discovered, where minor transgressions are disciplined by a lighter and more equitable
punishment; so that when their venial sins have been sufficiently suffered for, the purified spirits will be admitted to
Heaven.

A portion of the public services of the Catholic Church
is celebrated in Latin. The reason of this is because the
liturgy of the Church was anciently composed in that language, and a just reverence for antiquity induces her to
retain the form in which her prayers were originally
uttered. In this country all the prayers are translated
into English and printed, in the people's editions, together
with the Latin. The *Mass* is a series of Latin prayers,
during the utterance of which the consecrated host is offered to God by the officiating priest. The term Mass
itself is derived from the concluding words of this solemn
and imposing rite, which are "*Ite, missa est.*" In the
great cathedral churches of Europe the ceremonies connected with this portion of Catholic worship are solemn,
imposing, and sublime in a pre-eminent degree, and the
spectacle has often led the most thoughtless and irreverent
minds to pious and penitent emotions.

Notwithstanding the prevalence of Protestant sects and churches, the Roman Catholic Church is still more numerous than any other single denomination. Her members may be said, at a rough guess, to amount to a hundred millions. In the United States they have increased with a steady and rapid pace during the last fifty years, till at the present time they are one of the leading denominations. The spirit of this ancient and venerable church is aggressive, and her aspirations for extension never cease. But we believe that all those fears which some timid Protestants profess to entertain, of future danger to American liberty from the encroachments of the Church of Rome, are most preposterous and absurd; for that Church has enough to do to protect and preserve her own interests and security, without having any means, even if she possessed the will, to interfere with the rights and interests of others.

EVANGELICAL LUTHERAN CHURCH.

ONE of the oldest of the Protestant churches, and in Europe one of the most distinguished, is the Evangelical Lutheran. There are probably more historical incidents of interest and importance connected with the early career of this sect, than belongs to any other. The name or title by which they are designated—the term *Lutheran*— was first applied to them by their opponents, the Roman Catholics. When Luther met Dr. John Eck, the Romish theologian, in his celebrated debate at Leipsic, 1519, the latter endeavored to stigmatize the friends of the Reformer, and to turn both him and them into ridicule, by calling them Lutherans, in opposition to Catholics and Christians The term thus used in the first instance as one of reproach, became universally prevalent among the enemies and friends of the new sect; and it has since become renowned and esteemed for the honorable and memorable associations connected with it. The other title which Lutherans apply to themselves—that of Evangelical—is the one

which Luther and his followers originally claimed, when
they abandoned and renounced what they held to be the
errors and abominations of the Romish Church.

The birth of the Lutheran denomination may with some
fitness be dated from the year 1507, in which Luther then
a monk, and twenty-four years of age, first discovered a
Latin Bible among the rubbish of his convent library,
from the perusal of which he derived his novel and then
almost unknown ideas in reference to the doctrinal system
of Protestant theology. During ten years he continued
to investigate and study the Scriptures, at the end of
which period, in 1517, he made his first public foray into
the territories of Rome, by attacking the sale of Indulgences, which at that time was carried on by Tetzel, in
the vicinity of Luther's residence. Luther refused abso-
lution, as a priest, to those who had bought forgiveness of
their sins with money from Tetzel. A violent controversy
ensued between Luther and Tetzel, in reference to this
business, in which the former gained an overwhelming
advantage. His violent conduct, however, excited the indignation of the authorities of the Catholic Church, and
the Papal Court decreed that his writings should be publicly burnt. In return for this compliment, Luther collected together some of the standard works of the Romish
Church and burnt them, together with the condemnatory
bull of the Pope, in the view of the inhabitants of the city
of Wittenberg. To punish this audacity, the Pope fulminated another bull or decree, excommunicating the refrac-
tory and contumacious priest. Thus the breach was made
irreparable, and the career and independence of the new
sect were formally and publicly begun.

The first churches, or religious organizations connected
with this new sect, were established in Saxony. The
monarch of that State, the Elector Frederic, became a
patron of Luther at the commencement of his career : and
as the Reformer was one of his subjects, being professor
at Wittenberg, his favorite University, his protection was
of immense value. Soon Reformed and independent

churches were established in every city and town of
Saxony; from Saxony the new faith spread rapidly into
Hanover, Wurtemburg, Prussia, and many of the minor
principalities which constituted the then Germanic Empire.
The views of Luther even extended into France and England, into Denmark and Sweden; and it may with truth
be asserted that the most potent and efficient enemy which
the Roman Catholic Church has ever met with, during the
progress and vicissitudes of many centuries, was "Brother
Martin," the Monk of Eisleben, the illustrious founder of
Lutheranism.

The history of the Lutheran Church in Europe presents
two very marked and prominent features. Her conflicts
have been divided between those which she waged with
the Church of Rome, and those which were carried on
within her own bosom by the disputes and everlasting
differences of her own members. Debate and disturbances
seem indeed to have been the natural and normal state of
this sect during their whole past history. Even before
the death of Luther, the opinions of Melanchthon, his most
intimate and trusted friend, became so widely dissimilar
from his own, that a coldness of feeling ensued between
them. The various diversities of sentiment, among the
Lutherans, were somewhat harmonized by the memorable
Diet at Augsburg, at which the Confession or creed known
by that name was set forth, as the system of doctrine
which the Lutheran Churches then entertained. At a
subsequent period efforts were made to terminate the disputes which raged between the Lutherans and the Catholic
Church; and the Reformers prepared a revised edition of
the Augsburg Confession, called the *Smalcald Articles*, in
which some concessions were made toward the Romish
system. These purposes of conciliation ended in nothing.
Luther died in 1546, in the sixty-second year of his age,
and he left his followers an inheritance of great peril; for
they soon became involved in the horrors of war with the
Emperor Charles V., who was then champion of the
Romish Church and of its supremacy. The Elector of

Saxony and the Landgrave of Hesse were the political and military heads of the Protestant party. The Emperor, suddenly surrounded by the armies of the Protestants at Innspruck, in 1552, was compelled to make some important concessions to the Protestant leaders, which are known by the epithet of the Treaty of Passau. The Protestants eventually wrested from the Emperor an edict, by which he finally decreed and allowed that all those who had adopted the Confession of Augsburg should thenceforth be free from the ecclesiastical jurisdiction of the Roman pontiff, and were at perfect liberty to ordain laws for themselves in reference to all matters pertaining to their religious belief, discipline, and worship; and all the inhabitants of the German Empire should be permitted to judge for themselves in religious matters; and that whoever should injure or persecute them, or any of them, on account of their opinions, should be treated as enemies of the Empire, and disturbers of its peace.

At a subsequent period in the history of the Lutheran Church, another creed was added to their standards, in addition to those which we have already named, in order to aid in healing disputes and controversies which had arisen among her members and her theologians. This was called the *Formula of Concord*, which differs in some respects from the Augsburg Confession. The two catechisms of Luther, the Larger and the Smaller, also hold the rank of authority with the members of this sect; so that the symbolical books which contain their creed, when taken altogether, are of enormous size and volubility. The consequence is that the utmost diversity of opinions exists among the Lutherans in the various countries of Europe where they prevail. Every possible shade of sentiment and belief can be found among them, from the semi-Romish "old Lutheran," who, like Luther, adheres to the doctrine of consubstantiation, to the semi-Infidel, who, like Strauss, Paulus, Rohr, and the other modern rationalistic theologians of Germany, deny the inspiration and miracles of the Scriptures. In this country the same tendency to diversity of sentiment exists among the Lutherans, though it is not carried out to the same extremes; and a certain degree of uniformity, together with considerable liberty, prevails among them here.

From the period of Luther's labors the church which he represented gradually spread over a large part of northern Europe. In 1525, it became the established Church of Saxony. In 1527 the Lutheran doctrines were introduced into Sweden, with the sanction of the monarch, Gustavus Vasa Ericson. Lutheranism was introduced into Denmark in 1527, under the reign of Frederic I., whence it was carried into Norway, Lapland, and other countries of the extreme North. During the progress of half a century after Luther's death, his doctrines were proclaimed by able and learned advocates in the Netherlands, in Poland, in France, besides in all those German States and communities which we have already named.

In Europe the Lutheran Church is at the present time the most numerous of all the Protestant sects. Her members number eight millions in Prussia, two millions in Austria, two millions in Saxony, one million in Wurtemberg, one million in Hanover, two millions in the smaller German States, two millions in Denmark, four millions in Norway and Sweden, two millions and a half in Russia, half a million in Poland, and a hundred and twenty thousand in the Netherlands. Lutheranism is the established religion in more separate States and kingdoms than is any other Protestant Church. There are more universities connected with this denomination than any other Protestant sect can boast of; for nearly all the great seats of learning in Germany exist in connection with that sect, and are served by professors, who, for the most part, are Lutherans. Yet it must not be inferred from this fact that there is any unity of opinion among these numerous associations of learned and scientific men; for their belief exhibits the utmost possible differences. It no more implies unity or harmony of belief between people, to say of them in Europe that they are all Lutherans, than it would imply similarity of appearance and of character, to say of certain other people that they were all Swiss or all Frenchmen.

The Lutheran Church in Germany has produced, during the several centuries of its past existence, a greater numof learned and illustrious scholars than any other sect, either Romish or Protestant. It would be absurd to begin any enumeration of even a portion of these; for they would form a catalogue of many hundreds. Her clergy in Europe are the most learned, as a body, in theological science, of any sect in the world. At a time when candidates for the priestly office in England and Scotland were admitted, without their being able to understand a single word of the Hebrew, in which the original of the Old Testament is written—and the knowledge and interpretation of which are indispensable to every well-read theologian, or even intelligent preacher—at that time the Lutheran churches in Germany required, and still require, in all their candidates for the sacred office, a perfect acquaintance with the original languages of the Scriptures, and an equally accurate knowledge of every other department of theological science. It must be admitted that the three most influential and powerful sects in Europe at the present time, and since the Reformation, have been the Church of Rome, the Reformed Church of England, and the Lutheran Church in Germany.

We will now proceed to sketch the history of this last in the United States, and set forth the doctrines and usages which now predominate among her members and preachers.

The first religious assemblage of Lutherans which ever existed in the United States was composed of a few immigrants from Holland, who came to New York about 1630, a few years after the landing of the Pilgrims on Plymouth Rock, and while the colony of New York still remained under the jurisdiction of the Dutch. They belonged originally to the small community of Lutherans who lived in Holland, and who fled to this country probably to escape the horrors of the Thirty Years' War, which at that disastrous period threatened to exterminate Protestantism from Germany and the Netherlands. Their first minister was named Fabricius, who arrived in 1669, and who preached for them during eight years. Their first church was a log building erected in New York in 1671, for which a stone edifice was afterwards substituted.

The next settlement of Lutherans in this country was that of the Swedes on the Delaware, at Philadelphia, in 1636. They continued to hold their religious services in their native language for many years; after this the prevalence of the English around them, the difficulty of obtaining native preachers from Sweden, and the fact that the other then existing Lutherans of this city held all their public exercises in the *German* language, induced the Swedish Lutherans to apply to the Protestant Episcopal Churches for a supply of ministers. This request was readily complied with; and the consequence was, that in the progress of time the whole congregation were transferred to the Episcopal Church, and were formally united with that body.

The German Lutherans commenced to immigrate to this country about the year 1700, and gradually spread over a large portion of New York, Pennsylvania, Maryland, and Virginia. In 1710, three thousand of them came from the Palatinate and settled in New York. In 1733, a large number established themselves in Georgia, at a place which they called Ebenezer. These were driven from Saltzberg, in Bavaria, by the persecutions of the Jesuits, who then exercised an absolute supremacy in that kingdom. This colony was supplied with native ministers from Germany, and they have ever since been a prosperous and highly respected community. When George Whitefield traveled in this country, he visited the Lutheran Churches in Georgia, and was much pleased with their piety and usefulness; and besides preaching for them, presented them with a bell for one of their churches, as a token of his esteem. The descendants of these people still adhere to the religion of their forefathers, and are connected with the flourishing Lutheran Synod of South Carolina and the adjacent States.

The most numerous and prosperous colonies of Lutherans were located in Pennsylvania; and about the year 1742 they began to assume their first importance and prominence in the community. It was in that year that the great patriarch of American Lutheranism reached this' country. This was the Rev. Henry Melchior Mühlenberg, a remarkable man in every respect, one of the most useful and distinguished persons in the history of this sect in this country. He is the direct ancestor of the well-known family of Mühlenbergs which still exists, and has produced several men of eminence in the pulpit, in politics, and in the battle field. Previous to 1742, the Lutherans in Philadelphia worshiped in connection with a few members of the German Reformed Church, in a small log house, in the lower part of Arch street. Mühlenberg, having been sent out from the University of Halle, in Germany, as a missionary to supply the wants of the Lutherans here, immediately commenced his labors, and these he continued with great success during nearly half a century. He was admirably adapted in every respect for his difficult post. He was one of the most learned men of his time, and could preach fluently in German, English, Dutch, French, Latin, and Swedish. He was also thoroughly versed in Greek, Hebrew, and several of the cognate Oriental languages. He was one of the most laborious and indefatigable of men. Probably no missionary every toiled in this country with more unremitting effort than he. Often he preached four and five times on a Sunday, and in as many languages. He traveled extensively, and wherever his services were needed among the stray communities of Lutherans through the middle States, he was prompt and ready to bestow them. As might be expected, his work prospered; he himself became greatly esteemed, and acquired an immense influence in the community.

Through his instrumentality the first Lutheran Synod which ever convened in this country was held at Philadelphia, in 1748. At that time there were only eleven preachers belonging to the sect in the United States, with fifteen congregations, and a community of fifty thousand people. During the Revolutionary war the Lutherans were zealous in the support of the cause of liberty. A son of Dr. Melchior Mühlenberg was a General in the Continental army; and the Germans were prompt, according to their means, in assisting the good cause. Zion's church, their largest edifice then, and even still, in this country, located at Fourth and Cherry streets, in this city, was occupied at one time (in 1778) by the British army as a hospital. Their oldest church, that of St. Michael, at the corner of Cherry and Fifth streets, was also used by the British as a garrison church in the morning of Sunday; though the congregation were allowed to occupy it in the afternoon. These outrages were continued until the final expulsion of the invaders from the precincts of the city of Penn.

After the Revolutionary war the Lutherans began to increase rapidly, not only by the growth of their native members, but by foreign immigration. In 1786, they had about twenty-five ministers; and the number of the churches and pastors gradually grew, until, in the year 1820, the most important event in their career which ever occurred in this country took place. This was the establishment of their General Synod, by which the five or six separate District Synods which had previously risen into existence, in various portions of the country, were consolidated and united into one chief body. The results of this arrangement were soon felt, and were found to be highly beneficial. The General Synod served to give harmony, consistency, and unity to the various portions of the church which were scattered over the several States; and this result was much needed. The members of the sect, who immigrated to this country, came from the various Protestant States of Germany, and they brought with them the peculiar opinions and usages to which they had been accustomed at home. These are different and dissimilar in most of those States; and the result would very naturally follow here, that considerable difference of opinion should prevail among the aggregate masses on every point of doctrine and worship. It is but due to the Lutherans to say that, though harassed by this tendency to diversity and discord, they have gradually coalesced into a degree of uniformity and homogeneity which could hardly have been expected. Yet one cause of this result is to be found in that *indifference* to church matters which gradually prevailed among many of them, when their attention became diverted toward the opportunities for acquiring wealth with which they were favored in this country. A large proportion of them, devoted to their pecuniary interests, did not *care* what became of the church of their forefathers; and by giving twenty-five cents a year, to secure their right of burial, many of them became indifferent to the prosperity and welfare of that faith for which their forefathers had fought and suffered, and for the possession of which many of them had deserted their native land, and had ventured upon the perils and deprivations of a howling wilderness.

One of the first fruits of the establishment of the General Synod was the erection of the Theological Seminary at Gettysburg, Pa., intended to prepare the young men of the church for the ministry. This is the most important institution connected with the Lutheran sect in this country, and was established in 1825. It is provided with large and commodious buildings, and with one of the best theological libraries in the country. The President of this institution is Rev. S. S. Schmucker, D. D., who was elected its first professor in 1825; who still continues, after the lapse of thirty-three years, to fill the important duties of his office, and is the most eminent Lutheran theologian in this country. There are two other professors connected with the institution, completing the usual routine of the most thorough theological instruction. A large portion of the library was obtained by Dr. B. Kurtz from some of the universities and clergy of Germany and Denmark. As an auxiliary to the seminary, Pennsylvania College was founded at the same place in 1827, Dr. Schmucker and Thaddeus Stevens, Esq. being instrumental in procuring the charter of the institution from the Legislature. A branch of this college, and one of the most meritorious portions of it, is the Medical College in Ninth street, below Locust, in Philadelphia.

The Schmucker family, like that of the Mühlenbergs, holds a prominent place in the history and development of the Lutheran Church in this country; there being no less than *eleven* persons of the connection who have been, or now are, clergymen of that sect. The younger members of this family usually write their names "Smucker," for the sake of convenience and brevity. Other eminent names occur in the history of the Lutheran Church in this country, such as those of Dr. Helmuth, formerly pastor of Zion's Church in Philadelphia; Dr. Kuntze, one of the best Oriental scholars of modern times; Rev. Drs. Kurtz, Brunholtz, Handschuch, Lochman, Geissenhainer, Quitman, (father of the late General Quitman of Mexican fame,) Schæffer, Demme, Mayer, and Bachman, of Charleston, the greatest of American entomologists.

In addition to the institutions at Gettysburg the Lutherans have a seminary at Columbus, Ohio; another at Hartwick, New York; others at Lexington, South Carolina, and at Springfield, Ohio. They have Education, Home Mission, Foreign Mission, and other benevolent societies. At present they number twenty-two synods, fifteen of which are connected with the General Synod. They have about five hundred ministers, fourteen hundred congregations, and a hundred and forty thousand regular communicants. They hold, in point of numbers and influence, a very respectable position among the secondary denominations of this country.

In Europe the Lutheran Church is governed by bishops,

and by superintendents, whose functions are the same as those of diocesan bishops; but in this country parity exists in their ministry, and each preacher is regarded as a bishop.   In other words, their church government is Presbyterian; and their doctrines, or the doctrines which are entertained by the great majority of them, are termed Evangelical.   They believe in the Trinity, the Deity of Christ and of the Holy Spirit, the vicarious atonement, and the fall of man; but they discard the doctrine of Predestination and Absolute Decrees of God respecting Man's Salvation.   They hold to Justification by Faith alone; to the necessity of good works, nevertheless; and to the eternity of future hell-fire for the finally impenitent.   Their opinions exhibit the greatest diversity on the subject of the Lord's Supper; some of them adhering to the dogma of Consubstantiation, as taught by Luther; while others hold that the bread and wine are merely commemorative symbols of the broken body and shed blood of Christ. Luther declared to the last his belief in Consubstantiation. In one of his later works he says: " I should have wished to have denied the real presence of Christ in the Eucharist, in order to confound the Papists.   But so clear and strong are the words of Scripture which establish it, that in spite of my inclination so to do, and though I strained every nerve to reach the point, yet I could never persuade myself to doubt or deny it."   Hence the "old Lutherans," who profess to be *strict* Lutherans, adhere to this opinion; though their numbers in this country are comparatively few.   The vast majority, however, go to the opposite extreme, strip the Eucharist of all mystery, and invest it only with a commemorative efficacy.   The Lutherans also differ about "old and new measures," some being opposed to prayer meetings and other revival ways and means; while others adopt the Methodist method of converting sinners, and sometimes carry their usages to the utmost possible limits.   These Lutherans are, however, found chiefly in the western States.   They claim the liberty to believe and reject the Augsburg Confession, which is the principal creed of the sect, when they please and as far as they please. The rationalistic Lutheran theologians of Germany, many of whom are the most learned men of the age, assert that they carry out the great principle of the Reformation—that of private judgment in religious matters—to its full and legitimate extent; and thus each one of them has a creed of his own. There are a few German Lutheran Churches in *this* country who belong to this wing of the sect, some of whom are Unitarians, and others as good as Infidels and Rationalists. But with these heretics the main body of the Lutheran Church hold no communication whatever, regarding their sentiments with horror and condemnation.

GERMAN REFORMED CHURCH.

The German Reformed Church, as it exists both in Europe and in this country, is historically descended from the Swiss churches which were established in the sixteenth century, through the instrumentality of the distinguished reformer, Ulric Zwingli. The original seat of the sect was in Switzerland; but many of these churches exist in the various Protestant States of Germany, as well as in this country.

Zwingli was the contemporary of Luther. He commenced his reforming zeal nearly at the same time, and was led to the adoption of his Protestant sentiments by a process somewhat similar to that used by Luther. He was born at Wildhaus, in the canton of Schweitz, in January, 1484. At an early age he exhibited proofs of superior intelligence; and his parents, who were poor, made every effort to give him the benefit of a learned education. He was intended for the priesthood, as the best avenue which could then be found for the display of talent and the gratification of ambition. In due time he was ordained as a Roman Catholic priest, after having completed his studies at the University of Basle. In 1506 he became the parish priest of Glaris, a village near his native Wildhaus, and here he commenced to study and examine the Scriptures with special reference to the absurdities which were committed by the pilgrims who at that time traveled to the venerable shrine at Einsidlen, which, by some imposture or other, had at that time acquired a widely-spread notoriety. By opposing this local superstition, he invited and incurred the condemnation of his ecclesiastical superiors; while at the same time he acquired great popularity among the multitude as a young man who was able and determined to exercise some freedom of thought. His growing fame at length procured for him the post of preacher in the cathedral church of Zurich. This event occurred in December, 1518. He was an eloquent speaker; and though while at Glaris his morals had not been any better than they should be, this defect was overlooked and gradually overshadowed by his superior abilities as an orator.

Meanwhile Luther was carrying forward the Reformation of Wittenberg, and the new doctrines which he propounded and defended found a ready and an able advocate in Zwingli. The latter preached one novelty after another as fast as he became convinced, by a careful examination of its Scriptural authority, until he had gone over the whole ground of Protestant theology. During the progress of these labors many of the Swiss cantons became the partizans of the Protestant cause; and the centre of the new faith remained at Zurich, of which city Zwingli was the leading and most powerful intellect. In some respects, and on several important points, Zwingli differed from Luther, especially in regard to the nature of the Lord's Supper. For the purpose of comparing their views, and, if possible, of forming an ecclesiastical and religious union, they held several conferences together; but in both cases the rude and resolute manner in which the Saxon Reformer insisted on his own peculiar and unmodified opinions as being the only and the immutable truth, and his determination not to depart a single jot from his previously expressed sentiments, rendered all prospect of accommodation utterly hopeless, and sadly disappointed the charitable hopes which Zwingli had reasonably entertained on the subject

Zwingli, therefore, proceeded to carry on his reforms in Switzerland in entire independence of the movements of Luther. One canton after another declared in favor of the Reformation, until all, save five of them, ranged themselves on that side of the dispute. The names of those which refused to do so were Uri, Lucerne, Schweitz, Unterhalten, and Zug. It is probable that, had the Reformer lived longer, he might have been able to extend his doctrines among the inhabitants of these cantons also; but in October, 1531, a religious war was declared between the cantons of opposite faith, and Zwingli went forth as chief chaplain in the army of his confederates. He was slain at the battle of Cappel, and thus prematurely terminated a career which might have ultimately led to very important and permanent results. Zwingli was an inferior man to Luther in every sense. He was his inferior in native genius, in learning, in boldness, in eloquence, in the extent and grandeur of the arena on which he labored, in the results which he produced, in the fame which he acquired, and in the completeness and duration of his public career. Notwithstanding these disadvantages, Zwingli occupies a very honorable place in history, as the founder of the German Reformed Church.

After the death of Zwingli, his place as the head of this church was assumed by a much greater man than himself —by John Calvin—who resided at Geneva, and rendered that city the head and centre of Swiss Protestantism. Calvin differed from Zwingli on several points; especially on the nature of the Lord's Supper, and on the proper nature of church government. Zwingli regarded the Eucharist merely as a commemorative symbol of Christ's death; while Calvin taught that the worthy communicant received, in the bread and wine, the actual body, blood, and bones of Christ. As to church government, Zwingli was in favor of subjecting the church to the civil authority, so far as her temporal and secular affairs were concerned;

while Calvin contended that in all things, both temporal and
spiritual, the church ought to be wholly free and separate
from the civil power. Calvin never succeeded in persuad-
ing the Swiss, much less any German community, to receive and adopt his views of church government, though
they were doubtless founded in truth and justice.

The German Reformed Church in the United States
took its rise about the year 1720, when the first immigrants who belonged to that sect came to this country.
These settled in Eastern Pennsylvania; but other churches
were gradually formed in various portions of this State,
and subsequently in Virginia, Maryland, New Jersey, and
the Carolinas. In this country their church government
is essentially Presbyterian. Some of the congregations
of this sect are in a flourishing condition; though they
never have had any very large churches, nor have they
had any eminent or distinguished persons among their
membership. In this respect, as well as regards numbers,
wealth, and social influence, they have always been inferior to the Lutheran and Dutch Reformed churches.

The creed of this sect is set forth in the Heidelberg
catechism. Their doctrines are regarded as orthodox, believing as they do in the Trinity, the vicarious atonement,
and other fundamental points of Protestant theology.
The Heidelberg Catechism was drawn up in 1563, and
adopted at the city of that name. Its purpose was to effect
a compromise between the Reformed Churches of Switzerland and Germany; and it was composed by several eminent and learned men who represented several different
parties. These were Dr. Zacharias Ursinus, who was a
disciple of Melanchthon, Dr. Casper Olevianus, a follower
of Calvin; and the Elector Frederic III., sovereign of the
Palatinate, of which Heidelberg is the capital, who was a
disciple of Zwingli. This catechism says nothing about
the cardinal doctrine of the imputation of Adam's sin to
his posterity; the atonement is regarded as general, in
opposition to Calvin's opinion; and the theories of Calvin
and Zwingli about the Lord's Supper are so mingled, that

a compound of the two is made. It also teaches that mankind cannot repent without the assistance of the Spirit of God; yet it admits that when the Spirit impels and urges men to repent, they have the power to resist that impulse and act as free agents. The doctrine of Predestination was never received by the German Reformed Church, either in a formal manner, or by any great number of its members, until within a few years, in consequence of the existence of causes in this country to 'which we will now advert.

In the year 1844, the General Synod of the German Reformed Church resolved to send to Germany to procure the services of a German Professor for their Seminary, at Mercersburg, who would be better qualified than any of their native ministers to teach theology to their candidates for the clerical office. After some investigation they selected Dr. Philip Schaff, at that time an under-teacher, or *professor extraordinarius*, of theology in the University of Berlin, who had already acquired some reputation as a scholar and a man of ambitious energy, who seemed to possess peculiar qualifications for the vacant place. He accepted the invitation, removed to this country, and at once began to perform the duties of his office. Dr. Schaff is unquestionably a man of superior learning and ability; and the activity in elaborating ponderous books in the department of Church History, which he has since displayed, may well excite the astonishment and despair of American authors and scholars. His associate at Mercersburg was Dr. John W. Nevin, formerly a clergyman of the old school Presbyterian Church. Dr. Schaff brought with him to this country all his peculiar views in theology, which may be characterized as being strongly conservative, in opposition to everything like progress or freedom. His opinions are, in fact, very much like the Puseyite school in the Episcopal Church; having great reverence for the Romish Church, and entertaining very intense admiration for the usages and institutions of the Middle Ages, which he is horrified to hear ignorant people in this country call the "Dark Ages." No sooner had Dr. Nevin been brought within the range of his influence than he became a violent convert to Dr. Schaff's opinions, and the pair soon commenced between them the work of revolutionizing the whole system of belief and of church usage, which had till then prevailed in the German Reformed denomination in this country. Prominent among the antique novelties introduced by them was a singular and most preposterous theory in regard to the nature of the Lord's Supper, the peculiar features of which we will endeavor to explain. It was in substance as follows :

That, in the sacrament of the Supper, the glorified humanity of Christ, his body, bones, and blood, are actually present; that they are mysteriously united with the consecrated emblems ; and that they thereby become virtually and actually united with and received by the worthy communicant. This doctrine Dr. Nevin defended at length, in a work which he soon after published, entitled "The Mystical Presence;" and the title was well deserved, for never before nor since has the world seen so admirable a specimen of mysticism mystified. While asserting this doctrine, which, in reality, is nothing more nor less than Consubstantiation, Dr. Nevin declared, at the same time, that he rejected all idea of a "*local presence*" of the body and blood of Christ; contended that "the communion of the believer is *spiritual, and not material*—a participation of the Saviour's life." Yet how these assertions can be reconciled with those in which he contends for the actual presence of the *flesh and blood of Christ* in the Sacrament, as plainly as language could possibly make or express it, no one can imagine; and every reasonable person must come to the conclusion that the doctrine is one of those theological and metaphysical abstractions which more than once have been innocently foisted on the Christian Church by men of influence and reputation.

Accordingly, Drs. Nevin and Schaff went to work and endeavored to introduce this new doctrine —which they

contended, and with some truth, was the real doctrine of
Calvin—into the German Reformed Church. Few of the
ministers of the sect could fully comprehend what these
learned doctors meant; but as such able men as Schaff
and Nevin assured them that that was the doctrine both
of Calvin and of the Scriptures, they concluded that it
must be so, and inferred that all was right. Accordingly,
the several synods adopted resolutions approving of this
doctrine; and at the same time endorsing several other
theological crotchets—old-time, fossil, mediæval conceits
about the Church and the ministry, which Dr. Schaff had
imbibed when a student at the University of Tübingen,
which is the most antiquated and conservative Protestant
university in Europe, and teaches doctrines more than
semi-Romish.

The result of this resolution was that the new system
introduced into the German Reformed Church in this
country has destroyed much of the vitality which it had
previously possessed. The best men whom the Church
contained, such as Dr. Berg and Rev. S. Helfenstein,
withdrew in disgust; and since that period the denomination has made little progress. Dr. Schaff continues to write
enormous books at Mercersbug, which very few people
read; and lectures on theology to a seminary composed
of four or five students; while Dr. Nevin has retired from
the field, and enjoys his *dolce far niente* at Lancaster, in
this State. Some people assert, however, that he is
laboriously preparing to edify the world with another
immense volume in behalf of the Mystical Presence, the
mysticism of which he has been doing his utmost for some
years to illuminate.

In this country the German Reformed Church have
about two hundred and fifty ministers, and about five hundred congregations. They have a General Synod, and
various classics or district synods. Their literary institutions, such as Marshall College, and the Theological Seminary at Mercersburg—the former of which we believe is

now removed to Lancaster—are not very prosperous; yet many individual churches of the denomination are in a very flourishing condition.

THE BAPTIST CHURCH.

THOSE religious people to whom the term "Baptist" is applied, both in this country and in Europe, are divided into a variety of minor sects who are known by various epithets, such as Free Will Baptists, Free Communion Baptists, Seventh Day Baptists, and several others. The most extensive and important denomination of this class, however, are those known by the simple word "Baptists," and these are probably the most numerous and one of the most influential sects in the United States; and of these we propose to speak in this article.

The Baptists claim to be the oldest of the present divisions of Christendom, on the ground that their method of administering the right of baptism by immersion is the only one, as they contend, practiced by the apostles and the primitive Church, and the only one which ought to be practiced in succeeding ages. They hold that as baptism was and is the only method of admission to the Church, and as immersion is the proper way of administering this rite, those only can be members of the Christian Church who have thus been admitted. Consequently those who have been merely sprinkled are not baptized; and as, in the early ages, we hear nothing of infants being baptized, but only such as had first "believed," and were old enough to exercise *faith*, they therefore infer that adults only are suitable subjects for this rite, which incorporates them with the Church of Christ. It is undoubtedly true that the preponderance of proof is in favor of the position that baptism was, in the first instance, administered only by immersion; that the very word for baptism used in the Greek New Testament means plainly to "immerse," and not sprinkle; and that the ablest opponents of the Baptists have been compelled to admit that the argument drawn from the early practice of the Church is in their favor.

The history of the Baptists may therefore be said, in one sense, to begin with the apostles. But several generations after their day, the universal practice of the Church had gradually become changed, and the sprinkling both of infants and of adults had taken the place of the primitive rite. As a sect, or separate organization, they never existed for many ages, until the rise of Peter Waldo, in the twelfth century, who established the sect of the Waldenses among the mountains and valleys of Piedmont. One of the prominent doctrines which he and his followers believed was the impropriety of the baptism of infants, and the necessity of immersion to the validity of any baptism. Waldo commenced his reforming career in 1180; and during several centuries those who received his doctrine endured immense persecutions, according to the prevalent spirit of the times, from the Roman Catholic Church, which was then predominant throughout Europe.

Those Christians who adhere to "believers' baptism," in opposition to the sprinkling of infants, next appear as a sect, in the sixteenth century, under the epithet of the "Anabaptists of Munster." These were fanatics of the worst description, who did an infinite degree of harm, and met with a terrible fate; but they had no connection whatever with modern Baptists, except in the single fact that they immersed. The Munster Baptists may more properly be regarded as the predecessors of the modern Mennonites, who are indeed directly historically descended from them. In 1338, Walter Lollard, a Hollander of learning and distinction, who adhered to the doctrine of the Baptists, visited England, preached and made many converts, who were known by the epithet of "Lollards," after their leader. During the reign of Henry VIII., and Edward VI., they greatly increased in numbers; though subsequently, they were cruelly persecuted under Queen Mary. On one occasion as many as fourteen suffered death, rather than renounce their religious convictions.

Notwithstanding fire and sword, however, these people continued to increase, and gradually the name by which they were designated was changed from Lollard to Baptist; and they acquired more and more importance and influence. At length religious liberty and personal security were granted them by Cromwell, who had overthrown the pernicious tyranny of Charles I., and had established the Commonwealth. It was during the reign of Charles II., that those events occurred which planted the Baptist name and faith in the New World.

The chief instrument in producing this result was the celebrated Roger Williams, who was a native of Wales, and originally a clergyman of the Church of England. Becoming dissatisfied both with the doctrines and the government of that church, he determined to remove to the then infant colony of Massachusetts. His voyage terminated in February, 1631, and he first became a resident and a pastor at Salem. At that period he was a Puritan, and had not yet publicly announced his new views on the subject of Baptism. But when, some years afterward, he did so, he was expelled from the territory of the colony, and compelled to seek a new home elsewhere. Then it was that he and a few devoted followers removed to the region of country, then inhabited wholly by Indians, which now constitutes the State of Rhode Island. There he established the first regular Baptist Society in this country, at Providence, in March, 1639. Other societies were soon formed in other localities in the State, and the Baptists thus became the founders and chief citizens of one of the sovereign Commonwealths of this confederacy. During the progress of several centuries the denomination has gradually increased in all the States, and especially in the south, until at the present time, as their statistics show, they exceed in point of numbers every other sect in the community.

The doctrinal system of this denomination of Baptists, is Calvinistic and Orthodox. They believe in the eternal decrees of God, in reference to the salvation of the Elect, and hold that such as have been predestined to be saved from the foundation of the world *shall* be saved, and no others. At the same time their method of preaching is very earnest and practical—as much so as that of the Methodists—and they are very zealous in laboring for the conversion of sinners. It is to this fact that their remarkable increase in this country is to be attributed. They are also great proselytizers among the members of other churches, by means of arguments and reasonings in reference to the true nature and method of baptism. Their fundamental principle on this point is, that Christians should not admit anything as an article of belief or of duty which is not taught in the Scriptures, and sanctioned by the practice of the Apostles themselves. Every other doctrine or rite they hold to be a mere human invention. They apply this principle to baptism, and contend that both the teachings of the New Testament and the example of the Apostles are plainly in favor of "believers' baptism," in preference to infant sprinkling; the former is right, and the latter a wholly unauthorized innovation. In support of this doctrine they can array, besides Scripture proofs, a host of concessions and admissions which the most distinguished writers of other sects have made, which clearly admit the greater propriety of immersion, and thus concede the truth of the doctrine of the Baptists.

Nothing is more curious than the extraordinary fullness of these concessions from their opponents, and they are so remarkable that we will repeat a few of them. Bishop Burnet says: "To baptize means to plunge, as is granted by all the world." Calvin says: "The custom of the ancient churches was not sprinkling, but immersion." Bossuet admits that "the word baptize means to immerse, and the rite of immersion was observed by the ancient church." Dr. Doddridge says: "It seems the part of candor to admit that baptizing by immersion was most usual in early times." Whitefield declares that "the manner of baptism was by immersion." It certainly seems to be unaccountable that writers who are willing to

make admissions such as these, should still have adhered
to sects which practice the sprinkling of infants, and which
have wholly abandoned the practical observance of the
rite, the scriptural and apostolical authority of which they
do not deny.

Although Baptists place so much importance in the
mode of administering this rite, they do not go as far as
some other sects in their views of the miraculous *results*
of baptism when administered. They do not believe, with
the Roman Catholic and the Episcopalian, that it necessarily regenerates the nature of the baptized person ; and
they insist that unless repentance and faith accompany
this sacrament, it is of no avail, and produces no moral
benefit whatever. Baptism with them is a sign of the fellow-
ship of the recipient with Christ, of the remission of his
sins, and his heirship of eternal life; "*provided always,*" it
be accompanied with repentance and change of life. They
admit but one other sacrament, that of the Lord's Supper,
which they regard merely as a commemorative ordinance,
to remind Christians, till the end of the world, of the sufferings and death of Christ.

The Baptists further believe in the total fall and corruption of human nature, and in man's utter inability to
do anything whatever towards his own salvation. Hence
they hold to the doctrine of election ; because as God only
enables men to repent, and as but few *do* repent, it is inferred therefore that he aids but a few, leaving the balance
to the consequences of their own original sin, which
they inherited from old Adam through the fall, and of
their actual sins, which are the legitimate result of the
former.

The church government of the Baptists is purely congregational. Each society is a separate and independent
organization, and has entire control over all its own affairs.
They think that the apostolic churches were organized in
this way, and that these were proper models for the guidance of Christians in succeeding ages. Their church officers are bishops, or presbyters, who preach, and deacons

who assist and have charge of the temporal affairs of the congregation. Yet though the Baptists are Congregationalists or Independents in this respect, they long since felt the necessity and advantage of a certain degree of intercourse among their various churches, in different portions of the community; and hence they are accustomed to hold what are termed "Associations." When difficulties occur between a congregation and its pastor, a council of neighboring ministers is called together, who take the facts of the case into consideration, and give their opinion upon the merits. But their agency or influence is merely advisory; and they have no authority to prescribe any particular course of action in the matter, either to the church or to the preacher. The associations are composed of delegates from the congregations existing within certain limits, and they meet merely to consult together about the common interests of the churches, and to engage in religious exercises of more than ordinary earnestness and duration. Besides these associations they have "Conventions," which are composed of delegates from several associations, whose objects are to carry forward and promote the operations of the Missionary, Bible, Tract, and other benevolent operations of the sect; to give counsel and advice in doubtful and disputed cases, and to hold religious exercises.

Formerly the preachers of this denomination were inferior to those of several others in their literary and theological attainments. This defect has been greatly improved during the last few years. The Baptists have now under their care some of the best colleges and seminaries in this country. Among these are Brown University, at Providence, Rhode Island, over which the able Dr. Wayland presided for many years; Madison University, at Hamilton, New York; Georgetown College, at Georgetown, Kentucky; Newton Theological Seminary, at Newton, Massachusetts; and other theological institutions at Covington, Kentucky; Hamilton, New York; and New Hampton, New Hampshire. The consequence of the existence and operations of these various establishments has been to elevate the standard of literary merit among the clergymen of this church, until it is now nearly equal to that of any of their contemporaries.

In England the Baptists can boast of many distinguished men, prominent among whom were Bunyan, author of "Pilgrim's Progress;" John Gill, the Commentator; Robert Hall, the most eloquent preacher of his time, who declared, in reference to the voluminous works of Dr. Gill, that they were " a continent of mud ;" Dr. Ryland ; John Foster, the celebrated essayist ; and more recently, Mr. Spurgeon, at present the most popular preacher in London. In the United States the Baptists have also had some eminent men, among whom are Drs. William Staughton, Wayland, Judson, the missionary, Howard Malcomb, Barnas Sears, the learned Biblical critic, and Fuller, of Baltimore. The present statistics of this denomination show a vast increase during the last half century. In 1795 there were in the United States but nine hundred churches, eleven hundred preachers, and seventy thousand communicants. At the present time a sufficiently accurate computation gives them about ten thousand churches, six thousand ordained ministers, and nine hundred thousand regular members—which number, by including negroes in the Southern States, may readily be augmented to a sum total of one million. These estimates, we believe, much exceed those of any other denomination in the United States.

The Baptists are distinguished by their great zeal and enterprise in foreign missions. They have flourishing stations in Burmah, Siam, China, India, Ceylon, Australia, and Liberia; and some of the most successful missionaries of modern times have labored under the auspices. Such were Judson and Kinkaid, men of unsurpassed ability and usefulness in this difficult and self-denying enterprise. It is probable that, at the present time, ten thousand natives of the Asiatic countries just named are regular members of their missionary churches. In consequence of the fundamental differences between the Baptists and other Evangelical Christians on the subject of baptism, they have provided for themselves a new translation of the Scriptures, in which the word "baptize" is uniformly rendered "immerse," in accordance with their peculiar views on this subject.

SWEDENBORGIANS.

THE religious community founded by Emanuel Swedenborg is properly called the "New Jerusalem, or New Christian Church;" and while other sects boast of their antiquity, and of their connection and identity with the primitive apostolic Church, this sect regards it as a greater evidence of truth to possess the character of innovators, and to improve upon the old religion of previous ages. The peculiar nature of their doctrines has prevented them from becoming a very large or influential community; for there is a great deal of mystery, profundity, and difficulty involved in their belief, which makes the common understanding revolt from it.

Emanuel Swedberg was born at Stockholm, in Sweden, in 1688. His father, Jesper Swedberg, was first a chaplain in the army, and afterwards the Bishop of Skara, in West Gothland. Emanuel received a liberal education, and indicated his superior talents by his great success and proficiency in many departments of learning, especially in philosophy, mathematics, chemistry, anatomy, and languages. In 1716, he received from the king the appointment of Assessor Extraordinary of the Metallic College, in Stockholm. Several years afterward, in consequence of his abilities and services, the rank of a noble was conferred upon him, at which time he changed his name from Swedberg to the more sonorous one of Swedenborg. He thus became a member of the Equestrian Order, in Sweden, and took his seat in the Assembly of the States. He retained his office in the Metallic College from 1716 till 1747—a period of thirty-one years; and although a higher and more important office was then tendered to him, he declined it, in order that he might devote his whole attention to the exposition and propagation of the peculiar opinions which he had adopted. These opinions he made known, from time to time, in the many works which he published, all of which bear evidence of extraordinary intellectual powers, of great learning and industry, but at the same time of a visionary and imaginative tendency, which has no parallel in the history or development of the human mind. He lived to the great age of eighty-five, and died at London in 1772. He was universally esteemed for his personal qualities, admired for his learning and abilities; and he numbered among his intimate friends many of the most eminent persons of his time.

The sect founded by Swedenborg may be denominated the predecessors of the *Spiritualists* of the present day, though they greatly differ in many respects. They believe in communication with spirits, but not through the agency or medium of material substances, and such things as audible knockings. Swedenborg represented himself as the chosen herald of the second coming of Christ, not as the judge of the world, but as the revealer of new doctrinal truth, and of the practical results which those truths would produce upon mankind. It is in executing this commission that he was favored, as he thought, with frequent revelations from Heaven, and with intercourse with departed spirits, who communicated to him what he afterward revealed and taught to others. It is evident, from his whole history, that he himself was sincere, and was governed by no motive of a selfish or mercenary character in his conduct. He was rich, and did not seek profit. He was unambitious, and did not desire fame. He was unobtrusive and retiring, and shrank from the dignities and honors of this world. We must therefore infer that a desire to utter what he believed to be the truth, was his sole motive in proclaiming a new set of doctrines, which greatly astonished and startled his cotemporaries and all those who have since studied and examined them.

Communication with the spirit-world is the fundamental idea of the system of Swedenborg. By this means he

professed to receive his religious opinions; and the proofs
which exist to show that he really obtained superhuman
intelligence, are certainly remarkable. This intelligence
was not confined to religious matters, but extended also
to temporal and worldly affairs, which were, from their
very nature, palpable and unanswerable proofs that there
was something extraordinary in the man, which rendered
him different from other human beings around him. In
proof of this, we will narrate several of the events of this
character which occurred, and which are authenticated and
established beyond the possibility of a doubt.

In September, 1756, Swedenborg paid a visit to Gothenburg, and was the guest of one William Castel. Fifteen
other persons were invited to dinner. About ten o'clock
in the evening, Swedenborg left the company and withdrew. After a short time he returned, and seemed to be
much agitated and alarmed. The company immediately
perceived his state of mind, and inquired the cause of it.
He answered that he had been informed by his spiritual
agency that a fire had broken out in Stockholm, and was
at that moment raging with great fury; that the house of
one of his friends, whom he named, was already in ashes;
and that the conflagration was spreading rapidly. After
a short interval Swedenborg again retired, and returned
with a joyful countenance, with the intelligence that the
fire was then extinguished at the third door from his own
residence. The news of this reported conflagration rapidly
spread through Gothenburg, which is three hundred miles
distant from Stockholm. The governor of the city sent
for Swedenborg, and questioned him on the subject. He
described the fire with great minuteness, how it began, how
far it had extended, how it was suppressed, and some of the
incidents connected with its progress. A messenger had
been dispatched from Gothenburg to Stockholm to ascertain the truth or falsehood of the seer's revelation; and at
the earliest possible time, on the succeeding Monday, he
returned, bringing the most full and complete confirmation
of all the statements of Swedenborg, which were further

established by the royal courier, who soon after arrived at Gothenburg.

Another well attested and equally remarkable incident is as follows: Madam Hartville, the widow of the Dutch Plenipotentiary at Stockholm, was requested, a short time after her husband's death, to pay a certain goldsmith for a set of silver plate which her husband had purchased. The widow had good reason to believe that the bill had been paid during the lifetime of her husband, yet she was unable to discover any receipt or memorandum to that effect among his carefully-arranged papers. She was in great perplexity, as the sum in question was large; and at length a friend suggested to her that Swedenborg, whose alleged intercourse with spirits was a matter of general fame, should be consulted on the subject. She visited him and requested his aid. He promised to serve her; and three days afterward he called upon her, and informed her that he had conversed with her deceased husband. He further stated that the debt had been paid seven months before his death, and that the receipt had been put in a bureau in a certain apartment of her house. She replied that this bureau had already been thoroughly searched, and in vain. Swedenborg answered that the spirit had informed him, that the receipt would be found in a secret drawer in the left side of the bureau in question, which was hidden by the ordinary drawer, which must first be removed; and that, in that secret place, other important papers, connected with her husband's official correspondence, would also be found. An examination was immediately made in accordance with this direction, and the lost papers were discovered precisely as Swedenborg had designated.

The truth of these incidents is supported by unanswerable evidence; and many others, of similar character, and great clearness, occurred during Swedenborg's lifetime. It becomes a matter of interest to inquire what were the doctrines taught by a man whose spiritual insight seems to have been so remarkable; for all the opinions which he

taught he professed to have received from the same super-
natural and infallible mode of instruction.

Swedenborg did not believe, nor do his followers now
believe, that "all the tracts bound up in the Bible" are
necessarily inspired. They exclude from the inspired
books all the Epistles of the New Testament, yet they
read and receive them as writings of great interest and
value. Some of the sacred books they think contain
an internal sense, having been written according to the
"Science of Correspondences." Of this character is the
book of Job. The Swedenborgians also believe in a
Trinity; but it is not the Trinity of the Orthodox sects.
It is not a *Trinity of Persons*, but it resembles that Trinity which exists in man, who was created in the image of
God. In man there are the body, the soul or intellectual
essence, and the mode of operation. So Swedenborgians
say there is one God possessing a trinity of relations; the
Father is the spirit, the Son is the bodily form, the Holy
Ghost is the form of operation. They do not believe that
Christ is eternal as the *Son of God;* but that his Son-
ship only belongs to his nature, as it was born and existed in this world. Say they: Physiologists know that a
child receives his soul from his father, and his body from
his mother. Hence, as Christ had no human father, he
had nothing corresponding with a human soul, but was
animated directly and only by a divine nature.

Regeneration they believe to be merely the restoration
of the disarranged harmony of the soul, and bringing it
back to its original resemblance of the nature of God.
The object of the existence of the Christian Church in the
world is simply to aid in the accomplishment of this result. They do not regard the death of the body as a calamity or curse, but as a natural stage in the progress of
human beings, which puts an end to their probationary
state, and separates the soul from its material companion.
Immediately after death the spirit assumes a *spiritual
body* in place of the material body it has left behind. At
death men enter an intermediate state, in which their real

character is developed, according to the preponderance of
its moral tendencies. Those who possess a greater degree
of good than of evil qualities will be so developed and improved as to become perfect, and be ultimately admitted
to Heaven. Those in whom the evil is the greater, get
worse and worse, till they are consigned to endless perdition.

Swedenborgians deny the doctrine of election and reprobation, and believe that God has left salvation free to
all, and that all have an equal chance of attaining Heaven. Salvation, according to Swedenborg, is not salvation from punishment, but salvation from *sinfulness*. Those
who attain Heaven associate hereafter with angels, and in
their associations and spiritual employments the happiness
of Heaven consists. The wicked who finally enter endless
perdition become devils, or wicked angels, just as the redeemed finally become good angels in Heaven. None enter the other world entirely good, or entirely bad; yet
there is no repentance or reformation possible after death.
The final change and permanent situation of mankind in
the next world is accomplished by degrees; and during
its progress the departed are neither in Heaven nor Hell,
but in the " world of spirits," which enables them to have
intercourse, under certain restrictions, with human beings
in this world. They believe that there is a resurrection
after death, which is not the resurrection of the natural
or material body, but of the *spiritual* body from the natural. This resurrection, they think, generally takes place
on the third day after death, when the flesh becomes rigid
and putrefaction commences. They base this opinion on
the declaration of Saint Paul, that "*there is a natural
body and there is a spiritual body.*" When the spiritual
body rises from the material, it possesses spiritual organs;
and so all the things which exist naturally in the natural
world, *exist spiritually in the spiritual world.* Thus the
spiritual world is in fact a perfect counterpart of the natural or material world. There, spiritual things affect the
spiritual organs of men, as natural things affect their natural organs in this world. Hence Swedenborg was of

opinion that many persons who die, on their first awakening in the other world, do not know that they *are* in that world. But those who have their spiritual senses opened in this life, as was the case with him, are already able to see the spiritual persons and things of the other world, and hold communication with them, as he himself pretended to do. The resemblance between the things of the other world to those of this, is the foundation of that doctrine of "Correspondences," which is one of the leading principles of the system of Swedenborg. He also taught that every person carried into the future world his own future condition, his own heaven or hell, in the moral qualities which he possessed.

Swedenborg was a voluminous author, and it is the labor of a lifetime to become thoroughly acquainted with the mysterious and extraordinary doctrines which he taught, and to develope them to their full and legitimate extent. In consequence of the abstruseness of his system, his followers have never been numerous. Their form of worship is simple and devoid of ostentation; hence it has little whereby to attract the superficial and shallow. The leading man in the denomination in this country is Professor George Bush, the Biblical commentator. They have a few churches scattered throughout the Eastern and Middle States, and the aggregate number of their members in this country is about ten thousand. They are usually classed among the un-orthodox sects, in consequence of their views on the subject of the Trinity.

HICKSITE QUAKERS.

In the year 1827, a great schism occurred in the Quaker community in the United States. This event was brought about by the activity and the preaching of the celebrated Elias Hicks, who at that time succeeded in accomplishing a result to which the labors of several preceding years had been devoted. Hicks was a man of superior ability, a good speaker, and a reasoner of great logi-

cal acumen and power.   The tendency of his mind was
toward freedom and progress in religious belief; and having
become dissatisfied with some of the cardinal doctrines
which were held by the old Quakers, he commenced to investigate, to free himself from old trammels, to adopt new
conclusions, and to preach them in the various assemblages
of the Quakers which he attended.

The consequence of this course of conduct was that,
while on the one hand, he made adherents and converts
to his views, he excited the hostility and opposition of the
rest, and thus two parties were gradually formed in many
of the meetings or congregations throughout the Middle
and Northern States.   In April, 1827, the controversy
came to an open and public separation.   Various disputes
subsequently arose from time to time between the two
parties, some of which referred to doctrine, but more to
the possession of the property which belonged to the Quaker commmunity.   The Hicksites, regarding themselves
as the real Quakers, demanded possession of the meeting-
houses and graveyards of the sect—a requisition which
was resisted with great earnestness by the old Orthodox
Friends.

In the progress of time these disputes were settled in
various ways; in some instances the Hicksite, and in others
the Orthodox Quakers obtaining the victory.   The new
sect established meetings of their own in Pennsylvania,
New York, Ohio, Indiana, and Maryland.   Their dress,
language, church government, and usages are the same as
those of the opposite party, of which we will speak in another article.   In point of numbers, the Hicksites in this
country are about equal to the Orthodox, though in England the former are very few, and their existence there is
scarcely known.   In this country the Hicksites or Progressive Friends are not inferior to the other party in intelligence, wealth, and social influence; though, in consequence of their peculiar doctrines, they are looked down
upon by the various Orthodox sects with dislike and aversion, and are classed by them among the condemned and

anathematized communities, such as Unitarians, Universalists, and Swedenborgians.

The doctrinal peculiarities of the Hicksites are as follows: They assert that there is a tendency to progress and development in true Christianity, according to the teaching in Mark iv. 28: "There is first the blade, then the ear, after that the full corn in the ear." In following out this principle, they contend that they have arrived at the belief that the light of Christ, and of religious truth, is within them; that Christianity is wholly spiritual, the perfect ante-type of the visible, legal dispensation of the Old Testament; that under the gospel, the temple, the altar, the sacrifices, the water, the fire, and the entire worship, are spiritual, which require neither priest, nor book, nor ritual, nor outward ceremonies of any kind to render them efficacious and salutary. In a word, they carry out the doctrine of the entire spirituality of the gospel dispensation, to its utmost possible development.

The Hicksites also deny the doctrine of the Trinity. On this point they differ essentially from the Orthodox Quakers, who have been believers of the Trinity from the the first. Hicks argued with great earnestness and force against the doctrine, and his opinion on this subject was one of the chief grounds of the separation which occurred. He also denied the doctrine of satisfaction, or a vicarious atonement, and held that such a thing as "imputed righteousness" did not, exist. On both these fundamental points of orthodoxy the Hicksites are heterodox, and entirely alienated from other Quakers. They are not much more orthodox in their opinions respecting the inspiration of the Scriptures. They believe that these are profitable for doctrine and reproof, yet that they are an emanation only from the fountain of truth, not that fountain itself; that they are a dead letter unless accompanied by the light and influence of the inward monitor and the divine Spirit, and that their entire usefulness depends on the existence of the divine Spirit within the mind of the reader when perusing their contents.

As to *divine worship*, the Hicksites believe that to worship God in a formal manner, with regular and established ceremonies, is an abomination; and, like the Orthodox Quakers, they have frequently silent meetings, where nothing is either said or done. They have no singing or other outward worship, and they hold a hireling and mercenary ministry in greater abhorrence and disgust, if possible, than the Orthodox. The discipline which governs the community is the same in form as that of the other branch of the Quakers, consisting of monthly, quarterly, and yearly meetings. They marry, and are given in marriage, and bury, like other Quakers. They have Yearly Meetings in Philadelphia, New York, Genessee, Baltimore, Ohio, and Indiana; though like the other branch of the Quakers, they do not increase, but rather diminish in numbers with the progress of time. There is nothing in their system of worship or discipline which is adapted to win proselytes; and the energy and zeal of other sects are constantly attracting the young of both sexes to their more impressive or more edifying modes of worship and of association. It is the fashion of the orthodox religious sects to stigmatize the Hicksites as nothing better than outright infidels. This charge is very unjust and erroneous.

ORTHODOX CONGREGATIONALISTS.

The Orthodox Congregationalists constitute one of the most numerous and important sects in this country. They predominate throughout New England, and are identified with much that is excellent in New England intelligence, enterprise, wealth, and influence. The general principle which designates this sect in opposition to all others is, that they believe in the entire independence of each church or congregation of all other congregations; that each society is a complete whole within itself; and that no association or connection with any other church is necessary to constitute a community truly organized according to the apostolic model.

The first Congregational Church of which we have any record was one which was organized in England, by one Robert Browne, in 1583. His followers were first called "Brownists," from their leader; but, as their views were greatly abhorrent to the members of the English establishment, which was at that time flourishing under the royal favor of Elizabeth, they were immediately visited with persecution and broken up. Browne and a few followers escaped to Holland, and there organized another church in accordance with their views. After some years Browne returned to England, renounced his religious opinions and connections, and became, as his enemies said, openly immoral. Yet, in spite of his own apostasy, the doctrine which he had preached gradually acquired favor in England and about the time of the accession of James I. they numbered twenty thousand. At that period more stringent laws against dissenters were passed by that weak monarch, and the Brownists were compelled to flee, to escape the rod of persecution. Among their number was John Robinson, a man who afterwards became famous among them. He led another colony of his brethren over to Holland, and founded a Congregational Church at Amsterdam. Ten years elapsed, and, for various reasons, Robinson and his friends—prominent among whom were Elder Brewster, Bradford Carver, and Winslow—resolved to seek a freer home in America. It was about the year 1620, that they were able to execute their purpose; and the first feeble colony of exiles, after traversing the wide and stormy ocean, reached the memorable rock of Plymouth. In 1829 an additional colony was formed at Salem. Elder Brewster was the first pastor of the Plymouth church, and from that church colonists went forth from time to time, which established other societies based on the same principles of ecclesiastical government. Such were the churches at Marshfield, Duxbury, and Charlestown.

The principles on which New England Congregationalism was founded are as follows:—1. That no Christian church ought to contain more members than can conveni-

ently worship in one building.   2. That the true test of
membership in a Christian church is belief in Christ and
obedience to his precepts.   3. That any number of such
persons have the right to constitute themselves into a
separate church, and that such an organization will possess every necessary element of validity.   4. That, having
thus associated themselves together, they have the right
to elect their own officers and invest them with legitimate
functions.   5. That these officers are of three orders—
pastors or teaching elders, ruling elders, and deacons.
6. That elders being chosen, derive all their authority
from the members, and depend for its continuance on their
will and pleasure.   7. That all elders and all churches
are equal in the extent of their powers and privileges.
8. That the sacraments of the church are two—Baptism,
which is to be administered both to infants and adults, by
sprinkling, and the Lord's Supper, which is to be received
sitting at the table.   9. That Christians should not observe any holydays except the Sabbath, though they
might have occasional days for fasting and thanksgiving.
10. That the functions of the ministry and the rights to
preach may be validly bestowed upon any person chosen
for that purpose by the members and officers of any Christian church; that no clerical succession of any kind is
necessary for that purpose; that the ceremony of ordination does not in itself *confer* the functions of the ministry,
but that it is merely a *recognition* of the existence of those
functions, which are, in fact, already and solely conferred
on the preacher by his election by any Christian society
as their pastor.   11. That each congregation is totally independent, in all respects, both as regards its spiritual
and temporal affairs, of all other Christian churches.

The history of Congregationalism is closely identified
with the history of New England.   It extended more and
more widely as the country became more thickly settled.
In 1638, Harvard University was founded at Cambridge.
In 1646, common schools were established by law in
Massachusetts.   In 1648, the Cambridge Platform was

adopted by an assemblage of Congregational ministers, which set forth what is usually known as the Calvinistic system of theology.   At that time the number of churches of this sect in Massachusetts was thirty-nine; in Connecticut, four; in New Hampshire, three.   The Quakers first made their appearance in Massachusetts in 1656.   They were two women, who had fled thither from Barbadoes, hoping to find religious toleration and freedom in the land of the Pilgrims.   They were cruelly disappointed, were arrested and imprisoned for witchcraft, and afterwards sent back to Barbadoes.   Others arrived, three of whom were subsequently punished with death, though their only offence was their religious opinions.

In 1708, in consequence of various disputes on religious subjects which had, from time to time, agitated the religious community, an assemblage of ministers and elders convened at Saybrook, in Connecticut, who eventually adopted a confession of faith, which is generally known as the "Saybrook Platform," and is a symbol of great authority and importance among Congregationalists.   It differs from the Cambridge Platform in its teachings in reference to church government and discipline, and the desirableness of having ecclesiastical councils and associations, though the doctrinal opinions set forth are the same. In regard to the matter of associations, the modern Congregationalists believe that it is *useful* for neighboring churches to send their ministers and elders occasionally to a meeting for the purpose of consultation and religious exercises, and for the purpose of giving advice in reference to doubtful and difficult matters of doctrine or discipline which may be submitted to their examination and discussion; but these associations never possess any but mere advisory power, and the independence and supremacy of each separate congregation is carefully maintained.   It is also the custom now for the candidates for the ministry to be examined and ordained by these associations; whereas the custom formerly was, as we have said, for each congregation to ordain its own minister.

An important event in the history of New England Congregationalism was the appearance of Unitarianism among some of its most eminent clergymen. This event first occurred in 1760. In 1785 several churches in Boston openly avowed their Unitarian sentiments. Soon after Harvard University passed under the control of the new sect, and from that time till the present the progress of Unitarianism has been constant. The latter are also Congregationalists in their form of church government; and hence it is that the Congregationalists are frequently designated at the present time by the single epithet of "Orthodox." Most of the chief colleges of New England—such as Yale, Dartmouth, and Amherst, and the best theological seminaries, such as those of Andover and Bangor—are under their control, and hold a high place among the literary institutions of the country. The Congregationalists at the present time number about sixteen hundred churches, about fifteen hundred ministers, and three hundred thousand communicants. Among their most eminent men have been Drs. Cotton Mather, Emmons, Edward Griffin, Leonard Woods, N. W. Taylor, and Moses Stuart.

ORTHODOX FRIENDS, OR QUAKERS.

THIS remarkable sect had its origin in England, about the middle of the seventeenth century. As is well known, their head and founder was George Fox, who was born in 1624, at Drayton in Leicestershire. He was the son of a weaver, a pious member of the Episcopal or Established Church. Fox, who seems to have been by nature of a devout turn of mind, received a religious education. His disposition towards solemnity and gloom appears to have been confirmed by the occupation of a grazier, to which he was consigned at an early age. While tending his sheep in solitude and silence, his thoughts dwelt upon the state of religion around him. He came to the conclusion that worldliness, formality, and vanity were the chief characteristics of the prevalent religion; and at the age of nineteen he felt convinced that he had received a divine command to separate and exclude himself from the wicked world, and devote his time to spiritual exercises. Accordingly, during five years he led a wandering, unsettled, and lonely life. At the end of this period, he began to preach his peculiar. doctrines. He first held forth at Manchester, in 1648, and so great was his zeal and earnestness, that he soon acquired many converts and adherents. The name by which they proposed to be known was that of "Friends,"a term taken from the third Epistle of St. John, i. 14: "*Our friends salute thee*," &c. But at Derby the epithet of "Quakers" was first applied to them, by way of contempt, on account of the fact that their voices in speaking were very tremulous, and because they shook and quaked prodigiously in their meetings, in consequence of their religious terrors and conscientious fears.

Persecution became the portion of Fox and his followers, from the commencement of their career. This was especially the case during the reign of Charles the Second, when licentiousness and folly reached an unparalleled extent in England. When James the Second ascended the throne, the severe laws against dissenters were relaxed, and the Quakers were protected from the penalties which they had previously suffered from their refusal to take an oath in judicial proceedings; their simple affirmation, instead of it, was received; and a plan was adopted by which the levying of tithes was reconciled to their peculiar scruples. Fox continued to labor with great zeal during his. whole life. He traveled twice to the continent, and once he visited America. In 1655, meetings of his disciples were held in Holland and several other countries, and at the time of his death his sect was a well known and highly respectable body.

Among the converts whom Fox had made, and whose personal qualities added distinction to his society, were Robert Barclay and William Penn. The former wrote the celebrated work entitled "An Apology for the Quakers."

Penn was more distinguished by his achievments as a politician and founder of the colony of Pennsylvania. Penn was born in London in 1644. He was of an opulent and distinguished family. Being sent to Oxford University, he was converted to Quakerism by happening to attend a sermon by one Thomas Lee, a zealous and able preacher of that faith. Soon afterward he was expelled from the University in consequence of his religious views. He was also discarded by his father, because he refused to take off his hat before the king and him. In 1668, Penn boldly came forth as a Quaker preacher, and soon after he was sent as a prisoner to the Tower, where he remained in confinement seven months.

An important event in the external progress of the Quakers was the establishment by Penn of the colony which still bears his name. Charles II. was indebted to the father of Penn, in a considerable sum of money; and this he paid off by granting to Penn the right and title to an immense tract of land in North America, then called New Netherlands. This territory Penn proposed to settle with colonists of his own religious belief. He drew up the constitution of his proposed colony, containing twenty-four articles, which, while they granted perfect religious liberty to all, embodied the spirit and principles of his own belief. In 1682, Penn first visited the province. He remained two years and then returned to England. Subsequently he returned to Pennsylvania, and resided for forty years in the colony which he had founded, his head-quarters being at Philadelphia, the capital of the new State. During this long period he nurtured the community around him with wise laws, and admirable regulations of all kinds. He lived in peace and friendship with the Indians; and Philadelphia prospered in an eminent degree. At that time nearly all the inhabitants were Quakers. In 1710, Penn returned to England, where he died July, 1718. Beside being the founder of one of the most remarkable and flourishing colonies which ever existed, Penn was an eminent Christian, a voluminous writer, and an influential statesman. Among the works which he wrote, were "The Sandy Fountain Shaken," "Innocency with Her Open Face," &c. The Society of Friends are greatly indebted to him for the favorable influence in their behalf which he exerted in England, as well as in the colony of Pennsylvania. Notwithstanding the recent attack of the historian, Macaulay, on the character and conduct of Penn, it is true beyond cavil that he was a wise, benevolent, and pious man.

The doctrines for which the Quakers contended through many persecutions, and which the "Orthodox" portion of them still generally entertain, are as follows: That God has given to all men sufficient internal light, by which they can, if they will, attain their salvation; that this light is as universal as the diffusion of sin; and is capable of leading all who have not the outward means of salvation, to a saving knowledge of the truth. They believe that God condemns none but such as refuse the means of salvation which have been offered to them.

They hold that the Scriptures are not the principal source of religious truth and knowledge, nor the primary rule of faith and conduct, yet that they are useful as far as they go. The chief source of spiritual instruction is the Holy Spirit, and the law of the spirit of truth which is engraven on the hearts of men; in other words, their consciences—which is the inner light. Nor do they believe that immediate revelations from God to men have ceased; but that a measure or portion of the Spirit of God is given to every one, at this day and till the end of time. They believe that as all spiritual knowledge comes directly from God, those who have a gift of preaching ought to preach; that they ought always to obey the impulse of the Spirit to that effect; and as women are as much the recipients of the Holy Ghost as others, they should also preach as well as men. They refer for proof of the truth of this doctrine to the fact that St. Paul speaks of women who had labored with him in the gospel; and that Philip had four daughters who prophesied.

Hence female preachers hold a prominent place in the public services of this sect; and they gratify their unconquerable dispositions *to talk*, as well in public as in private;—and generally their preaching has more intelligence and point in it than the preaching of the male Quakers.

They believe that all external ordinances and ceremonies, including Baptism and the Lord's Supper, should not now be observed by Christians; that they were only enjoined for a time; that they should be observed or commemorated only spiritually; that the baptism which should be applied is the baptism of the Spirit, of which John's baptism was a mere figure; and that the breaking of bread should not actually be repeated any more than the washing of the disciples' feet, or the anointing the sick with oil. This they hold, because, as the gospel dispensation was purely a spiritual institution, the external and visible observance of these or any other ceremonies is useless and inconsistent.

The Orthodox Quakers believe in the Trinity, the vicarious atonement of Christ, the constant presence of the Holy Spirit in the hearts of true believers, the fall of Adam, man's depravity and utter inability to save himself without the aid and inspiration of the Holy Spirit; and that men are justified, not by their own righteousness, but by the righteousness and the mediation of Christ. They believe in the divine inspiration of the Scriptures, and are fiercely opposed to a "hireling ministry." The latter personage is the object of their special hostility; and they regard those as little better than wolves and robbers who preach for money, and who generally govern their choice of a field of labor, as they say, in accordance with the greater or the less amount of salary which they can procure. In support of this doctrine they quote the language of Christ: "Freely ye have received, freely give;" taking no account whatever of that other Scripture which saith, "The laborer is worthy of his hire:" "He that ministereth at the altar should live of the altar."

The moral principles and maxims of the Quakers are those which are the most peculiar and singular. They regard it as wrong to use the ordinary terms of courtesy which are prevalent around them, such as "your honor," "your lordship," "esquire," nor do they ever pay formal compliments of any kind. They refuse to kneel or prostrate themselves to any human being, or even to bow the body or uncover the head. They condemn all superfluity or show in apparel, in the furniture of their houses, or in anything else. They forbid indulgence in all games and sports, all amusements and recreations, as being inconsistent with religious gravity; and they think that even jesting and vain talking are pernicious to the soul and partake too much of the spirit of the world. Yet wealth, the great pursuit of the world, they grasp at as eagerly as any one; and when they cheat one another, and are told of it, they excuse it by saying, "Friend, I merely outwitted thee." They think it unlawful to take an oath in courts of justice, to engage in war or conflicts of any kind, or to resist evil in any way. They are great opponents of slavery, and are more radical and extreme in their condemnation of this peculiar institution than any other Christian sect. Their religious assemblies are frequently what are termed "silent meetings." Unless the Holy Spirit directly move them, or any of them, to speak, they keep quiet and say nothing. Yet it is presumed that, during this interval, they are doing a good deal of thinking. They inculcate charity and benevolence toward all men; and as regards the members at least of their own community, they practice what they teach; for they generally help those who are in want, and relieve them from the miseries and inconveniences of poverty.

The Society of Friends is governed and regulated by a system which is different from that of any other denomination. They have a discipline which consists of four different grades of assemblies; the least and lowest are those which are called Preparative Meetings, where the matters of business which require the attention and action of the members of the society, are first proposed and arranged. These affairs are then referred to the second assembly, called the Monthly Meetings, which are composed of several Preparative Meetings, and have higher executive authority. The decisions of the Monthly Meetings are then referred to the Quarterly, composed of several Monthly Meetings, which have higher jurisdiction still. After these have made their decisions, they are referred to the Yearly Meeting, which includes a large number of Quarterly Meetings, which examines into the condition and interests of the whole body, and pronounces its final determination, from which there is no appeal. Moral discipline among the members is administered through the agency of "overseers," who keep an eye on their conduct, admonish the delinquent, and who report any improper conduct first to the Preparative Meeting, and also, if thought necessary, to the other higher meetings successively.

The principal Yearly Meetings belonging to the Orthodox Quakers are those which convene in London for England; in Dublin for Ireland; in Newport for Rhode Island and New England; in New York city for that State; that for Pennsylvania and New Jersey is held in Philadelphia; in Baltimore for Maryland and others; for Virginia, North Carolina, Ohio, and Indiana, in those States respectively. These various assemblies represent a body of actual members, who number about a hundred and forty thousand persons, which is a smaller aggregate than that which existed twenty-five years ago.

According to the views of Quakers, their children inherit naturally a birthright and membership in the church, and no ceremony or rite is used for the purpose of initiating them into the connection. This birthright they retain through life, unless they forfeit it by some act of immorality, or some violation of the disciplinary regulations of the sect. Marriages are all celebrated or enacted among their members in public meeting, without much circumlocution or ceremony, each party merely declaring that they accept the other as a husband or wife. This usage comports with the idea of the marriage relation which the Courts of Pennsylvania have decided to be the only legal one, namely, that marriage is simply a civil contract, and need not, to be valid, be invested with any ecclesiastical or clerical sanction.

It is somewhat singular that, while the Quakers condemn all kinds of established forms in religion, they themselves are the most rigid formalists in the world; for they go so far as to display a peculiar formality in their dress, in their mode of living, and even in their speech. This inconsistency results from the fact that, after all, it is impossible for any assemblage or society of persons to remain associated together, without some distinctive features and badges of identity and resemblance. But Quakers, in yielding to this law of our nature, adopt a formalism in regard to such things as render them objects of ridicule to the worldly portion of the community, and impede their increase and their usefulness.

ARMINIANS.

THE Arminians are those who hold the tenets of Arminius, a Protestant divine, born in Holland in the year 1560, and latterly a professor of divinity at Leyden.

Thinking the doctrines of Calvin in regard to free will, predestination, and grace, contrary to the beneficent perfections of the Deity, Arminius began to express his doubts concerning them in the year 1591; and upon further inquiry, adopted sentiments more nearly resembling those of the Lutherans than of the Calvinists. After his appointment to the theological chair at Leyden, he thought it his duty to avow and vindicate the principles which he had embraced; and the freedom with which he published and defended them, exposed him to the resentment of those that adhered to the theological system of Geneva.

His tenets included the five following propositions : *First*, That God has *not* fixed the future state of mankind by an absolute, unconditional decree, but determined, from all eternity, to bestow salvation on those who, he foresaw, would persevere to the end in their faith in Jesus Christ, and to inflict punishment on those who should continue in their unbelief, and resist to the end his divine assistance. *Secondly*, That Jesus Christ, by his death and sufferings, made an atonement for all mankind in general, and for every individual in particular: that, however, none but those who believe in him, can be partakers of this divine benefit. *Thirdly*, That mankind are *not* totally depraved, and that depravity does not come upon them by virtue of Adam's being their public head, but that mortality and actual evil only are the direct consequences of his sin to posterity. *Fourthly*, That there is no such thing as irresistible grace in the conversion of sinners. And *Fifthly*, That those who are united to Christ by faith may fall from their faith, and forfeit finally their state of grace.

Thus the followers of Arminius believe that God, having an equal regard for all his creatures, sent his Son to die for the sins of the whole world; that men have the power of doing the will of God, otherwise they are not the proper subjects of approbation and condemnation; and that, in the present imperfect state, believers, if not particularly vigilant, may, through the force of temptation, fall from grace, and sink into final perdition.

The Arminians found their sentiments on the expressions of our Saviour respecting his willingness to save all that come unto him; especially on his prayer over Jerusalem, his sermon on the mount, and above all, on his delineation of the process of the last day, where the salvation of men is not said to have been procured by any decree, but because they had done the will of the Father, who is in Heaven. This last argument they deem decisive; because it cannot be supposed that Jesus, in the account of the judgment day, would have deceived them. They also say that the terms used in the Romans respecting election, are applicable only to the Jews as a body, without reference to the religious condition of individuals, either in the present or future world.

The asserters of these opinions in Holland were vehemently attacked by the Calvinistic party, which was prevalent at the time; and in 1610 the Arminians addressed a petition to the States of Holland for protection, from which fact they derived the name of Remonstrants. In the year 1618, nine years after the death of Arminius, the Synod of Dort was convened by the States General, and a hearing given to both parties. But the Synod was succeeded by a shameful persecution of the Arminians.

THE MORAVIANS, OR UNITED BRETHREN.

CORRECTLY speaking, the Moravians are the oldest of the Protestant sects, inasmuch as they are historically descended from the first dissenters from the Roman Catholic Church. They may trace their origin to John Huss, the Bohemian Reformer, who, together with Jerome of Prague, created commotions and disturbances in the Mother Church, in Bohemia, in the fifteenth century, and who were afterward burned at Constance in return for their reforming zeal. The sect languished in obscurity and amid persecutions during several centuries, driven to and fro, with various and disastrous fortunes, until at length, in 1722, they besought the protection of a German nobleman, Count Zinzendorf, who possessed a large estate at Herrnhut, in Upper Lusatia. The Count gave them a secure asylum; permitted the whole community to settle within his jurisdiction; and from that period the prosperity and good fortune of the society take their date.

At Herrnhut the Moravian community was organized upon a novel plan, which combined social features of a marked and peculiar character, together with religious and theological unity. They formed a body which they supposed resembled the primitive apostolical congregations. They adopted as articles of faith what they regarded only as the fundamental and chief doctrines of Christianity; while their social arrangements provided for a community of goods such as is referred to in the Acts of the Apos tles in reference to one or two of the primitive churches. Zinzendorf seems to have been a man admirably adapted to the organization of the new sect; and he devoted not only his time and labor, but also his wealth, to the firm establishment of principles and arrangements on which the sect was based.

The doctrinal belief of the Moravians has always been a very undefined and unsettled one. They have constantly avoided much argument or dispute on these points; and the sect has maintained an ascetic aspect, which is very peculiar. Their distinctive features are pre-eminently of a moral and practical nature, and also of a social character, by which, indeed, they are widely distinguished from all other denominations. They profess to receive the Augsburg Confession—the symbol of the Lutheran Church—as the clearest statement of their religious belief, or of the belief, at least, of the majority of them; and hence, in the absence of any creed of their own creation, they point to that Confession as the one which comes nearest to their views.

The chief doctrinal opinions of the Moravians may be defined as follows: They believe in the inspiration of the Scriptures, and their ample sufficiency and authority as the sole revelation of divine truth. They believe in the Trinity, and give great prominence to the history, nature, works, sufferings, and death of Christ. They carefully avoid abstruse argument or discussion on every topic of theology; and endeavor to make practical piety the principal aim of all their religious teachings. They hold to the vicarious atonement; they reject the doctrine of absolute predestination; and they believe in a future state of rewards and punishments. Yet few of their doctrinal tenets are clearly or accurately defined; and very great liberty and variety of belief are allowed among them.

The most remarkable features connected with the Moravians refer to their social arrangements, and to the government of their society as a church. During the earlier period of their existence as a sect, they not only

practiced and observed a community of goods among all
the members, but even the marriages of the young people
were arranged in the most singular manner.   They were
not permitted to court and marry like other people, but
their matches were disposed of *by lot*.   No man or woman
knew who was to be the partner of his or her life, until
the moment before the indissoluble union took place ; and
we may well imagine the strange feelings which such a
disposition of matrimonial matters would frequently produce.   Sometimes the blooming and beautiful maiden
found herself tied to the object of her secret aversion and
contempt; and so also the vigorous and athletic young
man suddenly discovered that some feeble, deformed, and
sickly creature, of the opposite sex, had become his companion for life.   A more stupid and detestable mode of
arranging the domestic and social relations of any community, could not possibly be imagined ; and we think it a
fortunate circumstance that in later and present times,
the heads and leaders of the sect have had wit enough to
abolish so objectionable a feature of their discipline.

Where the Moravians form separate and distinct communities, their mode of living also is peculiar.   They banish
from among them all amusements of a sort which, as they
suppose, tend to produce worldliness and a neglect of the
growth of experimental piety, such as dancing, theatres,
balls, games of cards, and even the public promiscuous
assemblages of their own young people.   In the Moravian
communities in Europe, the unmarried men and boys all
reside together in buildings which are separate from the
rest ; and the same is true also of the unmarried women
and young girls.   The dwellings of the former set are
called the "Single Brethren's Houses;" those of the
latter the "Single Sisters' Houses."   In these dwellings
various trades and occupations are pursued, suitable to
men and women.   An elder or superintendent has absolute authority over each house, and all the inmates are
required to be industrious and well employed.   This arrangement exists in Europe in order to prevent the too

frequent meeting of the young people of the two sexes, and to diminish the disposition to early and precipitate marriages; but in this country this feature of the sect has been relaxed, and Moravians live like other people; asso-ciate with their neighbors and fellow-members; and the youth of the society are permitted to approach each other without restraint or apprehension. In this country the marriage by lot is also abolished, and Moravians have the same freedom of choice which other civilized people enjoy. They provide for the aged unmarried women, who are supported in the "Widows' Houses," when they are no longer able to maintain themselves. These employ their time in ornamental needle-work, which is sold, and the proceeds devoted to the support of the houses in which they reside. This arrangement prevails even in this country only where the sect live together in distinct and isolated communities, such as at Bethlehem and Nazareth in this State. The young people are carefully educated, and the schools of the Moravians are highly esteemed. The chief government of the communities is conducted by a Board of Elders, composed of both sexes. This Board generally decides all differences between the members of the community, of every sort. The Elders do not preach, that office being confined entirely to the regularly ordained ministers.

As a substitute for all sorts of amusement and social intercourse in these distinct Moravian settlements, public exercises are held every evening in the churches, which consist of reading the Scriptures, narrating accounts which have been received of the adventures of their absent missionaries in various portions of the world, and sacred music. The last occupies a very prominent part in the religious services of this sect, and is the chief attraction connected with their religious and social organization. They likewise observe and celebrate the leading festivals of the Protestant Churches, such as Christmas, Easter, and Pentecost. They also have a "Love Feast" previous to every communion, at which the whole congregation partake together of coffee, or chocolate, and cakes, in token of their fraternal feeling and union. On Easter morning the Moravians observe a ceremony which is peculiar to themselves:—they meet together in the grave-yard at sun-rise; religious services accompanied with music are held; and the death of all those members who have departed during the preceding year, is commemorated. They also endeavor at all times to divest death of its gloomy and repulsive attributes. Like the Quakers, they observe no outward signs of mourning; but unlike them their funeral processions proceed to the grave, accompanied with solemn instrumental music. Their grave-yards are usually laid out to resemble a garden; and the last long home of the living, or rather of the dead, is invested with everything which could diminish its mournful and repulsive aspects.

When members of the Moravian communities violate any of the duties which devolve upon them, or are immoral, the elders first reprove them, and expostulate with them. If this process does not reform them, they are then excluded from the Lord's Supper. If they still remain incorrigible, they are then expelled entirely from the society. The highest dignitaries in the church are the bishops, who ordain the ministers or preaching elders. They have also the order of deacons, into which young preachers are admitted at the commencement of their pastoral labors. The Moravians claim to have the unbroken apostolic succession from the time of Christ to the present, by tracing its current through the Bohemian Brethren, the immediate disciples of John Huss.

The most remarkable feature connected with this small yet respectable sect is the singular zeal which they have always exhibited in reference to missionary work. Possessing very limited resources, they have been extremely liberal in this respect. When Count Zinzendorf died, in 1760, after presiding over the community at Herrnhut for more than a quarter of a century, the whole concern was insolvent, although he had expended all his estates in the service of the denomination. Yet by subsequent thrift, these difficulties were surmounted, and immense sums have since been expended in the enterprise of evangelizing the world. They have but six thousand members in the United States, of little account in a pecuniary point of view; yet the same lavish expenditure for the heathen prevails among them here. Even in Europe their actual membership does not exceed fifteen thousand persons. In the United States the whole number of their congregations is twenty-three, and the number of their clergymen is twenty-five. They have here also two bishops, and four principals of schools. Their literary institutions are situated at Bethlehem, Nazareth, Lititz, in Pennsylvania; and at Salem, in South Carolina. A few churches of this sect exist in England, and several even in Ireland. Their missions at present are among the negroes in the Danish West India Islands, at Jamaica, Barbadoes, in Surinam, in Greenland, in Labrador, among the Hottentots and Caffres in Southern Africa, and among the Indians of Upper Canada and Arkansas.

THE METHODIST EPISCOPAL CHURCH.

THIS prominent and active denomination of Christians owe their origin, as a sect, to the celebrated John Wesley. This remarkable man was born in the year 1703, and was educated at Oxford University, in England. He entered the Established Church, and was duly ordained a priest, or presbyter. At first he had little more conception of the true nature of religion, or the real responsibilities of his office, than the majority of the clergy around him, who were a worldly, selfish, and dissipated set of men, in general, who knew much more about card-playing, fox-hunting, and theatre-going, than they did about the truths and duties of Christianity.

About the year 1729, John Wesley "became converted." He then saw what he supposed to be the horrors of the existing state of religion and morals in the Established

Church, and among its clergy of all ranks; and he determined, if possible, to effect a reformation. He proposed to accomplish this work, not so much among the clergy themselves as among the people. He discerned that the kind of preaching which at that time was prevalent in the churches was utterly useless in awakening sinners to a proper sense of their moral condition, and that the vast majority of the churches were nothing less than religious dormitories, where humdrum preachers were paid high salaries for putting people comfortably to sleep twice on Sundays. Wesley's first efforts were made in the vicinity of Oxford, where he soon rendered himself very unpopular with the astonished and disgusted authorities and students of the University. He had been converted by perusing the writings of William Law, the well-known mystic. His brother, Charles Wesley, shared his religious feelings. The term "Methodist" was applied to them by their enemies, in consequence of their orderly and composed demeanor. In 1735, among other persons who had joined them was George Whitefield, the celebrated pulpit orator. Yet a fundamental difference of opinion existed between Whitefield and Wesley, the former being a rigid Calvinist, and the latter an Arminian; and this difference of sentiment characterized the followers of each when they subsequently became associated in sects. In 1735, the two Wesleys visited Georgia in order to preach to the colonists; but no very important results followed this expedition.

After their return to England, the Wesleys continued their reforming labours in London, in 1739, and their zeal and success constantly attracted more of the public attention, and increased the number of their converts. No preaching like theirs had ever before been heard in England. Their purpose was to arouse the consciences of the people, and convince them of the necessity of a new life and a regenerated nature, in order to escape future perdition. The earnestness and sincerity with which they preached, produced prodigious results. Wesley established congregations in various portions of England. He himself was a great itinerant; and while he did not possess the same degree of eloquence which Whitefield displayed, he was equally successful in making converts. Yet he always claimed to be a member of the Protestant Episcopal Church; and this fact is proved by an incident which occurred some years after he began his career as a reformer. There was a famous man in that day, a prominent person in the ranks of elegance and fashion, named "Beau Nash," who, like all other dandies, was a hopeless fool. He happened to be present when Wesley preached at Bath, and going up to him before the sermon, he asked him, "By what authority he undertook to preach?" Wesley replied, "By that of Jesus Christ, conveyed to me by the Archbishop of Canterbury, when he laid hands on me and said, 'Take thou authority to preach the gospel.'" Nash replied that "he was acting contrary to the laws of the Church." "Did you ever hear me preach?" said Wesley. "No, sir," replied Nash, "I judge of you by common report." "Well, sir," answered Wesley, "I should be more charitable than to form my opinion of *you* by common report." This incident serves to show at once the severity of the preacher, the stupidity of the dandy, and Wesley's regard for his clerical authority, as obtained from the Protestant Episcopal Church, which he always highly valued.

Wesley ordained the new preachers of the sect which he gradually organized by virtue of this authority. Before the period of his death, in 1791, when he expired at the age of eighty-eight, his followers were numerous throughout England, though they generally belonged to the poorer classes of the community. His labors did a vast amount of good, not only among those who became members of his own communion, but also in the Established Church; for the zeal of these "Ranters," as they were frequently called, put to shame the hypocrisy, worldliness, and wickedness of the Established clergy, and showed both them and the people who attended their services the necessity of a reform at least in external propriety; and a few were led to sincere reformation and repentance, both of the clergy and the laity.

The first congregation of Methodists in the United States was formed in the city of New York in 1766. It was composed of a few Irish immigrants, who had become converts in their native land. Among them was a local preacher named Embury, who preached in his own house, at first, to an assemblage of five persons. Very soon their numbers increased, and it became necessary for them to obtain a larger place of worship. They next hired a rigging loft in William Street in that city, and continued their exercises. In the progress of time they found the accommodations afforded by this house insufficient; and the members, who were generally poor and obscure persons, petitioned the Mayor and other prominent citizens of New York for pecuniary assistance. This was afforded them, and in 1768 the Methodists obtained a lot on John Street, and erected a house of worship sixty feet in length and forty-two in width, which they named "Wesley Chapel." This was the first Methodist meeting house ever built in the United States, and their first sermon was delivered in it in October, 1768, by Mr. Embury. Immediately afterward the congregation sent a request to John Wesley that he would send them a more competent preacher. In answer to this petition, Richard Boardman and Joseph Pillmore sailed for this country and commenced to labor, the former in New York, the latter in Philadelphia. This event occurred in 1770.

From this auspicious beginning, the growth of Methodism in this country was rapid and extensive. The zeal of their preachers and members, the earnestness and excitement which characterized their religious exercises, their powerful appeals to the fears and hopes of their hearers, their whole system of church government and ecclesiastical discipline, which were then on a small scale, pretty much the same as they are now, were all admirably adapted to impress their audiences, to influence the less

intelligent and educated class of hearers, and to make converts among the multitude.

In 1771, Francis Asbury and Richard Wright were sent
out by Wesley to aid the infant sect. These persons traveled extensively throughout many of the colonies, preaching and making converts, and founding congregations. So
successful were they, that, in 1773, there were ten traveling preachers and more than eleven hundred members
connected with the churches. Probably no sect ever existed in the United States which increased *in numbers* as
rapidly as the Methodist; and the reason of this is the
fact that their method of religious worship is eminently
aggressive, and they use every possible means and expe-
dients which can be devised to impress the feelings of
their hearers. This peculiarity they very frequently carried to an absurd and pernicious extreme; and the loud
noises and the tumultuous disorder which sometimes characterized the public worship of the Methodists, were the
result of a "zeal without knowledge," the evil consequences of carrying a good thing to an unjustifiable degree
of perversion.

At the time of the Revolution the Methodists were a
well-known and numerous sect. After its conclusion some
trouble occurred among them, in consequence of their
separation from the Methodist churches in England. Previous to the Revolution, all the Methodist preachers who
were in this country were merely "lay preachers," and
had no power or authority to ordain any persons to the
ministry. It now became necessary to adopt some means
by which a valid commission might be obtained by the
American churches, for the purpose of ordaining men to
preach without being dependent upon their brethren in
England. At first, John Wesley had some scruples as to
his power or authority to comply with this desire, and some
doubts as to the propriety of the measure. At length,
however, all his doubts were removed; and in September,
1784, assisted by other Methodist preachers whom he had

himself previously ordained, he consecrated the Rev. Thos. Coke, a clergyman of the Church of England, as a Superintendent, and ordained Richard Whatcoat and Thomas Vasey to the office of elders, and sent them to the United States to carry on the work. These men itinerated through the country, established many churches in various States, and ordained many preachers as elders and deacons. Mr. Coke was, in fact, the Bishop of the church in this country, for the term "superintendent" was merely another name for bishop. The question here arises: How could Mr. Wesley, who had only received priest's orders, confer orders on another, while diocesan bishops only possessed that right, according to the views of the Church of England, to which Wesley still professed to belong? And, more especially, How could he, a mere presbyter, confer on another (Mr. Coke) the functions of an office which was higher than his own—those of a bishop? This objection, however, was answered by asserting that, in the New Testament, the functions and the offices of presbyters and bishops were the same; and that if a man were a presbyter he was also a bishop, and could confer upon another the office which he himself possessed. Yet to this position another objection applies, which is that this position is contrary to the teachings of the Church of England, to which Wesley professed to adhere in doctrine; and hence he should either have abandoned that connection, or renounced a theory which that church condemned.

Having thus obtained full authority, as they supposed, to ordain, and preach, and carry on a separate and independent organization, the Methodists of this country continued their career with greater success than before. In 1792, they held their first General Conference, having control over all the district conferences of the church. At that time there were two hundred and sixty-six regular preachers, and sixty-five thousand members, in the United States. New circuits had been formed in various portions of the country; and annual conferences had been organized in the different States, all of which sent delegates to the General Conference. At the present time the Methodists have about five thousand regular and traveling preachers, about nine thousand local preachers, and one million church members, of whom about two hundred thousand are negroes in the Southern States.

The *government* of the Methodist Church is an anomaly in itself, yet admirably adapted to promote the ends and views of the organization. They have bishops, whose jurisdiction extends over the whole church conjointly, and is not confined to any one particular State. They have also presbyters, or traveling and regular preachers, and local preachers and deacons. Their churches are divided into various *classes*, each class consisting generally of a dozen members. Each class is presided over by a class-leader. They have also *stewards*, who are chosen by the quarterly meeting conference, who have charge of all the moneys contributed by the members for the support of the preachers; and *trustees*, to whom is committed the care of the church property. The bishops are elected by the General Conference. The presiding elders have control over the several circuits and stations which compose a district. The "leaders' meetings" are attended by all the class-leaders belonging to one church or station. The preachers receive but a very small yearly salary. In the country and towns each one is allowed a hundred dollars for himself, a hundred for his wife, sixteen dollars for each child under seven years of age, and twenty-four dollars for each child above that age. A further allowance is made for the table expenses and fuel of the preacher's family. In cities, where such sums would be of little account for the support of a family, the sums allowed are generally much larger. The bishops receive no greater remuneration than the itinerant preachers.

During the last few years the Methodist clergymen have been generally better educated than they were formerly, and they have established and conducted several literary institutions for this purpose. They have the Wesleyan

University, located at Middletown, Connecticut; Dickinson College, at Carlisle; Allegheny College, at Meadville; and others of minor importance. Their most remarkable and valuable institution is their Book Concern, located in New York, which has published a vast number of religious works and accumulated an immense capital. The separation which took place between the Northern and Southern portions of the church, in consequence of differences on the subject of slavery, does not seem to have inflicted much injury on either branch.

The doctrines of the Methodists are well known. These do not differ from the teachings of other orthodox sects, except on two fundamental points. They are strenuous Arminians, holding to "free grace," or the theory that the offers of the gospel are made to all men alike, and not to an elect few; and that all may repent if they desire to do so. They also believe in "Christian Perfection," or the ability of Christians to attain such a state of holiness in this world that they will become entirely free and exempt from all moral turpitude. In many respects the Methodists are among the most zealous and useful of religious sects. Among their most eminent preachers have been Adam Clarke, Bishop Soule, Drs. Bascom, Durbin, Maffit, and Olin.

SAINT SIMONIANS.

CLAUDE HENRI, Count de St. Simon, of the ancient family of that name, born in 1760, was engaged during the greater part of his life in a series of unsuccessful commercial enterprises, a traveler, and in the early portion of his career a soldier in America; but having dissipated a considerable fortune, and being unable to draw the attention of the public to a variety of schemes, political and social, which he was constantly publishing, he attempted suicide in 1820. He lived, however, a few years longer, and died in 1825, leaving his papers and projects to Olinde Rodriguez. St. Simon's views of society and the destiny of mankind are contained in a variety of works, and especially in a short treatise entitled the *Nouveau Christianisme*, published after his death by Rodriguez. This book does not contain any scheme for the foundation of a new religion, such as his disciples afterwards invented. It is a diatribe against both the Catholic and Protestant sects for their neglect of the main principle of Christianity, the elevation of the lower classes of society; and inveighs against "l'exploitation de l'homme par l'homme," the existing system of individual industry, under which capitalists and labourers have opposite interests and no common object.

The principle of association, and equal division of the fruits of common labor between the members of society, he imagined to be the true remedy for its present evils. After his death these ideas were caught up by a number of disciples, and formed into something resembling a system. The new association, or St. Simonian *family*, *was* chiefly framed by Rodriguez, Bazar, Thierry, Chevalier, and other men of talent. After the revolution of July, 1830, it rose rapidly into notoriety, from the sympathy between the notions which it promulgated, and those entertained by many of the republican party. In 1831, the society had about 3,000 members, a newspaper called the *Globe*, and large funds.

The views of the St. Simonian family were all directed to the abolition of rank and property in society, and the establishment of associations, of which all the members should work in common and divide the fruits of their labor. But with these notions, common to many other social reformers, they united the doctrine, that the division of the goods of the community should be in due proportion to the merits or capacity of the recipient. Society was to be governed by a hierarchy, consisting of a supreme pontiff, apostles, disciples of the first, second, and third order.

It was not until about this period (1830) that they began to invest these opinions with the form and character of a religion; but shortly after having done so they went

into great extravagances. There was a disunion among
them as to the fittest person to preside over the society; and
consequently Messrs. Bazar and Enfantin divided, for
some time, the duties and dignity of the "Supreme Father," as he was termed. But on the 19th of November,
1831, Bazar and many others left the association, of which
Enfantin remained the supreme father. Their doctrines
and proceedings now became licentious and immoral to
the last degree. On the 22d of January, 1832, the family
was dispersed by the government. Enfantin and Rodriguez were tried on various charges, and imprisoned for a
year. The former afterwards collected again a part of
the society at Menilmontant; but it was dissolved for want
of funds. Some former members of the St. Simonian association attained places of rank and consideration; some
of the most extravagant traveled to the East; but Enfantin, we believe, has now no followers.

NEW SCHOOL PRESBYTERIAN CHURCH.

THE New School branch of the Presbyterian Church
claims to be a genuine and consistent descendant of the
Presbyterian Church as it exists in Scotland, asserting at
the same time that the Old School are the schismatics who
have departed from their ancient hereditary faith. According to this assumption, the history of the Presbyterian
Church in Scotland and the United States until the great
division of 1830, will apply to the New School Church as
well as to the Old; and hence we may fitly continue the
history of the former by commencing with the separation
in question, and describe the career of the New School
branch from that time till the present.

Previous to the year 1830, the Rev. Albert Barnes
was pastor of the Presbyterian Church at Morristown,
New Jersey; and while residing there he preached and
published a sermon on "The Way of Salvation," which
excited remark, as it seemed to teach a theory somewhat
different from that set forth in the "Confession of Faith."

The matter, however, attracted but little attention until Mr. Barnes received a call from the First Presbyterian Church of Philadelphia, inviting him to assume the pastoral charge of it. The case was discussed by the Presbytery of Philadelphia in April, 1830; and at length the call was admitted by that body according to Presbyterian usage, but accompanied by a protest against it, which was signed by twelve members. After Mr. Barnes' removal to Philadelphia, a complaint was made by the aforesaid twelve to the "Synod of Philadelphia," based on the protest which they had previously made, setting forth the fact that Mr. Barnes had been settled and received by the Presbytery, notwithstanding the fact that he had taught heretical doctrines in the sermon entitled "The Way of Salvation," and demanding an investigation of the case. The matter was fully discussed in the Synod; after which the whole subject was referred back again to the Presbytery. The latter debated the questions involved at great length; and, after due deliberation, expressed their disapproval of the doctrine defended by Mr. Barnes, and appointed a committee to confer with him for the purpose of convincing him of his error, and bringing him back to a knowledge and confession of the truth.

Mr. Barnes and his friends appealed from this decision to the General Assembly, in 1833. The questions involved, both of doctrine and discipline, were fully investigated by that body, who eventually reversed the proceedings of the Synod of Philadelphia, and confirmed the acts of the preceding year. This decision brought the dispute again before the Synod for final examination, and the result was that the Synod annulled the decisions of the General Assembly, and dissolved the Second Presbytery of Philadelphia, which the Assembly had organized in accordance with the wishes of the friends of Mr. Barnes. After some further attempts to compromise and arrange the existing difficulties, which were unsuccessful, the contest was brought to a crisis by the action of the Rev.

George Junkin, a member of the Presbytery of Newton, who preferred a charge against Mr. Barnes in a regular and formal manner, before the Second Presbytery of Philadelphia, to the effect that he had taught dangerous errors and heresies contrary to the word of God, in his recently published "Notes on the Romans." After a full investigation of the charge, with all that endless volubility of argument and harangue which generally characterizes the meetings and the proceedings of Presbyterial bodies, the accused was acquitted by a decisive majority. This decision of course satisfied nobody who was of the opposite opinion; and an appeal was at once taken to the Synod of Philadelphia, which convened in 1835. After another interminable outlay of speeches, the Synod reversed the decision of the Presbytery, and condemned it as contrary to truth and righteousness, while they censured Mr. Barnes' new doctrines as contrary to the teachings of the Presbyterian Church, and in opposition to the instructions of the word of God; and they further suspended Mr. Barnes from the functions of the ministry. From this sentence Mr. Barnes of course appealed to the General Assembly of 1836.

When this body met, they were deluged with all manner of "complaints," "appeals," "protests," and "memorials," having reference to this dispute. Eventually, after one of the most protracted and violent discussions known in the history of the churches in this country, the Assembly rescinded all the acts of the Synod of Philadelphia, absolved Mr. Barnes from all censure, removed the sentence of suspension which had been pronounced upon him, and proclaimed in substance that the theories which he taught in his aforesaid books were in accordance with Scripture and the standards of the Presbyterian Church. This decision only increased the alienation and bitterness which already existed between the two parties in the Church, and it was evident that these troubles would not end there. The differences which divided the two belligerent parties may be described in brief as depending upon,

or resulting from, the way in which they severally interpreted the "Confession of Faith," one party adhering to
a *strict* interpretation, and the other a more *lax and liberal*
one.   Both factions now prepared themselves for a grand
and decisive conflict in the ensuing General Assembly of
1837.

A week previous to the opening of the Assembly, an in-
formal Convention of Ministers was held in Philadelphia,
for the purpose of comparing views and discussing the
matters in litigation.   This convention sent the result of
their deliberations to the General Assembly, immediately
after its opening, in a document which was entitled a
"Testimony or Memorial," and in it they condemned as
erroneous a long list of subjects, which they supposed
would probably come up for subsequent discussion—such
as sixteen doctrinal errors, ten departures from the order
of the Presbyterian Church, and five invasions of Christian discipline.   They also set forth their views of some
necessary reforms, which comprised measures such as these:
The abolition of the Plan of Union which then existed with
the Congregationalists, and which had been adopted in
1801; the discontinuance of the American Home Missionary and Education Societies; the separation from the
church of all presbyteries and synods which contained un-
sound and disorderly members; the separation from the
church of all presbyteries and synods which were not organized on strictly and exclusively Presbyterian principles;
and the requisition on all candidates for the ministry that
they shall make an explicit acceptance of the Confession
of Faith and Form of Government of the Presbyterian
Church.

The Convention having sent in their memorial to the
Assembly of 1837, the latter approved of all its views
and suggestions, and carried out the "reforms" which it
had recommended.   The doctrinal views which the convention condemned and submitted to the Assembly were also
censured and pronounced in opposition to the teachings
of the Presbyterian Church.   As the document which sets

these alleged errors forth is one of the most extraordinary and remarkable which has ever been elaborated in the history of any Christian church, and as it is rarely to be found at the present time, we will insert it for the edification of our readers :

" I. God would have been glad to prevent the existence of sin in our world, but was not able, without destroying the moral agency of man ; or, that for aught which appears in the Bible to the contrary, sin is incidental to any wise moral system.

"II. Election to eternal life is founded on a foresight of faith·and obedience.

" III. We have no more to do with the first sin of Adam than with the sins of any other parent.

"IV. Infants come into the world as free from moral defilement as was Adam when he was created.

" V. Infants sustain the same relation to the moral government of God in this world as brute animals, and their sufferings and death are to be accounted for on the same principle as those of brutes, and not by any means to be considered as penal.

"VI. There is no other original sin than the fact that all the posterity of Adam, though by nature innocent, or possessed of no moral character, will always begin to sin when they begin to exercise moral agency.   Original sin does not include a sinful bias of the human mind and a just exposure to penal suffering.   There is no evidence in Scripture that infants, in order to salvation, do need redemption by the blood of Christ and regeneration by the Holy Ghost.

" VII. The doctrine of imputation, whether of the guilt of Adam's sin, or of the righteousness of Christ, has no foundation in the word of God and is both unjust and absurd.

" VIII. The sufferings and death of Christ were not truly vicarious and penal, but symbolical, governmental, and instructive only.

" IX. The impenitent sinner by nature, and independently of the renewing influence or almignty energy of the Holy Spirit, is in full possession of all the ability necessary to a full compliance with all the commands of God.

"X. Christ never intercedes for any but those who are actually united to him by faith; or Christ does not intercede for the elect until after their regeneration.

"XI. Saving faith is the mere belief of the word of God, and not a grace of the Holy Spirit.

"XII. Regeneration is the act of the sinner himself, and it consists in a change of his governing purpose, which he himself must produce, and which is the result, not of any direct influence of the Holy Spirit on the heart, but chiefly of a persuasive exhibition of the truth, analogous to the influence which one man exerts over the mind of another; or regeneration is not an instantaneous act, but a progressive work.

"XIII. God has done all that *he can do* for the salvation of all men, and man himself must do the rest.

"XIV. God cannot exert such influence on the minds of men as shall make it certain that they will choose and act in a particular manner, without impairing their moral agency.

"XV. The righteousness of Christ is not the sole ground of the sinner's acceptance with God; and in no sense does the righteousness of Christ become ours.

"XVI. The reason why some differ from others in regard to their reception of the gospel is, that they make themselves to differ."

The Convention pronounced these " errors unscriptural, radical, and highly dangerous," which in "their ultimate tendency, subvert the foundation of Christian hope, and destroy the souls of men."

The session of the General Assembly of 1837, was not long enough to complete the schism of the church, and the final dissolution did not take place till the meeting of that body in 1838. Besides the irreconcilable doctrinal differences which existed between the two opposing factions, other causes of dispute arose. The Moderator of the Assembly refused to entertain a motion which was made to receive the Commissioners who had been chosen and sent from the four Synods of Genesee, Geneva, Utica, and the Western Reserve, because the members of those Synods were not supposed to be rigidly Presbyterian, and because their correspondence with the Assembly had been previously suspended by a vote of the Assembly of 1837, in accordance with the suggestion of the "Convention" already referred to. When this extreme degree of rigor was exhibited by the Moderator of the General Assembly, the New School party deemed that the proper time had at length arrived for them to secede and separate themselves from a body of whose acts and views they so little approved. Accordingly it did so; they withdrew from the Assembly, organized themselves in the edifice of the First Presbyterian Church, (Mr. Barnes',) elected a Moderator and clerks, and thus commenced a separate and independent ecclesiastical existence, which still continues to the present day. They are sometimes termed the "Puritan" party in the Presbyterian body, in opposition to the "Scotch" party, which term is applied to the Old School faction. The General Assembly of the former meet once in three years, that of the latter once each year.

Since this memorable separation, the two Churches have greatly flourished; though the Old School have increased more rapidly than the New. The differences of doctrine between them may be described simply thus: the New School are not quite as extreme Calvinists as the opposite party; though the distinction between them is in truth so slight, that it is almost impossible to define it clearly. Both parties claim to be purely Calvinistic, and disclaim any admixture of Arminianism in their views. They differ most materially on the subject of slavery. As a large majority of the members of the Old School Church live in Southern States, that Church has declared authoritatively by her Synods and Assembly that slavery is right, allowable, and even an institution recognized and permitted in the Scriptures. As a large majority of the members of the New School Church live in Northern and Western States, that Church has decided by its several tribunals that slavery is utterly wrong, condemned by the word of God, atrocious, and justifiable by no law human or divine. The literary institutions of the New School Church are the Theological Seminaries at Auburn, the Union Seminary in New York city, Lane Seminary at Cincinnati, that at Marysville, Tennessee, and the Western Reserve College, Ohio. The General Assembly has under its jurisdiction twenty synods, about one hundred and five presbyteries, fifteen hundred ministers, two thousand churches, and about two hundred thousand regular communicants. Among the eminent men belonging to the New School Church are Drs. Nathan S. S. Beman, Ezra Stiles Ely, Albert Barnes, Lyman Beecher, and Edward Robinson.

THE DUTCH REFORMED CHURCH.

THE Protestant religion was established in Holland in the year 1573, after that country had achieved its liberties, and thrown off the yoke and tyranny of Spain, through the agency of the heroic William of Nassau, Prince of Orange. Previous to this period the doctrines of the Reformation had been gradually introduced, and isolated churches had been formed throughout all the United Provinces; but it was not till the period just named that the Protestant religion became established and recognized by law. It then took the name of the Dutch Reformed Church, and became the national religion of North Holland.

The first members of this communion who existed in this country were the original settlers and inhabitants of Albany and New Amsterdam, in the colony of New York. The name of the latter town was subsequently changed to that of New York—the predecessor of the present vast metropolis of wealth, vice, misery, and mud, of this country.

Soon after the arrival of the Dutch immigrants in the colony of New York, they sent to the Classis or Synod of Amsterdam, desiring that they might be supplied with ministers. This request was conveyed by several captains who were in the service of the Dutch West India Company, who at that time visited the port of New York. The Classis of Amsterdam took the matter into consideration, and finally selected several young clergymen to visit the distant colony and reside in it.

The first Dutch Church in the United States was erected in New York, on the spot now occupied by the Battery, at the foot of Broadway. Other authorities, however, contend that a small religious edifice had been built shortly anterior to this, near the lower end of Stone Street, about the year 1620. Another church was afterward constructed, in 1642, in what was then the Fort. The next in the order of time was a church erected by Governor Stuyvesant on his farm, or, as it was called in the Dutch language, his bowery. It is from this source that the celebrated street now known as the Bowery, in the city of New York, derived its appellation. The first ministers who supplied these churches, and preached only in the Dutch or Hollandish language, were Dominies Bogardus and J. and S. Megapolensis. These clergymen came from the Classis of old Amsterdam; and it was this fact which afterward gave rise to the fierce and long dispute which subsequently ensued between the Dutch churches of New York and the Classis of Amsterdam, when the latter claimed the right of exercising an absolute jurisdiction over the Dutch churches in the colony. Two parties arose in those churches, one of which was in favor of recognizing the claim of the Classis of Amsterdam, and the other in favor of regarding the churches in New York as perfectly free and independent of foreign jurisdiction. According to the view of those who were in favor of the Amsterdam Classis, all questions of devotion and discipline, and all casses of ecclesiastical controversy, were to be sent over to the old country for adjudication; and all young candidates for the ministry should be sent there also to be educated and ordained. These obligations were regarded as a great and unnecessary burden by the Native American party in the church, and were strenuously opposed by them. The controversy which ensued was one of the longest and most determined which has occurred in the history of religious denominations in this country. At length the zeal of the parties expended itself; a compromise was gradually adopted; and the authority and dominion of the foreign Classis dwindled down till at last it amounted to nothing more than a recogition of fraternal alliance.

The Dutch Reformed Church remained the leading sect in New York till about the year 1670, when the Protestant Episcopal Church began to attain a superior power and importance. In 1664 the province was surrendered by the Dutch to the English monarch, and from that period the tide of influence turned; although the majority of the inhabitants of the colony were Dutch, and were connected with the Dutch church. As might naturally be expected, an intense spirit of jealousy arose between the two churches in New York, which has not even yet entirely passed away. In 1693 the project began to be mooted by the then Governor Fletcher, of making the Episcopal Church the established religion of the colony; he proposed that all the citizens should be taxed, without exception, for its support; and in a short time, through his agency, the Assembly passed a law to that effect, which attained the purposed end in the counties of New York, West Chester, Richmond and Queen's. This state of things continued from 1694 till the year 1776—a period of eighty-two years. The Dutch Reformed Churches, beside maintaining their own preachers, were compelled by taxes to aid in the support of the clergymen of the Church of England. This miniature copy of the ecclesiastical despotism of the established church in England continued to exist until the outbreak of the American Revolution, when it fell to the ground, along with many other detestable monuments of the avarice, tyranny and ambition of Great Britain.

After the Revolution, the Dutch Church in New York began to flourish greatly. About the year 1771, Dr. John H. Livingston appeared upon the stage of action; and his superior talents and influence were thenceforth devoted, during a long life, to the promotion of the interests of this church. His is the most eminent name which occurs in the history of the Dutch Reformed sect in this country. He was to them what Dr. Henry M. Muhlenberg was to the Lutheran Church. Dr. Livingston was a man of unusual ability, of great prudence, and was admirably adapted to accomplish much good in the then formative and transition state of the Dutch Reformed Church. He, together with other men of like views and spirit, went to work and drew up a plan of church government for the future and independent control of the churches. The leading men in the sect at that time were Livingston, Hardenberg, Roosevelt, Westerlo, Romeyn, and Schoonmaker; and these having approved the form of discipline and government which Dr. Livingston had prepared, it was submitted to a convention of all the ministers and elders of the church in this country, and was ultimately approved by them. A copy was then sent to the great Classis of Amsterdam, in Holland, by whom it was also approved. By the attainment of this happy result, the harmony and unity of the churches were promoted, and the most favorable results attained.

The next important step in the progress of this church was the establishment of a college for the education of young ministers. Of this institution Dr. Livingston was elected President. In 1784 the old and almost defunct Queen's College, which was located at New Brunswick, was revived by the Classis; and their new college was incorporated into it. That institution, after various vicissitudes, still continues to exist, with a considerable share of prosperity. Its public buildings, libraries and philosophical apparatus, are all on a liberal scale. From the year 1816 till 1825, its exercises were wholly suspended, in consequence of pecuniary embarrassments. The eminent and venerable Dr. Milledoler was for many years afterward its President, and the worthy successor of Dr. Livingston. This establishment, which has a theological department connected with it for the purpose of educating young clergymen, is the chief literary institution belonging to the Dutch Reformed Church. In New York city some of the congregations of the sect are very numerous and wealthy; and they number among their members many persons occupying the highest positions of influence and importance in the community.

The doctrinal system held by the Dutch Reformed Church is that of extreme and ultra Calvinism. They believe in the Predestination of a few of the human family to eternal life, and the reprobation of a vast majority of them to eternal misery. They hold to the limited atonement of Christ; to man's entire and total moral corruption; to his utter inability to repent, unless it be in accordance with a divine and eternal decree to that effect; and to the final perseverance of the Saints—that is, if a person be once converted, it is impossible for him to fall away and come short of salvation. These doctrines were proclaimed by the great Synod of Dort, or Dordrecht, which convened in 1618, and were promulgated there in thirty-seven articles. They are the same as those which are set forth in the Heidelberg Catechism, which is the symbol of the German Reformed Church. The Dutch Church believes in the inspiration and sufficiency of the Scriptures as a rule of faith and practice for Christians. There is, in fact, no difference in doctrine between this sect and the Old School Presbyterian Church. Nor do they differ as to church government; for both believe in the parity or equality of all ordained ministers, and both are governed by Synods and a General Assembly, or what is the same thing, by Classes and a General Synod. Each congregation has its session, or consistory, which is equivalent to the vestries of other churches. The Deacons are entrusted generally with the secular affairs of the congregation. The only essential difference between the Dutch Reformed and the Presbyterian churches is, that, in the former, the Ruling Elders are always chosen to serve for *two years*, whereas in the latter they are elected for life.

The Dutch Church in this country holds a prominent place among the secondary sects. Her preachers are generally well educated; though sometimes clergymen are admitted from other denominations who are deficient in suitable theological attainments. They have twenty Classes, or Synods, and a General Synod. The number of members, or of persons who attend the churches of this sect, is about a hundred thousand. There are three hundred organized congregations and two hundred and ninety ministers in the United States. Among them are some clergymen of distinction, such as Drs. Bethune, De Witt, Knox, Milledolèr and Brownlee. Among the past and present laymen of the Church, the distinguished names occur of Van Rensselaer, Freylinghuysen, Roosevelt, Schuyler, Stuyvesant, and others. This sect has always been remarkable for its liberality of feeling toward other orthodox sects; and it is a singular fact that the Rev. Mr. Vesey, the first rector of Trinity Church in New York, was inducted into his office, in 1697, in the Dutch Church, in Garden street; that two Dutch clergymen, Messrs. Solyn and Nucella, officiated on the occasion; and that Mr. Vesey afterward conducted his public services in the Dutch Church, until the building of Trinity Church, which was then in progress, was completed. In 1779, during the Revolutionary war, the Dutch Church in Garden street was seized by the British troops and used as a hospital; on which occasion the vestry of Trinity Church reciprocated the favor, and tendered to the Dutch congregation the use of St. George Church for the purpose of holding their religious services therein. We doubt very much whether the Episcopal Church would exhibit the same fraternal feeling anywhere at the present day, to any of the "dissenters," even in their direst necessity.

HUGUENOTS.

In French History this name was given in the sixteenth century to the Protestants or Calvinists of France. The writers of that time were not acquainted with the true derivation of this popular epithet, to which they assigned various absurd etymologies. It is undoubtedly a corruption of the German "Eidgenossen," signifying the Swiss confederates.

The Huguenots arose in the year 1560, and greatly increased until the year 1572, in the reign of Charles IX., when at the feast of Bartholomew on the 24th of August, nearly eighty thousand Protestants were massacred in France, by the decree of this king. Twenty-six years afterwards, Henry IV., caused the Edict of Nantz to be passed, which enabled the Protestants to worship God agreeably to the dictates of their consciences. Their privileges were thus enjoyed by them to the time of the voluptuous and sensual reign of Louis XIV., when they were again persecuted, their churches destroyed, and thousands put inhumanly to death. From the best authorities it is said that near one hundred thousand were driven out of their own country during that reign.

Vast numbers found an asylum in England, who brought with them the manufacture of silks, which became a great source of wealth to the government of England. Many found refuge in the United States, particularly in South Carolina, and their descendants are among the most respected of American citizens.

THEOPHILANTHROPISTS.

This title was assumed by a society formed at Paris during the first French revolution. It is a compound word, derived from the Greek, and implies a profession of adoration towards God and love for mankind.

The object of the founders of this sect was to establish a new religion in the place of Christianity, which had been formally abolished in France by the Convention, and had lost its power over the minds of large classes of the people. The Directory granted these philosophical sectarians the use of ten parish churches in Paris, where they held meetings for religious service; at first on the Decadi, or revolutionary holiday, afterwards on Sunday. Their system of belief was a pure Deism; their service a simple liturgy, with some emblematical ceremonies. The following inscriptions were placed upon their altar:

FIRST INSCRIPTION.—We believe in the existence of a God, in the immortality of the soul.

SECOND INSCRIPTION.—Worship God, cherish your kind, render yourselves useful to your country.

THIRD INSCRIPTION.—Good is every thing which tends to the preservation or the perfection of man.

Evil is every thing which tends to destroy or deteriorate him.

FOURTH INSCRIPTION.—Children, honor your fathers and mothers. Obey them with affection. Comfort their old age.

Fathers and mothers, instruct your children.

FIFTH INSCRIPTION.—Wives, regard in your husbands the chiefs of your houses.

Husbands, love your wives, and render yourselves reciprocally happy.

"The temple most worthy of the divinity, in the eyes of the Theophilanthropists," said one of their number, "is the universe. Abandoned sometimes under the vaults of heaven to the contemplation of the beauties of nature, they render its author the homage of adoration and gratitude. They nevertheless have temples erected by the hands of men, in which it is more commodious for them to assemble and listen to lessons concerning his wisdom. Certain moral inscriptions, a simple altar on which they deposit, as a sign of gratitude for the benefits of the Creator, such flowers or fruits as the season affords, and a

tribune for lectures and discourses, form the whole of the
ornaments of their temples."

The attempt on the part of the Theophilanthropists to
found a new religion was a failure. In 1802, they were
forbidden the use of the churches of Paris by the consuls,
and then. ceased to exist.

GNOSTICS.

GNOSTICISM was a philosophical system of religion
which prevailed in the East during the first four centuries
of our era, and exercised great influence upon Christian
theology, giving birth to numerous and widely-diffused
heresies, and insinuating itself under a modified form even
into the writings of the most orthodox fathers. The origin of the system is involved in considerable obscurity; in
its leading principles it seems to point to the Oriental
philosophy as its genuine parent, but it is objected to this
solution that the fathers refer it, together with the errors
similarly introduced by Platonism, to a Greek origin, and
appeal to the cosmogonies of Hesiod and others, as the
real exemplars, from which it is imitated. It is to be re-
marked, however, that the fathers were universally ignorant of the Oriental philosophy; from which we may conclude that their opinion upon such a point is not necessarily conclusive. A modern solution conceives Alexandria
to have been the central point to which the speculations
of the Greeks and the Orientals converged, and from
whence they frequently re-issued, after having undergone
the process of fusion into a common mass. It is certain
that Alexandria was, during the time we have spoken of,
a celebrated resort of Gnostic opinions, both within and
without the Church.

The grand principle of this philosophy seems to have
been an attempt to reconcile the difficulties attending upon
the existence of evil in the world. Evil, it was supposed,
being the contrary of good, must be contrary to, and
therefore, the opponent of God; if the opponent of God,

then independent of him and coeternal. From the many imperfections which are involved in all outward and sensible objects, it was held that matter must contain in itself the principle of all evil. The human soul on the contrary, which aspires after, and tends to a higher and more perfect development, was held to be the gift of the Supreme Deity, imparted to man for the sake of combating against the material principle, and with the prospect of finally subduing it. From the Supreme God on the one hand, and matter on the other, succeeding philosophers produced various fanciful genealogies of superior intelligences, under the name of Æons—a Greek word, signifying properly, periods; thus representing these divinities themselves by a name expressive of the time and order of their generation, much as in our current language the term reign, or government, is frequently put for the king or ministers governing. The Demiurgus who formed the world out of matter, appears to have been an Æon derived from the evil principle. He was also the God of the Old Testament, who was considered by the Gnostics to be an object of aversion to the One Supreme God, to counteract whose machinations the Æon Christ was sent into the world. This is the earlier and simpler system, which is attributed to Simon Magus; the number of the Æons was fancifully multiplied in latter times, and an extravagant theory of morals founded upon the system. The object of this principally was, as may be supposed, to depreciate the honor due to the body, as being a part of matter, and to elevate the thinking faculty, or at least, to remove it from all consideration of worldly things. The Gnostics imagined that by assiduous practice of certain mental and bodily austerities, they could obtain an intuition of the divine nature, and dwell in communion with it; and this part of their system is adopted to a considerable extent by Clemens Alexandrinus, whose opinions, as expressed in the *Pœdagogus*, are very similar to those of a Pietist of more modern times.

The Gnostics split in process of time into various sects,

distinguished rather by the different cosmogonies they invented, than by any variation in principle. Of these, the principal were founded by Carpocrates, Basilides, Tatian, and Valentinus. The system did not survive the 4th century. The Christians seem sometimes to have adopted the general designation of Gnostics.

MORMONS OR LATTER DAY SAINTS.

NOTWITHSTANDING the general abhorrence and contempt with which the Mormons are regarded by all other religious sects, they adhere pertinaciously to their claim to be the true church ; and are in no degree daunted or discouraged by the universal hostility which is manifested against them. Their pretensions, and the prominent place which they have obtained in the history of religion, false and true, in the United States render it proper that we should include them in this work.

Joseph Smith, the founder of this remarkable community, was born in Sharon, Vermont, in December, 1805. In his youth his parents removed to Palmyra, New York, and he commenced his public career in the vicinity of that place. He never enjoyed the benefit of much education ; to "read, write, and cypher" was the extent of his scholastic attainments. He pretended that in September, 1823, he was favored with a divine vision, in which he saw a light, brighter than the noonday sun, and that an angel from heaven stood before him in person, who informed him that he was chosen by Christ to proclaim a new religion, an improvement upon the old Christianity ; that the end of the world, the latter day glory, was approaching, of which he (Smith) was appointed to be the herald and the forerunner. He was also informed that certain golden plates, containing a new revelation, and a record of the history of the Aborigines of this continent, were buried at a certain place under ground ; and he was commissioned to obtain, read, and interpret them, and proclaim their contents to the world.

It is pretended that these plates contained the Book of Mormon, which has since become well known. Smith began to give himself out, after this, as a teacher sent from God. His immediate relations and friends were those to whom he first preached; and after some time and labor, he succeeded in converting five of them to his creed. The first regular organization of a Mormon church took place in April, 1830, in the town of Manchester, New York. The translation of the contents of the golden plates, which were written in an unknown and mysterious language, Smith professed to accomplish by means of the " Urim and Thummim," the keys of light and knowledge which were miraculously imparted to him. The opponents of the Mormons, however, assert that the Book of Mormon is nothing more than a religious history, or romance, written by a person named Solomon Spaulding, who was a graduate of Dartmouth College, and became a clergyman, who afterward relinquished the profession and entered into commercial pursuits. Having removed to Ohio, he conceived the idea of writing such a work, and he spent three years in the execution of it. Two of the principal personages in the story are Mormon and Moroni, and from the former of these the book is named. In 1812 Spaulding brought the manuscript to Pittsburgh, and offered it to a bookseller named Patterson, for the purpose of publication. Before the matter could be arranged, Spaulding died, and the work remained in the possession of Patterson, who paid no further attention to it. After his death, in 1826, the manuscript fell into the hands of one Sidney Rigdon, by whose means it came under the inspection of Joseph Smith. From it Smith conceived the idea of founding a new sect, on the basis of the new revelation which this book was supposed to contain.

The Book of Mormon is an imaginary narrative of the early history of the American Indians, who, the writer endeavors to show, are the descendants of the ten lost tribes of the Jews. It gives a detailed account of their supposed journey from Jerusalem, both by land and sea, till their arrival in America, under the guidance of Nephi and Lehi. The identity of these two works was proved by the assertions under oath of several respectable persons who had heard Spaulding read portions of his manuscript, and who readily discovered that a perfect sameness and resemblance pervaded them. Yet the book answered the purposes of Smith admirably, for it was written in an antique style, was filled with Oriental allusions, and was singularly adapted to answer the preposterous end to which the Prophet subsequently appropriated it.

The great object which Smith professed to have in view in the establishment of his new sect was to prepare the way for the second coming of Christ to judgment, to usher in the millennium, and to gather a round him all those who, by belonging to his community, should be in a state of preparation to receive Christ, and thus become heirs of Heaven. His earnestness and zeal soon gathered around him a considerable number of adherents; and the first conference of all the "saints" was held in June 1830, at Fayette, N. Y. The palpable absurdity and falsehood of the whole concern soon surrounded Smith and his associates with many and bitter enemies, and they found it necessary to remove. They first emigrated to Kirkland, Ohio; but here their sojourn was short. After a few weeks they proceeded further west, and halted in Jackson county, Missouri. Here Smith resolved to found the "New Jerusalem." The surrounding country was beautiful, game and fish of all kinds were abundant, and everything seemed propitious for the purposes of the new prophet. Moreover, the Almighty had informed Smith, by a direct "revelation," that this spot was the one which was agreeable to him as the future home of the saints, and predestined for that purpose. A site for the temple was laid out and dedicated. Subsequently a printing press was obtained, and a paper commenced, called the *Evening and Morning Star*. At this time Smith's followers amounted to several hundreds. But soon the new sect was again surrounded and assailed by persecution; serious charges were made against their morals; the people around them rose in a mob; public indignation meetings were held; some of the Mormon leaders were taken, tarred, and feathered; and at last the whole community were expelled from the county. The greater portion of them took refuge in the neighboring county of Clay, where for a time they obtained a precarious resting place.

The Mormons remained in this locality about four years, at the end of which time their enemies became so determined and resolute in their persecutions that a new flight became necessary to their safety. On one occasion they were attacked by an armed band of several hundred persons at a place known as "Hawn's Mill," when twenty persons were killed and wounded. Threats were made to exterminate the whole community, and it became absolutely necessary for them again to remove. Then it was that these persecuted fanatics selected the place which they afterwards termed Nauvoo, Illinois, as their headquarters. The "saints" numbered at this period about ten thousand persons, including women and children; and soon afterward they increased to fifteen thousand by the addition of immigrants from the Eastern States and England. At Nauvoo they immediately commenced to lay out and build a regular town, to erect a temple, and provide other edifices suitable to their future plans and purposes. They had purchased the land on which the new town was erected; and as none but Mormons sought a residence among the inhabitants of the place, the whole community was of one mind, and the Mormon leaders possessed not only supreme religious influence, but all the secular and political power.

The temple which was erected at Nauvoo, was an extraordinary building. The foundations were laid in April, 1841, Joseph Smith officiated on the occasion. It was built of polished white limestone, being a hundred and thirty-eight feet in length, and eighty-eight in breadth. lt was surmounted by a spire a hundred and seventy feet nigh. In the course of several years the Mormons erected two thousand houses, public schools, and buildings; had established a paper known as the *Times and Seasons*, and had sent forth a large number of missionaries and elders to Europe and other distant countries to make converts. The success of some of these emissaries was extraordinary. Orson Hyde, and Heber C. Kimball, converted and baptised two thousand persons in England and Scotland during the course of a single year; though all their converts were among the lowest and most ignorant classes of the community.

Nauvoo and the Mormons thus continued to grow at a rapid rate; but with prosperity came its usual concomitants in such cases—spiritual pride and internal dissensions. It was about this period that Sidney Rigdon, one of the twelve apostles, first proposed and asserted the doctrine of the plurality of wives as being a part of the true Mormon creed. It is but justice to Joe Smith to say, that he was opposed to this innovation, and that it was not till after his death that it became a fully recognized and admitted principle and practice of the Mormon community. Rigdon was subsequently expelled from the church; but he had gained a large number of followers in his views, and a dangerous schism followed his exit. But the chief trouble of the Mormons at Nauvoo arose from the fact that, led on by Smith and his confederates, they assumed an independent jurisdiction in Nauvoo, refusing to acknowledge the authority of the State of Illinois within their limits; and a law was passed by the municipal authority of Nauvoo, severely punishing any stranger who, within the limits of the city, should use any disrespectful language toward the prophet or his religion. So great had the arrogance of these fanatics become, that, in 1843, Smith was publicly nominated and proposed by them as a candidate for the Presidency of the United States.

Various acts of injustice and tyranny gradually incensed the community in Illinois against the Mormons, which ultimately led to furious hostilities, and to the death of Smith and several of his leading associates. They were

arrested and confined at Carthage on the charge of destroying the office of a newspaper named the *Expositor*,
which had been commenced at Nauvoo by an anti-Mormon;
and also on the charge of treason against the authority
of the State of Illinois. While confined on this charge,
an infuriated mob attacked the jail; fire-arms were used;
and Smith, in attempting to escape through a window, was
struck by many balls, and fell to the ground a corpse.
Thus ended the life and personal career of one of the most
extraordinary men of the age, who without learning or
culture, or real ability of any kind, but by the mere force
of boundless craft and impudence, succeeded in establishing a sect which has obtained no obscure place in the history of the present century, and which bids fair to exist
for several generations to come.

It was after the death of Smith that Brigham Young,
the present leader of the Mormons, first assumed a prominent place in their community. He succeeded in being
chosen to the Presidency of the sect, in the defunct prophet's place; and he has since managed to retain his
supremacy. He resembles his predecessor in many important respects—in his want of education, his impudence,
his craft and cunning, and his ability to control the opinions and actions of his co-religionists. But the death of
Smith did not appease the vengeance of the enemies of
the Mormons. New persecutions were commenced, which
resulted finally in an attack on Nauvoo, and the expulsion
of the Mormons from Illinois in January, 1846. They
now resolved to seek a home beyond the Rocky Mountains. They had heard of the desirable features of a tract
in the distant and unoccupied territory of Utah, named
the Great Salt Lake Valley, and thither they determined
to travel. Four thousand persons constituted the company, who under the guidance of Brigham Young, commenced and completed this long and laborious journey.
In July, 1847, they reached Great Salt Lake Valley, and
began to build the town which they still inhabit.

The career of the Mormons since their removal to Utah

is so familiar to the public that it is unnecessary for us to dwell upon it here. We will conclude with a brief statement of their doctrines. They believe in the Trinity, entertaining on this point the orthodox Christian theory. They deny that men will be punished in any way for Adam's sin, or that they *fell* in consequence of Adam's transgression. They believe that all mankind may be saved by Christ's atonement, and by the use of the sacraments and ordinances of the Mormon church. These ordinances they hold to be Faith, Repentance, Baptism by Immersion, Laying on of hands, and the Lord's Supper. They believe that the true church should be organized like the apostolic church, with Apostles, prophets, elders, teachers, evangelists, &c., who should possess, like them, the power to work miracles, to heal the sick, &c. They hold that the Scriptures are inspired, and that the Book of Mormon is equally so, and possessed of an authority and sanctity similar to that of the Bible; that Israel will be literally " gathered in ;" that Christ will reign in person a thousand years on the earth; that his head-quarters will be with the Mormon saints, wherever they may be at the time of his advent; and that when he comes there will be a new heaven and a new earth. In addition to these points, they hold to the literal resurrection of the body, a literal judgment, and the reigning of the saints with Christ over the whole earth.

But the most remarkable feature of the Mormon creed is their " spiritual wife" doctrine. This theory is based on the idea that the future kingdom of the saints is to consist solely of their own posterity, and hence the more children a " saint" has, the more heirs of glory are created; and that women may become heirs of heaven also, by becoming "*sealed*" to a saint, and entering paradise with him. This *spiritual* relation, however, always involves the usual incidents which accompany ordinary marriage, and it is in fact nothing but a subterfuge to excuse and justify the monstrous sensual excesses of polygamous life, in which they indulge. Some of the saints are said to have as many as twenty, others thirty, and others even forty wives; and the having of more than one wife is the generally prevalent custom among the inhabitants of Salt Lake City. It is probable that the whole Mormon community now dwelling in Utah territory may amount to forty thousand persons; and the sum total of the sect throughout the world cannot, by the most liberal estimate, exceed a hundred thousand.*

NECESSARIANS.

THAT scheme which represents all human actions and feelings as links in a chain of causation, determined by laws in every respect analogous to those by which the physical universe is governed, is termed the Doctrine of Necessity. This doctrine has been attacked and defended with great zeal, in almost every period of speculative inquiry since the Reformation.

The inductive method of research, applied by Bacon and his contemporaries to the phenomena of nature, led very soon to the adoption of a similar method in reference to the phenomena of mind. The discovery, or rather the distinct re-assertion, of the law of association by Hobbes, and the ready solution which it appeared to furnish of states of consciousness, which, without it, would have seemed capricious and unaccountable, encouraged many philosophers to attempt its application to every province of the human mind. It is only in connection with this fact that the prevalence of Necessarian views in modern times can be adequately explained.

Without venturing an opinion on the merits of the question at issue, between the advocates of free will and of necessity, we are sufficiently assured of the historical fact, that the distinction between man and nature, between the actions of a self-conscious agent and the workings of

---

* See the Social, Religious, and Political History of the Mormons, from their Origin to the Present Time. Edited and Completed by Samuel M. Smucker, A. M. New York, 1857.

blind, unintelligent powers, was considered by the great philosophers of antiquity as the groundwork of their systems of morality, and as involved in the very conception of moral science. It was natural that this distinction should be felt to be a barrier to the progress of the exclusively empirical psychology to which we have alluded. To the historians of man's nature, the necessity of his actions appeared in the light of an hypothesis which lay at the very foundation of their inquiries, precisely as the natural philosopher is compelled to assume the regular recurrence of the same outward phenomena under the same circumstances.

The psychologist considers the states of which he is conscious, merely as they are related to each other in time; and, thus considered, it seems to him a mere identical proposition to assert that all that can be known of them is the order of their succession. If their succession were arbitrary or uncertain, nothing could be known of it, and the science which he professes could no longer have an existence.

It is in this consideration, rather than in the dialectic subtleties by which the doctrine has been sometimes defended, that the real strength of the Necessarian lies. So long as he can maintain the merely phenomenal character of human knowledge, he can reduce his opponents to the dilemma of either denying the possibility of mental science altogether, or of admitting the existence of those uniform laws which are its only object.

BAXTERIANS.

IN ecclesiastical history, the name of Baxterians is applied to those theologians, who adopted the sentiments of Richard Baxter on the subject of grace and free will, forming a sort of middle way between Calvinism and Arminianism. They never formed, strictly speaking, a sect, and the name is now disused; nevertheless, similarly modified opinions are common among Presbyterians at this day.

With the Calvinist, Baxter professes to believe that a certain number, determined upon in the divine councils, will be infallibly saved; and with the Arminian he joins in rejecting the doctrine of reprobation as absurd and impious; admits that Christ, in a certain sense, died for all, and supposes that such a portion of grace is allotted to *every* man as renders it his own fault if he does not attain eternal life.

Among Baxterians are ranked both Watts and Doddridge. Dr. Doddridge, indeed, has this striking remark: "That a being who is said not to tempt any one, and even swears that he desires not the death of a sinner, should *irresistibly* determine millions to the commission of every sinful action of their lives, and then with all the pomp and pageantry of an universal judgment condemn them to eternal misery, on account of these actions, that he may promote the happiness of others who are, or shall be irresistibly determined to virtue, in the like manner, is of all incredible things to me the most incredible!"

Baxter, who was born in Shropshire, England, in 1615, was an extraordinary character in the religious world. He wrote about one hundred and twenty books, and had above sixty written against him. His "Saint's Rest" is a work with which every intelligent Christian, of whatever denomination he may be, should be familiar. Though he possessed a metaphysical genius, and consequently sometimes made a distinction without a difference, yet the great object of most of his productions was peace and amity. Accordingly his system was formed, not to inflame the passions and widen the breaches, but to heal the wounds of the Christian church, under which she had long languished.

As a proof of this assertion, we take the following affecting declaration from the narrative of his own Life and Times: "I am deeplier afflicted at the disagreements of Christians, than when I was a young Christian; except the case of the infidel world, nothing is so sad and grievous to my thoughts as the case of the divided churches! And therefore, I am the more deeply sensible of the sinfulness of those who are the principal cause of these divisions. Oh, how many millions of souls are kept by their ignorance and ungodliness, and deluded by faction, as if it were true religion! How is the conversion of infidels hindered, Christ and religion heinously dishonored! The contentions between the Greek church and the Roman, the Papists and the Protestants, the Lutherans and the Calvinists, have woefully hindered the kingdom of Christ!"

THE SECEDERS OR ASSOCIATE REFORMED.

THE history of this sect, which is a prominent branch of the great Presbyterian family, illustrates forcibly the effects which result from that prodigious spirit of controversy and contention which has often characterized the Scotch churches. This sect arose in 1733, and was occasioned by the delivery of a sermon by the Rev. Ebenezer Erskine, at the opening of the Synod of Perth and Stirling, in Scotland, in which he condemned the then recent laws passed by General Assembly in reference to the settlement of ministers. He was afterward arraigned for trial, was censured, refused to submit to the censure, and then seceded from the Presbyterian or Established church. He, with half a dozen other ministers, formed themselves into a new and distinct body, which they called the "Associate Presbytery." They also published a document, in which they set forth their views and their motives for making the secession, which they called their Testimony.

A few years elapsed, and in 1746 a controversy arose among them in regard to the "Burgher's Oath," some of them contending that the taking of this oath was wrong, the others maintaining that it was right. They split into two parties eventually, who were known by the names of the Burghers and the anti-Burghers, each claiming to be the true Secession church. In 1796 the Burgher party again divided and underwent a sub-split, in consequence of a dispute among them in reference to the powers of the civil magistrate. One party was called the "Old Light Burghers," and the other the "New Lights." In 1806 the anti-Burghers were also agitated and eventually divided by a dispute on the same subject, and the two parties into which they formed themselves were called the "Old" and "New Light" anti-Burghers. Subsequently the fever for schisms subsided, and a contrary tendency took place among these people. The New Light Burghers and the anti-Burghers united in one body; and it is a curious circumstance that this union took place in the very same building in Edinburgh in which seventy years before the original separation had occurred. In 1837, the Old Light Burghers returned to the Established Church of Scotland. Such repeated divisions and subdivisions present no very favorable illustration of Christian unity and forbearance.

In 1751, the anti-Burgher Synod of Scotland determined to send several ministers of their sect to the United States, to supply the wants of a few members who had emigrated to this country. Several preachers were appointed, who eventually refused to obey the injunction. The Synod then, in 1752, indignantly passed a resolution to the effect that, should any minister or licentiate thereafter refuse to remove to the American colonies after they had been appointed by the Synod so to do, they should be expelled from the clerical office. This was an act of ecclesiastical tyranny which was a disgrace to the Christian name; for unless the Synod professed to act in the choice made directly under Divine inspiration, there could be no certainty that their resolution was infallible and always demanding unqualified obedience.

Accordingly, in 1752, the Rev. Messrs. Gellatly and Arnot were appointed to this mission, and they soon after reached this country. The latter, however, was not sent out to remain permanently, but to make a tour of observation in regard to the state of the sect in this country, and then return to Scotland. In the next year Rev. James Proudfit came over. In 1770, there were about ten ministers of this denomination in this country, who constituted what they termed the Associate Presbytery of Pennsylvania. From this date the churches and members of the Associate Reformed sect continued steadily to increase in the Middle States.

After the American Revolution, the scattered churches of this sect made an effort to consolidate themselves under an ecclesiastical government. In 1782, their ministers accordingly associated together, and took the title of the "Associate Reformed Synod of North America," and adopted a set of articles containing their doctrinal opinions. These were chiefly as follows: That Christ died only for the elect; that the gospel is addressed indiscriminately to all mankind; that the righteousness of Christ is the only ground of salvation; that civil government originates with God the Creator, and not with Christ the Mediator; that the administration of providence is given into the hand of Christ, and that the civil magistrates are appointed to execute the purposes of God's government and providence, and to promote the welfare of his spiritual kingdom; that the law of nature and the moral law taught in the Scriptures are the same, though the latter expresses the will of God more fully and clearly; and that therefore all magistrates should be governed by the teachings of Scripture in the performance of their functions; that no religious test, further than an oath of fidelity, should be required of the civil magistrate, except where the people make a religious test a condition of government; that the Westminster Confession of Faith, the Catechisms and Directory of Worship, shall be the future standards of the Church; that the American churches shall be independent of the Scotch Ecclesiastical Courts. The peculiar tone of these articles, which gave such prominence to the duties and relations of the *civil magistrate*, arose from the nature of the endless quarrels and squabbles which at that time agitated the members of the sect in this country, and which received an undue importance in the minds of the churches, in consequence of the controversies of which they were the everlasting theme.

In the history of all the American sects, a prominent event in their career is the establishment of a theological seminary, which should serve as a nursery for the preparation of the young men of the Church for the ministry. This remark applies to the Seceder denomination which we are now describing. In 1802, the leading preachers of the sect resolved to establish such an institution; and Dr. John M. Mason, the most eminent man among them, was appointed to visit England and Scotland, and solicit funds for the purpose. He did so, and obtained about six thousand dollars, which were chiefly appropriated to the purchase of a library. In 1804, the plan of the seminary was completed, and Dr. Mason was elected Professor of Theology. The institution was located in the city of New York, and we believe it was the first theological seminary ever established in this country. Under the direction of Dr. Mason it attained considerable success; but its prosperity was greatly inspired by subsequent events.

In 1822, a proposition was made by certain members of the Secession Church, and of the Dutch Reformed Church, that an union between the two sects should be effected. After some discussion on both sides the plan was abandoned, and another substituted in its place. This was an union between the Seceders and the Presbyterians. Resolutions favorable to the union were passed, both by the General Synod of the former, and by the General Assembly of the latter. The Seceders, as a denomination, were opposed to the union; but the library of the seminary in New York was immediately removed to Princeton, apparently to prevent the possibility of losing so valuable an acquisition. The Seceder Synod of New York refused to acquiesce in the union, and demanded the return of the books. This demand was refused; but the decision of the Courts afterwards restored the plundered property to its rightful owner. Subsequently this seminary was re-established at Newburgh, in New York, and Dr. Joseph McCarroll was appointed professor. This sect have another theological seminary at Allegheny city, in this State, of which Dr J. T. Pressley is the chief professor ; and another at Oxford, Ohio, presided over by Rev. Joseph Claybaugh, D. D.

The Associate Reformed Church at present exists in many of the middle and western States. They have about two hundred and fifty ministers, three hundred congregations, and about thirty thousand members. They are regarded as the most rigid and extreme of all the Calvinistic sects ; their form of worship is very simple ; and they condemn the use of any hymns but David's psalms in the public singing of the church. They oppose instrumental music, and even choirs ; the singing being always led by a precentor or clerk. Its character is generally such as to set on edge the teeth of any one who has the least fondness for the melody of sweet sounds. The Seceders are remarkable for the everlasting length of their sermons. These are rarely less than an hour and a half, or two hours in duration ; and sometimes they have been known to continue even three. The consequence of this peculiarity is, as might have been expected, the greatest want of attention to the preacher on the part of the congregation ; and we have generally observed in Seceder churches that when the door is heard to open, the heads of the congregation turn round simultaneously, as if moved by machinery, to see who the new comer is. This sect can boast of having had among its ministers one of the most gifted of American divines, Dr. John M. Mason, whose superior for powerful and masterly eloquence has never stood in the American pulpit.

FREE COMMUNION BAPTISTS.

The Free Communion Baptists are a small sect in this country, whose distinctive feature is, that they are willing to allow Christians of all denominations to partake with them of the Lord's Supper, while the other Baptist denominations are all in favor of "close communion." A few churches of this persuasion existed in England, and the celebrated Robert Hall believed in free communion. He wrote a tract in defence of his opinion, in which he says : "It is too much to expect an enlightened public will be eager to enrol themselves among the members of a sect which display much of the intolerance of Popery without any portion of its splendor, and prescribes as the pledge of conversion, the renunciation of the whole Christian world." Elsewhere he remarks : "I would not myself baptize in any other way than by immersion, as the ancient mode, because it best represents the meaning of the original term employed, and the substantial import of this institution ; and because I should think it right to guard against the spirit of innovation, which, in positive rites, is always dangerous and progressive; but I should not think myself authorized to baptize any one who had been *sprinkled in adult age.*" The testimony of Robert Hall, in favor of free communion, did not, however, accomplish much for the dissemination of his views in England and the sect never attained a regular and distinct organization there.

The Free Communion Baptists exist chiefly in this country. About the year 1800 the first church of this faith was established in Herkimer county, New York, by a certain Elder Corp, who remained its pastor till his death, in 1838. Other congregations were gradually gathered in different portions of New York and Pennsylvania, by various preachers, prominent among whom were John Farley, Nath. Dickerson, Easterbrook, Hunt, Rowland, and Dodge. The growth of this sect has, however, never been very rapid or extensive. They now have about fifty preachers, sixty churches, and three thousand communicants. Their church government is strictly congregational, although they have a General Conference, Yearly Conferences, and Quarterly Meetings, whose duties and powers are only advisory, without any power to alter or revoke the decisions of the churches. They believe in the

Trinity and in the Atonement, and originally they held to the doctrine of absolute decrees and the perseverance of the saints, though they have in later times practically abandoned these views. The public washing of the feet of the members in meeting was one of the most prominent and important usages in this sect ; though more recently, inasmuch as this observance gave rise to much ridicule and opposition, they virtually abandoned it, in accordance with a resolution, adopted by their General Conference in 1831, which provided that " all persons in connection with us shall have a free and lawful right *to wash their feet or not*, as they may best answer their conscience to God." We should suppose, however, that in warm weather it would be desirable, in view of several important considerations, that they should practice the affirmative of this alternative.

FREE WILL BAPTISTS.

ANOTHER minor denomination of Baptists are known by this title, which designates their most prominent characteristic. They believe in the freedom of the human will, in opposition to the Calvinistic theory, which is entertained by all the other Baptist communities. This sect was commenced in 1780, in New Hampshire, by a Baptist preacher named Benjamin Randall, who had been converted by George Whitefield. Randall imitated Whitefield in his endeavors to promote revivals, and he made a number of journeys, during the progress of which he preached with great success. He founded a large number of churches, and spread the new sect through Maine, New Hampshire, Vermont, Rhode Island, and Massachusetts. He died in 1808. The sect is governed by a General Conference, which was organized in 1827. They have also Yearly and Quarterly meetings, subordinate to the first. Their preachers are rarely men of much education, though they are very earnest and zealous. They have about twelve hundred churches, one thousand preachers, and sixty thousand communicants. They have a theological institution at Whitestown, New York, beside several academies in different parts of the country. They take considerable interest in foreign missions, and have three stations in Orissa, a province in Hindostan. They are numbered among the orthodox sects, believing in the Trinity, total depravity of man by nature, the vicarious atonement, &c. Their church government, like that of all the sects which bear the Baptist name, is congregational or independent. They have a printing establishment at Dover, New Hampshire, which publishes religious books, and they issue several newspapers and magazines, which are devoted to the propagation and defence of their peculiar doctrine. A prominent feature of the sect is their violent condemnation of negro slavery, and their great zeal in the use of those contrivances and measures which tend to promote and carry on popular revivals and religious excitements.

WHIPPERS.

THIS denomination originated in Italy, in the thirteenth century, and was thence propagated through almost all the countries in Europe. The society that embraced this new discipline, ran in multitudes, composed of persons of both sexes, and all ranks and ages, through the public streets, with whips in their hands, lashing their naked bodies with the most astonishing severity, with a view to obtain the divine mercy for themselves and others, by their voluntary mortification and penance. This sect made their appearance anew in the fourteenth century, and taught, among other things, that flagellation was of equal virtue with baptism and other sacraments; that the forgiveness of all sins was to be obtained by it from God, without the merit of Jesus Christ; that the old law of Christ was soon to be abolished, and that a new law, enjoining the baptism of blood to be administered by whipping, was to be substituted in its place.

A new denomination of Whippers arose in the fifteenth

century, who rejected the sacraments and every branch of external worship, and placed their only hopes of salvation in *faith* and *flagellation*.

MILLENARIANS.

THE Millenarians are those who believe that Christ will reign personally on earth for a thousand years; and their name, taken from the Latin, *mille*, a thousand, has a direct allusion to the duration of this spiritual empire. The doctrine of the Millennium, or a future paradisaical state of the earth, is not of Christian, but of Jewish origin. The tradition is attributed to Elijah, which fixes the duration of the world in its present imperfect condition to six thousand years, and announces the approach of a sabbath of a thousand years of universal peace and plenty, to be ushered in by the glorious advent of the Messiah. This idea may be observed in the epistle of Barnabas, and in the opinions of Papias, who knew of no written testimony in its behalf. It was adopted by the author of the Revelations, by Justin Martyr, by Irenæus, and by a long succession of the Fathers. As the theory is animating and consolatory, and when divested of cabalistic numbers and allegorical decorations, probable even in the eye of Philosophy, it will, no doubt, always retain a number of adherents.

But as the Millennium has during some years past attracted the attention of the public, we shall enter into a short detail respecting it:

Mr. Joseph Mede, Dr. Gill, Bishop Newton, and Mr. Winchester, contend for the personal reign of Christ on earth. To use that prelate's own words, in his Dissertations on the Prophecies:—"When these great events shall come to pass, of which we collect from the prophecies, this is to be the proper order:—the Protestant witnesses shall be greatly exalted, and the 1260 years of their prophesying in sackcloth, and of the tyranny of the beast, shall end together; the conversion and restoration of the

Jews succeed; then follows the ruin of the Othman Empire; and then the total destruction of Rome and Antichrist. When these great events, I say, shall come to pass, then shall the kingdom of Christ commence, or the reign of the saints upon earth. So Daniel expressly informs us, that the kingdom of Christ and the saints will be raised upon the ruins of the kingdom of Antichrist, vii. 26, 27 :— 'But the judgment shall sit, and they shall take away his dominion, to consume and destroy it unto the end: and the kingdom and dominion, and the greatness of the kingdom under the whole heaven, shall be given to the saints of the Most High, whose kingdom is an everlasting kingdom, and all dominions shall serve and obey him.' So, likewise, St. John saith, that, upon the final destruction of the beast and the false prophet, Rev. xx., Satan is bound for a thousand years; 'and I saw thrones and they sat on them, and judgment was given unto them; and I saw the souls of them that were beheaded for the witness of Jesus Christ and for the word of God; which had not worshipped the beast, neither his image; neither had received his mark upon their foreheads or in his hands; and they lived and reigned with Christ a thousand years. But the rest of the dead lived not again till the thousand years were finished. This is the first resurrection.' It is, I conceive, to these great events, the fall of Antichrist, the re-establishment of the Jews, and the beginning of the glorious Millennium, that the three different dates, in Daniel, of 1,260 years, 1,290 years, and 1,335 years, are to be referred. And as Daniel saith, xii. 12 :—'Blessed is he that waiteth and cometh to the thousand three hundred five and thirty days.' So St. John saith, Rev. xx. 6 :—' Blessed and holy is he that hath part in the first resurrection.' Blessed and happy indeed will be this period; and it is very observable, that the martyrs and confessors of Jesus, in Papist as well as Pagan times, will be raised to partake of this felicity. Then shall all those gracious promises in the Old Testament be fulfilled—of the amplitude and extent, of the peace and prosperity, of the glory and happiness of the church in the latter days. Then, in the full sense of the words, Rev. xi. 15:—shall the 'kingdoms of this world become *the kingdoms* of our Lord, and of his Christ; and he shall reign for ever and ever.' According to tradition, these thousand years of the reign of Christ and the saints, will be the seventh Millenary of the world: for as God created the world in six days, and rested on the seventh; so the world, it is argued, will continue six thousand years, and the seventh thousand years will be the great Sabbatism, or holy rest to the people of God. 'One day (2 Peter iii. 8) *is* with the Lord as a thousand years, and a thousand years as one day.' According to tradition, too, these thousand years of the reign of Christ and the saints, are the great day of judgment, in the morning or beginning whereof, shall be the coming of Christ in flaming fire, and the particular judgment of Antichrist and the first resurrection; and in the evening or conclusion whereof, shall be the *General Resurrection* of the dead, small and great; and they shall be judged, every man according to their works."

This is a just representation of the Millennium, according to the common opinion entertained of it, that Christ will reign personally on earth during the period of one thousand years. But Dr. Whitby, in a Dissertation on the subject; Dr. Priestley in his Institutes of Religion; and the author of the Illustration of Prophecy, contend against the literal interpretation of the Millennium, both as to its nature and duration. On such a topic, however, we cannot suggest our opinions with too great a degree of modesty.

Dr. Priestley, entertaining an exalted idea of the advantages to which our nature may be destined, treats the limitation of the duration of the world to seven thousand years as a Rabbinical fable; and intimates that the thousand years may be interpreted prophetically: then every day would signify a year, and the Millennium would last for three hundred and sixty-five thousand years. Again he supposes that there will be no resurrection of any individuals till the general resurrection; and that the Millennium implies only the revival of rational religion.

HUMANITARIANS.

THIS term has been applied to those who deny the divinity of Christ, and assert him to have been a *mere man.* This, however, is more than the word properly signifies, and the term Psilanthropist, or Humanitarian, has been suggested as conveying the idea more accurately.

One of the ablest of modern Humanitarians is the Rev. Theodore Parker, minister of a Unitarian church in Boston, Mass. The following extracts from one of his discourses will convey some idea of his views:

"Alas! what men call Christianity, and adore as the best thing they see, has been degraded; so that if men should be all that the pulpit commonly demands of them, they would by no means be Christians. To such a pass have matters reached, that if Paul should come upon the earth now, as of old, it is quite doubtful that he could be admitted to the Christian church; for though Felix thought much knowledge had made the Apostle mad, yet Paul ventured no opinion on points respecting the nature of God and the history of Christ, where our pulpits utter dogmatic and arbitrary decisions, condemning as infidels and accursed all such as disagree therewith, be their life never so godly. These things are notorious. Still more, it may be set down as quite certain, that if Jesus could return from the other world, and bring to New England that same boldness of inquiry which he brought to Judea; that same love of living truth, and scorn of dead letters; could he speak as he then spoke, and live again as he lived before, he also would be called an infidel by the church; be abused in our newspapers, for such is our wont, and only not stoned in the streets, because that is not our way of treating such men as tell us the truth.

"Such is the Christianity of the church in our times. It does not look *forward* but *backward.* It does not ask truth at first hand from God; seeks not to lead men directly to him, through the divine life, but only to make

them walk in the old paths trodden by some good, pious
Jews, who, were they to come back to earth, could as
little understand our circumstances as we theirs.   The
church expresses more concern that men should walk in
these peculiar paths, than that they should reach the goal.
Thus the means are made the end.   It enslaves men to
the Bible ; makes it the soul's master, not its servant ;
forgetting that the Bible, like the Sabbath, was made
for man, not man for the Bible.   It makes man the less
and the Bible the greater.   The Saviour said, Search the
Scriptures ; the Apostle recommended them as profitable
reading ; the church says, Believe the Scriptures, if not
with the consent of reason and conscience, why without
that consent or against it.   It rejects all attempts to hu-
manize the Bible, and separate its fictions from its facts;
and would fain wash its hands in the heart's blood of
those who strip the robe of human art, ignorance, or folly,
from the celestial form of divine truth.   It trusts the imperfect Scripture of the Word, more than the Word itself, writ by God's finger on the living heart.

"The church itself worships not God, who is all in
all, but Jesus, a man born of woman.   Grave teachers,
in defiance of his injunction, bid us pray to Christ.   It
supposes the soul of our souls cannot hear, or will not
accept a prayer, unless offered formally, in the church's
phrase, forgetting that we also are men, and God takes
care of oxen and sparrows, and hears the young ravens
when they cry, though they pray not in any form or
phrase.   Still, called by whatever name, called by an
idol's name, the true God hears the living prayer.   And
yet perhaps the best feature of Christianity, as it is now
preached, is its idolatrous worship of Christ.   Jesus was
the brother of all.   He had more in common with all
men, than they have with one another.   But he, the
brother of all, has been made to appear as the master of
all ; to speak with an authority greater than that of Reason, Conscience, and Faith ;—an office his sublime and
Godlike spirit would revolt at.   But yet, since he lived

divine on the earth, and was a hero of the soul, and the noblest and largest hero the world has ever seen, perhaps the idolatry that is paid him is the nearest approach to true worship, which the mass of men can readily make in these days. Reverence for heroes has its place in history; and though worship of the greatest soul ever swathed in the flesh, however much he is idolized and represented as incapable of sin, is without measure below the worship of the ineffable God; still it is the purest and best of our many idolatries of the nineteenth century. Practically speaking, its worst feature is, that it mars and destroys the highest ideal of man, and makes us beings of very small discourse, that look only backward.

"The influence of real Christianity is to disenthral the man; to restore him to his nature, until he obeys Conscience, Reason, and Religion, and is made free by that obedience. It gives him the largest liberty of the Sons of God, so that as faith in truth becomes deeper, the man is greater and more divine. But now those pious souls who accept the church's Christianity are, in the main, crushed and degraded by their faith. They dwindle daily in the church's keeping. Their worship is not Faith, but Fear; and Bondage is written legibly on their forehead, like the mark set upon Cain. They resemble the dwarfed creed they accept. Their mind is encrusted with unintelligible dogmas. They fear to love man, lest they offend God. Artificial in their anxiety, and morbid in their self-examination, their life is sickly and wretched. Conscience cannot speak its mother tongue to them; Reason does not utter its oracles; nor love cast out fear. Alas, the church speaks not to the hearty and the strong; and the little and the weak, who accept its doctrines, become weaker and less thereby. Thus woman's holier heart is often abased and defiled, and the deep-thoughted and true of soul forsake the church, as righteous Lot, guided by an angel, fled out of Sodom. There will always be wicked men who scorn a pure church, and perhaps great men too high to need its instructions. But what shall we say when the church, as it is, impoverishes those it was designed to enrich, and debilitates so often the trusting souls that seek shelter in its arms?

" Alas for us! we see the Christianity of the church is a very poor thing; a very little better than heathenism. It takes God out of the world of nature and of man, and hides him in the church. Nay it does worse; it limits God, who possesses heaven and earth, and is from everlasting to everlasting, restricting his influence and inspiration to a little corner of the world, and a few centuries of history, dark and uncertain. Even in this narrow range, it makes a deity like itself, and gives us not God, but Jehovah. It takes the living Christ out of the heart, and transfigures him in the clouds; till he becomes an anomalous being, not God, and not man; but a creature whose holiness is not the divine image he has sculptured for himself out of the rock of life, but something placed over him entirely by God's hand, and without his own effort. It has taken away our Lord, and left us a being whom we know not; severed from us by his prodigious birth, and his alleged relation to God, such as none can share. What have we in common with such an one, raised above all chance of error, all possibility of sin, and still more surrounded by God at each moment, as no other man has been? It has transferred him to the clouds. It makes Christianity a Belief, not a Life. It takes religion out of the world, and shuts it up in ·old books, whence, from time to time, on Sabbaths, and fast days, and feast days— it seeks to evoke the divine Spirit, as the witch of Endor is fabled to have called up Samuel from the dead. It tells you, with grave countenance, to believe every word spoken by the Apostles—weak, Jewish, fallible, prejudiced, mistaken as they sometimes were—for this reason, because forsooth Peter's shadow, and Paul's pocket handkerchief, cured the lame and the blind. It never tells you, Be faithful to the spirit God has given; open your souls and you also shall be inspired, beyond Peter and Paul it may be, for great though they were, they saw not all

things, and have not absorbed the Godhead.   No doubt the
Christian church has been the ark of the world.   No
doubt some individual churches are now free from these
disgraces ; still the picture is true as a whole.

"The Christianity of the Church is a very poor thing ;
it is not bread, and it is not drink.   The Christianity of
Society is still worse ; it is bitter in the mouth, and poison
in the blood.   Still men are hungering and thirsting,
though not always knowingly, after the true bread of life.
Why shall we perish with hunger ?   In our Father's house
is enough and to spare.   The Christianity of Christ is
high and noble as ever.   The religion of Reason, of the
Soul, the Word of God, is still strong and flame-like, as
when first it dwelt in Jesus, the chiefest incarnation of
God, and now the pattern-man.   Age has not dimmed the
lustre of this light that lighteneth all, though they cover
their eyes in obstinate perversity, and turn away their
faces from this great sight.   Man has lost none of his
God-likeness.   He is still the child of God, and the father
is near to us as to him who dwelt in his bosom.   Conscience
has not left us.   Faith and hope still abide; and love
never fails.   The Comforter is with us; and though the
man Jesus no longer blesses the earth, the ideal Christ,
formed in the heart, is with us to the end of the world.
Let us, then, build on these.   Use good words when we
can find them, in the church or out of it.   Learn to pray,
to pray greatly and strong; learn to reverence what is
highest; above all learn to live; to make Religion daily
work, and Christianity our common life.   All days shall
then be the Lord's day; our homes the house of God, and
our labour the ritual of Religion.   Then we shall not glory
in men, for all things shall be ours; we shall not be im-
poverished by success, but enriched by affliction.   Our
service shall be worship, not idolatry.   The burthens of
the Bible shall not overlay and crush us; its wisdom shall
make us strong, and its piety enchant us.   Paul and Jesus
shall not be our masters, but elder brothers, who open the
pearly gates of truth, and cheer us on, leading us to the

Tree of Life. We shall find the Kingdom of Heaven and enjoy it now, not waiting till death ferries us over to the other world. We shall then repose beside the rock of ages, smitten by divine hands, and drink the pure water of life as it flows from the Eternal, to make earth green and glad. We shall serve no longer a bond-slave to tradition, in the leprous host of sin, but become freemen, by the law and spirit of life. Thus like Paul we shall form the Christ within; and, like Jesus, serving and knowing God directly, with no mediator intervening, become one with him. Is not this worth a man's wish; worth his prayers; worth his work, to seek the living Christianity; the Christianity of Christ? Not having this we seem but bubbles,—bubbles on an ocean, shoreless and without bottom; bubbles that sparkle a moment in the sun of life, then burst to be no more. But with it we are men, immortal souls, heirs of God and joint heirs with Christ."

THE PROTESTANT EPISCOPAL CHURCH.

THE Protestant Episcopal Church, both in England and in the United States, is one of the most important which exists in either of those countries; its only rival in influence, wealth, and eminence, being the great Presbyterian body, strictly so called. The origin of the Episcopal Church dates from the sixteenth century; and it took its rise in England when that licentious man and tyrannical monarch, Henry VIII., swayed the sceptre of that realm. Henry VIII., as is well known, indulged himself with six wives, several of whom he executed, as the most convenient means of getting rid of them, when they were no longer able to gratify or attract his fickle passion. When the Pope refused to grant him a divorce from Catherine of Arragon, Henry first conceived the idea of throwing off the papal influence and power in his kingdom; and the charms of Anne Boleyn deserve the praise of having been the real cause of the introduction of the Reformation into England. The Pope excommunicated Henry on account of his marriage with that lady; and the breach which was thus begun was eventually widened and made irreparable by the violent acts of resistance to the papal power, and innovations in ecclesiastical matters, which the King and his ministers afterward continued.

These events began in 1534. Cranmer was the chief agent of Henry in reforming the English Church and making it anti-Romish in doctrine, ceremony, and discipline. When Henry died, in 1547, the work thus begun was very incomplete; but during the short reign of his son and successor, Edward VI., the Reformation was carried on energetically. This prince was pious, amiable, and intelligent. He invited men from abroad who were distinguished for learning and personal merit, and also for their attachment to the doctrines of the Reformation, that they might remove to England and use their influence in spreading the reformed faith in his dominions. Among these men were the celebrated Martin Bucer and Paul Fagius. But this career was prematurely terminated by the death of Edward in 1553, when he was succeeded by his sister Mary, the daughter of Catherine of Arragon, Henry's first wife. This princess was a Roman Catholic. Her own disposition was extremely despotic and cruel, and she exerted all her influence to restore the Roman Catholic Church to its pristine power and supremacy throughout her dominions. To accomplish this result, barbarous tortures and even death were used as means of coercion. Among the persons who suffered from the persecutions of this relentless bigot, were Archbishop Cranmer, and the good Bishop Latimer. The former of these, however, deserved little pity, for he was nothing better than a deceitful and unprincipled courtier, who had himself burnt several Roman Catholics during the reign of Edward VI., when he was in power; and, though his name is prominent in the history of the Anglican Church, he was one of the most time-serving, ambitious, and contemptible of men, who in fact richly *deserved* his ultimate fate.

Queen Mary, whom the Protestants generally call

"Bloody Mary," died in 1558, and she was succeeded by the great Elizabeth, a daughter of Henry VIII., under whose reign the Reformation of the Church of England was completed. This monarch delighted to be called the "Virgin Queen," and her virginity is alleged by her admirers to have continued during a lengthy reign of nearly half a century; but those who scrutinized her conduct with impartiality and sagacity, assert that her lovers were numerous, and her intrigues with her favorites continual. Yet she had the cunning to conceal the *proofs* of her indulgences, in a great measure, from the notice of her cotemporaries, and to maintain the rigid semblance of virtue as far as her external conduct was concerned. During the reign of Elizabeth, the English Church was completely separated from the authority of the Church of Rome. Her mass was abolished, though the English Prayer Book, which was then prepared and introduced into all the churches of the establishment, is in a great measure composed of the prayers of the Roman Catholic Mass, translated into English. A very large proportion of the rites and ceremonies of the Papal Church were abolished; among them were auricular or secret confession, the celibacy of the clergy, extreme unction, the use of tapers in churches, prayers in Latin; and the sacraments were reduced from seven to two, though a number of the chief holidays and feasts of the Catholic Church, such as Christmas, Easter, and Lent, were retained. Elizabeth loved pomp and splendor in public worship, as she did in everything else; and this taste of hers gave form and character to the Anglican Church, which was firmly and permanently established in England during her reign. She was a princess of superior ability; but she was selfish, vain, deceitful, ambitious, and cruel. The great stain which will forever deform her character, and pollute it through everlasting ages with a crimson hue, which not all the waters of great Neptune's ocean can wash away, was her judicial murder of Mary, Queen of Scots, for whose execution she could show no just reason whatever. Even though Mary had approved of conspiracies which her friends had formed against Elizabeth, those conspiracies were only devised and contemplated after the English Queen had deprived her of her liberty, and of all hope of regaining it, thus justifying her in attempting by all possible means to escape from the deadly grasp of her adversary.

The Protestant Church in England remains to this day, very much as Elizabeth left it. The doctrines which it teaches are those known as the Thirty-nine Articles, the contents of which we will enumerate hereafter, as being the same which are held by the Protestant Episcopal Church in this country. The form of government is a hierarchy, being composed not only of three orders in the ministry—deacons, presbyters or priests, and bishops—but she has also two archbishops, those of Canterbury and York. The former of these is the Primate of all England, and possesses an extent of power, and displays a degree of splendor, little in harmony with the poverty and simplicity of the primitive apostles and first teachers of the Christian faith.

The first Episcopalians who ever existed in the United States were members of the colony of Virginia, and the first church of this sect in this country was built at Jamestown, in that colony, in 1607. The rector's name was Hurst. In 1610, he was succeeded by the Rev. Mr. Buck. Several years afterward, other parishes were established in the vicinity of Jamestown, and other English clergymen came over to supply their spiritual wants. After the lapse of a century, about the year 1720, there were more than fifty Episcopal churches in Virginia. At the era of the Revolution these had increased to the number of a hundred in Virginia alone. During the Revolution many of the churches fell into decay, and were abandoned, so that at the present time their number does not much exceed those which then existed.

The first English Episcopal Church in Pennsylvania was built in Philadelphia about the year 1685. It is narrated as an extraordinary fact that, in 1700, the Rev. Mr.

Evans, a missionary of the Church of England, performed the prodigious feat of converting five hundred Quakers to the church within the short space of two years; in reference to which achievement we would here observe, that the "Friends" must have been much less tenacious of their peculiar opinions then, than they have generally been since. After the Revolution, there were but six Episcopal clergymen and fifteen parishes in Pennsylvania. The successive bishops who have exercised the functions of the Episcopate in this State have been as follows: Dr. Wm. White, who was consecrated on the 4th of February, 1787, and died in 1836; Dr. H. U. Onderdonk, who was consecrated Assistant Bishop on the 25th of October, 1827, was superseded for dram-drinking on the 21st of October, 1844, and died in 1858; and Dr. Alonzo Potter, who was consecrated on the 23d of September, 1845.

Several of the Protestant Episcopal Churches in Delaware are of very ancient date. Delaware did not become a separate State till 1704; and from that period till the Revolution several of those churches continued to exist dependent on supplies of clergymen from Pennsylvania. In 1817, there remained but two clergymen of this sect in that State. In 1844, the parishes were seventeen, and the clergy ten. On the 12th of October, 1841, Rev. Alfred Lee was consecrated Bishop of the diocese.

In Maryland, the first church of this denomination was erected in 1675. In 1692, the whole colony contained thirty-one parishes. For many years the Roman Catholic Church was the dominant power in the State; though the utmost religious freedom was granted by them, as long as they remained in the majority. In 1792, the number of Protestant Episcopal parishes in the State was about forty. In 1844, their number had increased to about one hundred. The first Bishop of the church in Maryland was Rev. T. J. Clagget, who was consecrated in September, 1792. After him succeeded Bishops Kemp, Stone, and Whittingham. The last was consecrated in September, 1840.

In Massachusetts the Episcopal Church took its rise at an early period, the first congregation being gathered there in 1679. The churches grew in number until after the era of the Revolution, when the mysterious and potent rise of the Unitarian faith gradually persuaded the more learned and intelligent portion of the community in Boston and its vicinity, and both clergymen and people avowed themselves believers in the new faith, and severed their connection with the old. By this means, also, some of the church edifices became alienated from the Episcopal service, and were devoted to the use and occupation of Unitarian clergymen. The history of " King's Chapel," one of the oldest churches in Boston, is an illustration of this remark. Four Bishops have successively presided in the diocese of Massachusetts—Drs. Bass, Parker, Griswold, and Eastburn; the last having been consecrated in December, 1842. In 1844, the number of parishes under his jurisdiction was forty-eight; the number of clergymen was sixty.

It is in the State of New York that the Protestant Episcopal Church in this country has flourished most extensively. The first parish was formed in New York city, in 1697, the Rev. Mr. Vesey being the rector. He continued to perform the duties of his office during the amazing period of more than fifty years. In 1752, there were twenty parishes in the colony, and they grew rapidly. By the bounty of Queen Anne, a very large amount of property was conferred on Trinity parish, in the city of New York, which increased in value from year to year, until now it amounts to the sum of many millions. A large portion of the surplus revenue of this bloated and opulent corporation has been spent in building churches, and in assisting feeble parishes throughout the State of New York—thus contributing to the increase of churches. In 1838, it was found necessary to divide the diocese into those of Eastern and Western New York. In 1844, the number of parishes in Eastern New York was one hundred and sixty-four; those of Western, were one hundred and sixteen. The whole number of clergymen in the State, at that time, was three hundred. New York has had six Bishops—Drs. Provost, Moore, Hobart, B. T. Onderdonk, (suspended in Jan. 1845, also for dram-drinking,) Potter, and De Lancey—the last of whom officiates in the diocese of Western New York. He is the only bishop consecrated there since the separation. In the city and State of New York, this sect are very greatly superior to all others in influence and wealth. The enormous resources of Trinity Church have aided very effectually in producing this result; and it cannot be denied, in spite of all the slanders and the opposition which that church has had to endure, that its means have generally been expended in a judicious and commendable manner.

The first Episcopal Church in New Jersey was founded by the Rev. John Talbot, in 1705. After the lapse of fifty years, the number of parishes amounted to only sixteen, and the clergy to eight. In 1844, the parishes were forty-six, and the clergy fifty. The church has never flourished very much in this State, in consequence of the operation of several unfavorable influences. She has been unfortunate in the choice of at least one of the two bishops who have exercised their episcopal functions there. Rev. John Croes was consecrated in November, 1815, and died in 1832. His successor was the well-known Dr. George W. Doane, who was consecrated on the 31st of October, 1832. Two of his consecrators were Bishop Onderdonk, of New York, who was afterward deposed, and Bishop Ives, of South Carolina, who has since become a convert to the church of Rome.

This sect claims to be intensely orthodox; and their views *are* of that character, according to the generally prevalent estimate of what orthodoxy is. This term "orthodox," which simply means *sound*, or *true* in the faith, is arrogated to themselves by certain denominations of Christians, just as the epithet Catholic is appropriated by others; but the mere assumption of this title is no evidence, in itself, of the truth or the falsehood of the doc-.

trines which are identified with it.   *Orthodoxy* is in`reality
very often, though not always, the indication of extreme
conservatism, sometimes of superstition and belief in theories which are abhorrent to enlightened reason and the
dictates of common sense.

The Protestant Episcopal Church teaches the doctrine
of the Trinity, or the existence of three coëqual persons
in one God.   As this doctrine is well understood by most
readers, it is unnecessary for us to dwell upon it.   This
Church further holds, that the Scriptures contain all that
is necessary to salvation.   By the Scriptures are meant
the Canonical Books of the Old and New Testament, to
the exclusion of those writings which are regarded as un-
canonical or apocryphal.   Yet, though this is the authorized
theory of the Church, there are two ways in which Episcopalians apparently contradict it.   One way is that in
which the more enthusiastic members of the Church reverence and magnify the Prayer Book, which is chiefly a
translation from the Roman Missal; and it is also well
known that the Prayer Book was ordained to be used in
churches, together with the Book of Homilies, because in
the reign of Queen Elizabeth, the priests in England were
generally so ignorant, and'many of them so dissolute, that
they could neither preach nor pray without having the book
before them.   The other way by which the *plenary inspiration* and sufficiency of the Scriptures are practically nullified,
is by the opinion of many of the clergymen of the Church,
that the traditions of the primitive Fathers are, after all,
of great use, and in some instances absolutely indispensable, to a proper understanding of the meaning of Scripture.

This Church believes in the total and absolute fall of the
whole human family, in the fall of Adam.   In Eden, the
progenitor of the human race was perfectly pure, holy,
upright; both mind, soul, and body, were perfect and fault-
less in every respect.   He fell by transgressing the Divine
command not to touch *that* tree of the knowledge of good
and evil; and by his fall not only did his own nature, both

intellectually and morally, become totally, radically, and thoroughly corrupt, incapable of thinking a good thought, or doing anything save what was detestably wicked: but with Adam his whole race fell also, and by inheriting his wicked nature, incurred the penalties which that nature deserved. In other words, Adam was the federal or representative head of all his descendants; they are responsible for what he did, and are fated to suffer for it; though possibly, had they been there to counsel and advise, they might have done their utmost to persuade the progenitor of the human race not to transgress the divine command. But coming afterward into the world, they are compelled to take it precisely as they find it.

Our readers are aware that the whole system of Orthodox Christianity hinges around the Remedy which God has provided for the purpose of curing the miseries and calamities produced by the fall of Adam. In other words, the atonement made by Christ, the second Adam, is the means which God has devised in order to rescue the human family from the consequences of the fall. Sects differ very materially on this head, as to the nature of the atonement and its extent. There are two parties or divisions on the subject, one of whom believe that the atonement of Christ, his sufferings and death, were intended for the benefit and actual use of the whole human family; while the other school teach that the benefits and efficacy of Christ's death are confined to a predestined few. In the Protestant Episcopal Church there has always been a division on this subject; and both of these theories have prevailed among the clergy and laity. The High Church, from the time of Archbishop Laud down to the present time, have always been *Arminian:* that is, they believe that Christ died for the redemption of the whole world; that all may be saved who choose to repent and believe; and that all who hear the Gospel possess the power, within themselves, to repent and believe. They do not believe to the same enormous extent in the total ruin and depravity of human nature; but think that man still possesses the power and freedom of his will to a degree which is necessary to enable him freely to accept or to reject the offers of the Gospel. They contend that where there is no freedom of choice and of action, there can certainly be no responsibility; and that where there is no responsibility, there can be no guilt or innocence, and therefore no real desert, either of future reward or punishment.

The Low Church party, however, have always held the doctrine of Calvin in its strictest sense, believing that the real effectual purpose of the atonement is limited to an elect few, who are predestinated from all eternity to be saved; and who, therefore, if the purpose of God concerning them is not to be defeated, *must inevitably repent*, in order to become worthy of the salvation which they will hereafter enjoy. This school holds to the total depravity and utter ruin of man's nature by the fall; and teaches that no man can make the least effort or motion towards repentance or piety, by his own unassisted strength. Consequently the elect are those whom God chooses as the objects of his partial favor; and by irresistibly impelling them to repentance and faith, fulfils his benevolent decree of salvation concerning them.

According to the teachings of this church, justification is produced solely by the merits of Christ applied to the believer. Yet good works are greatly commended; and a zealous Episcopalian is generally expected to show his piety and zeal by very liberal donations to his church, and by very industrious devotion to all the rites, ceremonies, and observances, which form a prominent part of her public worship.

This church believes in two sacraments—Baptism and the Lord's Supper. In baptizing, sprinkling is used, though it is admitted by many of the leading theologians of the sect that the primitive mode of administering the ordinance was by immersion. In the Lord's Supper, the consecrated emblems, bread and wine, are regarded with great reverence. It is in regard to this matter of the sacraments that this church more nearly approximates to the

Church of Rome; inasmuch as these rites are regarded with a degree of mysterious and solemn consequence, which to a still greater extent is prevalent in the Catholic Church. By the Episcopal Church, Baptism is regarded as a proof of the election of the baptized in Christ, to eternal life ; an evidence of their adoption as sons of God, of their being ingrafted into the body of Christ, and a sure guarantee of pardon, regeneration, and ultimately of salvation. This is the extreme High Church view.

In regard to the presence of the body and blood of Christ in the Eucharist, the *prevalent* theory is, that his body and blood are present really and truly, though they are in a *spiritual* manner presented to and received by the communicant ; or he receives the body and blood of Christ objectively, from without himself, and subjectively, that is, by faith within himself. The effects and the benefit of the Lord's Supper are regarded as of great importance ; for as by Baptism the spiritual life of the recipient is *begun,* so by the Supper it is nourished, strengthened, and perpetuated, till it culminates at last in the attainment of eternal life.

The doctrine concerning *the church* is a prominent one with Episcopalians. The church is the whole number and body of the faithful, of whom Christ is the head and centre ; the members of which are the heirs of the salvation procured by him ; to whom all the promises of the Gospel belong ; to whom the sacraments and benefits of the new covenant appertain ; who have the true apostolical succession and ministry, and with whom Christ has promised to be and to remain until the end of the world. According to this theory, those who are not members of the church are aliens, and have no claims to the benefits of the Gospel nor any hope of future salvation ; and as the Protestant Episcopal Church is *the* church, the plain English of the doctrine held by this sect is simply that all those who are not Protestant Episcopalians are excluded from the kingdom of heaven.

Uncharitable and detestable as this conceit may be, it is

really and practically held by the High Church faction. The late Bishop George W. Doane, for instance, strenuously taught it. It has long been a complaint which has with justice been urged against a portion of the Protestant Episcopal sect that they, an exceedingly small minority of professing Christians, unchurch the whole of the rest of Christendom.

A prominent characteristic of this church is its observance of various rites which the majority of Protestants regard as of no importance. Advent is the beginning of the ecclesiastical year, and comprises four Sundays previous to the 25th of December. It is used as a preparation for the appearance of Christ in the flesh. Christmas, or Nativity Day, is the next and greatest festival, as commemorating the birth of Christ. This festival always occurs on the 25th of December; whereas it is well known that the best and most learned chronologists assert that Christ, instead of being born in December, first saw the light of this breathing world during the summer. After Christmas comes St. Stephen's Day, St. John's, that of the Holy Innocents, the Circumcision of Christ, the Epiphany or the Manifestation of Christ by the star in the East. Great among these ecclesiastical contrivances is Lent. Because our Lord fasted forty days in the wilderness, Episcopalians believe that they must imitate his example and punish themselves with unusual fasting, religious services, and other deeds of piety during a similar period. The first day of Lent is known by the epithet of Ash Wednesday, because in primitive times Christians sometimes sprinkled their heads with ashes. The last week of Lent is called Passion Week, because it commemorates the sufferings of Christ on the cross. Palm Sunday occurs during this week; and the whole of Lent is terminated by Good Friday, which commemorates the crucifixion of our Lord. Then comes Easter Sunday, which signalizes Christ's resurrection. Forty days after is Ascension Day, on which our Lord ascended to Heaven. Ten days after that is Whit Sunday, which is the same as Pentecost, on which the Holy Spirit descended. The whole winds up with Trinity Sunday, which celebrates the existence and the influences and the works of the Triune God.

It is somewhat curious that not a solitary word is said in the Scriptures in reference to the observance of any such holidays and festivals. On the contrary, Christ would seem to have taught a different principle of Christian practice when he abolished and superseded the Jewish law and ritual, in which such observances are prominent and essential. On the other hand, it is urged that the Primitive Church (not the Apostolical Church) observed these or similar festivals, and that it is well to follow their example and imitate their spirit. *Chacun à son goût.* Very conclusive arguments can doubtless be urged on both sides of this disputed and difficult question.

The Protestant Episcopal Church in the United States occupies the first rank among Christian sects for several important characteristics. Her members are unrivaled for their liberality and taste in the erection of church edifices, and for the liberal support which, as a general thing, they give to their clergy. Meanness, parsimony, and similar defects, cannot be charged upon the members of this church; at the same time they are distinguished for their intelligence and mental cultivation; and were such a thing as an established church possible in this land of equality and freedom, it is certain that this church would be admirably adapted to such a high and ambitious relation. The clergymen of this sect are generally well educated; and among their literary and professional accomplishments, not the least in importance is the skill with which they read the prayers in public worship, and the grace with which they often manage "to trill the r's." It is no small glory to this sect that, in this country, many of those men who have been most distinguished in the annals of war and of statesmanship, have belonged to it; and by their private virtues and public fame have greatly increased its influence.

THE GREEK CHURCH.

THE Greek Church comprises the great bulk of the Christian population of Russia and Greece, Moldavia and Wallachia, besides various congregations scattered throughout the provinces of the Turkish and Austrian empires, who acknowledge the Patriarch of Constantinople as their head.

The opinions of this church bear considerable affinity to those of the Latin, or Roman Catholic. The fundamental distinction is the rejection of the spiritual supremacy of St. Peter, and the denial of any visible representative of Christ upon earth. In the view which it takes of the Holy Ghost it is also at variance, not only with the Roman Catholic church, but with Protestants.* It recognizes, however, the seven sacraments; authorizes the offering of prayer to the saints and Virgin; and encourages the use of pictures, though forbidding the use of images. It holds in reverence, also, the relics and tombs of holy men; enjoins strict fasting and the giving of alms, looking upon them as works of intrinsic merit; and numbers among its adherents numerous orders of monks and nuns. It allows, however, the marriage of its secular priests, and rejects auricular confession. It holds that modified form of the Roman doctrine of the eucharist, which is denominated Consubstantiation; and apparently entertains some confused notions of a purgatory, in consideration of which it offers prayers for the dead. It administers baptism by immersion.

The services of this church consist almost entirely of ceremonial observances.

Preaching and the reading of the Scriptures form but a small part of them; the former, indeed was at one period altogether forbidden in Russia.

The origin of the separation which has now prevailed for many hundred years between two such important sec-

---

* The variation consists in the idea, that the Holy Ghost proceeds from the Son alone, and not from the Father and the Son.

tions of Christendom as the Latin and Greek churches, approaching so near as they do in many of their fundamental principles, is to be attributed to the rival pretensions set up by the bishops of the two imperial cities, Rome and Constantinople, and dates almost from the foundation of the latter capital. The Roman branch continued, however, still powerful in the East, and the intrigues of the papal see were frequently successful; until in 1054, the mutual excommunications pronounced upon each other by Leo IX. and Cerularius, caused the final separation which has continued to the present day.

WILKINSONIANS.

THE followers of Jemima Wilkinson, who was born in Cumberland, R. I. In 1776, she asserted that she was taken sick and actually died, and that her soul went to heaven. Soon after, her body was reanimated with the spirit and power of Christ, upon which she set up as a public teacher, and declared she had an immediate revelation for all she delivered, and was arrived to a state of absolute perfection. It is also said she pretended to foretell future events, to discern the secrets of the heart, and to have the power of healing diseases; and if any person who had made application to her was not healed, she attributed it to his want of faith. She asserted that those who refused to believe these exalted things concerning her, will be in the state of unbelieving Jews, who rejected the counsel of God against themselves; and she told her hearers that was the eleventh hour, and the last call of mercy that ever should be granted them; for she heard an inquiry in heaven, saying, "Who will go and preach to a dying world?" or words to that import; and she said she answered, "Here am I—send me;" and that she left the realms of light and glory, and the company of the heavenly host who are continually praising and worshipping God, in order to descend upon earth, and pass through many

sufferings and trials for the happiness of mankind.   She
assumed the title of the *universal friend of mankind.*

Jemima made some converts in Rhode Island and New
York, and died in 1819.   She is said to have been a very
beautiful but artful woman.

MYSTICS.

THIS denomination derived their name from their maintaining, that the Scriptures have a *mystic* and *hidden
sense*, which must be sought after, in order to understand
their true import.   They derived their origin from Dionysius, the Areopagite, who was converted to Christianity,
in the first century, by the preaching of St. Paul at
Athens.   To support this idea, they attributed to this
great man various treatises, which are generally ascribed
to writers who lived at a later period, particularly to a
famous Grecian Mystic, who, it is said, wrote under
the protection of the venerable name of Dionysius, the
Areopagite.

This denomination appeared in the third century; and
increased in the fourth.   In the fifth century, they gained
ground in the eastern provinces.   In the year eight hundred and twenty-four, the supposed works of Dionysius
kindled the flame of Mysticism in the western provinces.
In the twelfth century, they took the lead in their method
of expounding the Scriptures.   In the thirteenth century,
they were the most formidable antagonists of the school-
men; and towards the close of the fourteenth century,
they resided, and propagated their sentiments, in almost
every part of Europe.   In the fifteenth and sixteenth centuries, many persons of distinguished merit embraced their
tenets.   In the seventeenth century, the radical principle
of Mysticism was adopted by the Behmists, Bourignon-
ists, and Quietists.

The ancient Mystics were distinguished by their professing pure, sublime, and perfect devotion, with an entire

disinterested love of God, and by their aspiring to a state of passive contemplation.

The first suggestions of these sentiments have been supposed to proceed from the known doctrine of the Platonic school, which was adopted by Origen and his disciples, that the divine nature was diffused through all human souls, or, in other words, that the faculty of reason, from which proceeds the health and vigor of the mind, was an emanation from God into the human soul, and comprehended in it the principles and elements of all truth, human and divine.

They denied that men could, by labor or study, excite this celestial flame in their breasts. Therefore, they disapproved highly of the attempts of those, who, by definitions, abstract theorems, and profound speculations, endeavoured to form distinct notions of truth, and to discover its hidden nature. On the contrary, they maintained, that silence, tranquillity, repose, and solitude, accompanied with such acts of mortification as might tend to attenuate and exhaust the body, were the means, by which the hidden and internal word was excited to produce its latent virtues, and to instruct men in the knowledge of divine things. For thus they reasoned:

They, who behold, with a noble contempt, all human affairs, who turn away their eyes from terrestrial vanities, and shut all the avenues of the outward senses against the contagious influence of an outward world, must necessarily return to God, when the spirit is thus disengaged from the impediments which prevent this happy union: and in this blessed frame, they not only enjoy inexpressible raptures from their communion with the Supreme Being, but also are invested with the inestimable privilege of contemplating truth undisguised, in its native purity, while others behold it in a vitiated and delusive form.

The apostle tells us, that *the Spirit makes intercession for us*, &c. Now, if the Spirit prays in us, we must resign ourselves to its motions, and be swayed and guided by its impulses, by remaining in a state of mere inaction.

As the Rev. William Law, who was born in 1687, makes a distinguished figure among the modern Mystics, a brief account of the outlines of his system, may perhaps be entertaining to the readers.

He supposed that the material world was the very region, which originally belonged to the fallen angels. At length, the light and spirit of God entered into the chaos, and turned the angels' ruined kingdom into a paradise on earth. God then created man, and placed him there. He was made in the image of the Triune God, a living mirror of the divine nature, formed to enjoy communion with Father, Son, and Holy Ghost, and live on earth, as the angels do in heaven. He was endowed with immortality; so that the elements of this outward world could not have any power of acting on this body. But, by his fall, he changed the light, life, and spirit of God, for the light, life, and spirit of the world. He died, the very day of his transgression, to all the influences and operations of the spirit of God upon him, as we die to the influences of this world, when the soul leaves the body: and all the influences and operations of the elements of this life were open in him, as they are in any animal, at its birth into this world. He became an earthly creature, subject to the dominion of this outward world; and stood only in the highest rank of animals.

But the goodness of God would not leave man in this condition. Redemption from it was immediately granted; and the bruiser of the serpent brought the life, light, and spirit of heaven, once more into the human nature. All men, in consequence of the redemption of Christ, have in them the first spark, or seed, of the divine life, as a treasure hidden in the centre of our souls, to bring forth, by degrees, a new birth of that life, which was lost in paradise. No son of Adam can be lost, only by turning away from the Saviour within him. The only religion, which can save us, must be that, which can raise the light, life, and spirit of God, in our souls. Nothing can enter into the vegetable kingdom, till it has the vegetable life in it;

or be a member of the animal kingdom, till it has the animal life. Thus all nature joins with the gospel in affirming, that no man can enter into the kingdom of heaven, till the heavenly life is born in him. Nothing can be our righteousness or recovery, but the divine nature of Jesus Christ derived to our souls.

The arguments, which are brought in defence of this system, cannot easily be abridged in such a manner, as to render them intelligible. Those who are fond of mystical writings, are referred to the works of this ingenious author.

SIX-PRINCIPLE BAPTISTS.

By this name are designated those, who consider that the imposition of hands subsequent to baptism, and generally on the admission of candidates into the Church, is an indispensable pre-requisite for Church membership and communion. They support their peculiar principle chiefly from Heb. vi. 1, 2—" Therefore, leaving the principles of the doctrine of Christ, let us go on unto perfection; not laying again the foundation of repentance from dead works, and of faith toward God, of the doctrine of baptisms, and of laying on of hands, and of resurrection of the dead, and of eternal judgment."

As these two verses contain six distinct propositions, one of which is the laying on of hands, these brethren have, from thence, acquired the name of "Six-Principle Baptists," to distinguish them from others, whom they sometimes call "Five-Principle Baptists." They have fourteen churches in Massachusetts and Rhode Island.

MENNONITES.

The Mennonites were a society of Baptists in Holland, so called from Mennon Simonis, of Friesland, who lived in the sixteenth century. Some of them came to the United States, and settled in Pennsylvania, where a considerable body of them still reside.

The fundamental maxim of this denomination is, that practical piety is the essence of religion, and that the surest mark of the true Church is the sanctity of its members. They advocate perfect toleration in religion, and exclude none—unite in pleading for toleration in religion, and debar none from their assemblies who lead pious lives, and own the Scriptures for the word of God. They teach that infants are not the proper subjects of baptism; that ministers of the gospel ought to receive no salary; and that it is not lawful to swear, or wage war, upon any occasion. They also maintain that the terms *person* and *Trinity* are not to be used in speaking of the Father, Son, and Holy Ghost.

The Mennonites meet privately, and every one in the assembly has the liberty to speak, to expound the Scriptures, to pray, and sing.

The Mennonites in Pennsylvania do not baptize by immersion, though they administer the ordinance to none but adult persons. Their common method is this: The person who is to be baptized, kneels; the minister holds his hands over him, into which the deacon pours water, and through which it runs on the crown of the kneeling person's head; after which follow imposition of hands and prayer.

Mr. Van Beuning, the Dutch ambassador, speaking of these "Harmless Christians," as they choose to call themselves, says: "The Mennonites are good people, and the most commodious to a state of any in the world; partly, because they do not aspire to places of dignity; partly, because they edify the community by the simplicity of their manners, and application to arts and industry; and partly, because we need fear no rebellion from a sect who make it an article of their faith never to bear arms."

DUNKERS.

Conrad Peysel, a German Baptist, was the founder of the Dunkers about the year 1724. Weary of the world, he retired to an agreeable solitude, within fifty miles of Philadelphia, that he might give himself up to contemplation. Curiosity brought several of his countrymen to visit his retreat, and by degrees, his pious, simple, and peaceable manners induced others to settle near him. They formed a little colony of German Baptists, which they call *Euphrata or Euphrates*, in allusion to the Hebrews, who used to sing psalms on the border of that river.

This little city forms a triangle, the outside of which are bordered with mulberry and apple trees, planted with great regularity. In the middle is a very large orchard, and between the orchard and these ranges of trees are houses built of wood, three stories high, where every Dunker is left to enjoy the pleasures of his meditations without disturbance. Their number in 1777 did not exceed five hundred, and since that period they have not multiplied greatly. They do not foolishly renounce marriage, but when married they detach themselves from the rest of the community and retire into another part of the country.

The Dunkers lament the fall of Adam, but deny the imputation of his sin to posterity. They use *trine* immersion (dipping three times) in baptism, and .employ the ceremony of the imposition of hands when the baptized are received into the church. They dress like Dominican friars, shaving neither head nor beard ; have different apartments for the sexes, and live chiefly on roots and vegetables, except at their love-feast, when they eat mutton. It is said no bed is allowed except in case of sickness, having in their separate cells a bench to lie upon, and a block of wood for their pillow ! They deny the eternity of future punishment—believe that the dead have the gospel preached to them by our Saviour, and that the souls of the just are employed to preach the gospel to those who have had no revelation in this life.

But their chief tenet is, that future happiness is only to be obtained by penance and outward mortification, so as that Jesus Christ by his meritorious sufferings became the

Redeemer of mankind in general, so each individual of the human race by a life of abstinence and restraint may work out his own salvation. Nay, it is said they admit of works of supererogation.

They use the same form of government and the same discipline as other Baptists do, except that every person is allowed to speak in the congregation, and their best speaker is usually ordained to be a minister. They have also deacons, and deaconesses from among their ancient widows, who may all use their gifts, and exhort at stated times.

THE JEWS.

THE origin of this ancient and remarkable people is traced to Abraham, who was chosen by the Almighty to be the father and progenitor of a favorite people, to whom the Deity promised to reveal his law and will, in preference to all the rest of mankind. The moral and ceremonial laws, which were given to govern them, are contained in the Pentateuch, or Five Books of Moses; and these present one of the most remarkable systems of ethics and worship which the world has ever seen. The contents of these books refer so exclusively to matters of a temporal and mundane character, that many persons have doubted whether the Jewish Scriptures really made any reference to a future state after death; and Bishop Warburton, in his famous work on the "Divine Legation of Moses," denies that any such doctrine was known to Moses or his successors.

The history of the Jewish people till the time of Christ is contained, to some extent, in several books of the Old Testament. When the Messiah came, they were divided into several religious sects: the Pharisees, who placed the substance and value of their religion in external forms and ceremonies; the Sadducees, who were remarkable for their incredulity; and the Essenes, who were distinguished by their austere sanctity. These sects are referred to in

10

the New Testament.   In more modern times, the Jews are
divided into two classes : the Caraites, who admit no rule
in religious matters except the strict letter of the law of
Moses; and the Rabbinists, who add to the law the traditions
and comments of the Talmud.

The capture of Jerusalem by Titus, and the first dispersion of the Jews after the advent of Christ, occurred
A. D. 70.   From that day till the present they have wan-
dered over the face of the whole earth, and have existed
in many countries under various circumstances.   They still
look for the advent and appearance of the promised Messiah.   The fact that their ancestors were the persons who
inflicted death upon Christ, has made them the subjects of
unjust persecution in almost all Christian countries; and
nowhere do they enjoy the same degree of religious freedom and the just and inalienable rights of man, so fully
and impartially as in the United States.

The first Jews who ever existed in this country became
residents of New York, then called New Amsterdam, about
the year 1660.   They were Portuguese and Spanish Jews,
who had fled in the first instance from the cruelties of the
Inquisition, in their native country, to the comparative
security of the Batavian Republic; and there becoming
acquainted with the greater benefits of a residence in the
United States, removed afterwards to New York.   They
gradually increased, and eventually built a small synagogue for themselves.   Several generations elapsed before
they attained to any great numbers, for till 1827 one place
of worship sufficed for all their community.   At that time
a second building was erected.   At present the city of
New York contains the largest Jewish community which
exists in this country, and ten synagogues are necessary for
their use.   They there number about ten thousand persons;
and particular localities, such as Chatham street, are in a
great measure occupied by them, either as residences or
places of business.

After New York, one of the oldest Jewish communities
which exist in this country was assembled in Newport,

Rhode Island, where there are still a synagogue and a burying ground. About the same period (1780) the first Jews began to settle in Philadelphia, and in several places in Maryland and Virginia. Only one State in the confederacy is tyrannical enough to withhold the fullest religious freedom and equality from Israelites, and that is one of the poorest and the least enlightened of them. In North Carolina the Constitution of the State forbids Jews the privileges of citizens, and to some extent restricts their worship.

In the United States the Jewish congregations are not governed by the same regulations, nor by the same ecclesiastical authorities, that prevail in Europe. There are in reality no Rabbis in this country, though the title is sometimes given by way of compliment. Each congregation is in a great measure free, makes its own rules and regulations, chooses its own minister, and his ordination consists in his election and induction into office, without any other ceremony. The Jews have no literary institutions here, devoted to the giving of instructions to their peculiar tenets. But they have several charitable establishments, which are liberally endowed. They have a religious periodical called the *Occident and American Jewish Advocate.*

In Europe many of the most eminent persons in modern times, in various departments of intellectual labor, have been Jews. In the German Universities some of the most learned of their linguists are members of this community. The celebrated church historian, Neander, was a Jew by birth, though he afterwards became a Christian. With the eminence of the Rothschilds in the department of finance, every one is familiar. The Jews of all classes are generally well read in the Hebrew language, and many of them in Hebrew literature. Prominent among their theological writings is the Talmud, already referred to. This is in substance a collection of doctrines and moral precepts. There are two works which bear this name, the "Talmud of Jerusalem," and the "Talmud of Babylon." The former is more ancient, but it is shorter and more obscure than the latter, which is clearer, more extensive, and is generally more highly valued by the Jews.

As an illustration of the horrible cruelties to which these people have been subjected even in recent times, we may adduce the following instances: Dr. Grant relates that, during his residence at Ooroomiah, in Persia, in 1840, a Jew was publicly burnt to death in that city, by order of the Governor, on the charge of killing the children of the Gentiles to obtain their blood to mingle with the bread of the Passover. Naphtha was poured over the body of the poor wretch, and the torch applied. He was instantly enveloped in flames, and died in the greatest agonies. In Meshed, another city of Persia, the same accusation was preferred against the Jews who resided at that place in 1839, in consequence of the mysterious disappearance of a Mahometan child. The inhabitants resolved upon the entire extirpation of the Jews in the place. The massacre began, and fifteen of them were slain. The rest, to avoid the same fate, embraced the alternative offered them of becoming Mahometans—with how much sincerity or admiration for their new faith, may readily be conceived.

The number of Jews throughout the world is not far from five millions. In the United States they do not exceed seventy thousand. They have synagogues in New York, Philadelphia, Newport, Charleston, Baltimore, Wheeling, Savannah, New Orleans, Cincinnati, St. Louis, and a few other places. There are a million of them in Poland and Russia ; half a million in Austria; a million in the Barbary States; and other large communities exist in the chief countries in Europe. It is a curious circumstance that the Catholic inhabitants of Spain and Portugal, who formerly persecuted the Jews with such horrid barbarity, are themselves the descendants of Jews, of those colonies which went forth from Palestine in the reign of Solomon, and paid tribute to that monarch.

The religious belief of the Orthodox Jews does not change. It may be stated as follows, in the language of the creed, which was drawn up for their use by Maimonides, an illustrious Rabbi, who lived in the eleventh century:

"I. I believe, with a true and perfect faith, that God is the Creator, whose name be blessed, Governor and Maker of all creatures, and that he hath wrought all things, worketh, and shall work forever.

"II. I believe, with a perfect faith, that the Creator, whose name be blessed, is *one*, and that such a unity as is in him can be found in none other, and that he alone hath been our God, is, and forever shall be.

"III. I believe, with a perfect faith, that the Creator, whose name be blessed, is not corporeal, nor to be comprehended with any bodily property, and that there is no bodily essence that can be likened' unto him.

"IV. I believe, with a perfect faith, the Creator, whose name be blessed, to be the first and the last, that nothing was before him, and that he shall abide the last forever.

"V. I believe, with a perfect faith, that the Creator, whose name be blessed, is to be worshiped, and none else.

"VI. I believe, with a perfect faith, that all the words of the prophets are true.

"VII. I believe, with a perfect faith, the prophecies of Moses, our master—may he rest in peace—that he was the father and chief of all wise men that lived before him, or ever shall live after him.

"VIII. I believe that the law was given by Moses.

"IX. I believe that the law shall never be altered, and that God will give no other.

"X. I believe that God knows all the thoughts and actions of men.

"XI. I believe that God will regard the works of all those who perform what he commands, and that he will punish those who have transgressed his laws.

"XII. I believe that the Messiah is yet to come, though he tarry a long time.

"XIII. I believe that there will be a resurrection of the dead, at the time when God shall see fit."

This is the doctrinal belief of what are now termed the Orthodox, or Conservative Jews. In recent times there has arisen a new school among them, who are termed Progressive, or Rationalistic, who differ in some of their sentiments from the other portion of the Jewish community.

ENGLISH SEVENTH DAY BAPTISTS.

THE doctrine that the seventh day of the week, and not the first day, is the true Sabbath of the Christian Church, has been entertained by many eminent divines, in various countries; but there are only two denominations who make that doctrine the peculiar and distinctive characteristic of their sect. These are the English and the German Seventh Day Baptists.

The former of these arose in England about the year 1650. At that time, or soon after, there were some eight or ten small congregations of them existing in that country. They were obscure, and of little importance. Prominent among their members was a preacher named Edward Stennet, who was persecuted by the authorities for his religious belief. The "Conventicle Act," which was then in full force, prevented these people even from holding any kind of religious worship in accordance with their peculiar views. Another of their preachers, Joseph Davis, was imprisoned for a long time. Francis Bawfield was in jail eight years, during the reign of Charles II., and eventually died in prison, on account of his attachment to principles which were in opposition to those inculcated by a luxurious, pampered, hypocritical, and worldly Church.

In 1665, the first Seventh Day Baptists arrived in this country from England. They were led by Stephen Mumford, and settled at Newport, Rhode Island. But here also they were called on to endure some persecution in consequence of their conscientious scruples in observing the first day of the week as the Christian Sabbath. The sect slowly spread into Connecticut, New Jersey, and New York. At the present time they exist in many of the

States, in small numbers; and they have about fifty congregations, forty ministers, and seven thousand communicants, in the United States. They are divided into four
associations—an Eastern, a Central, a Western, and a
South-Western. They have an Annual Conference, composed of delegates from these four associations; yet they
are Congregational in their Church government—each Society being in reality perfectly independent in the control
of its private and individual affairs. The officers of their
churches are pastors and deacons; the latter of whom are
chosen for life. They have a Literary Institution at De
Ruyter, established in 1837; also an Academy at Alfred,
in New York. In proportion to their numbers and means,
they are an active and enterprizing sect. They are regarded as orthodox, entertaining the doctrine of the Trinity, man's total depravity, the vicarious atonement, &c.
But their main distinctive doctrine is their strict observance of the Seventh day, or Saturday, as the Lord's Day.

In support of this usage and belief they urge some very
plausible arguments, of which the following are a specimen.
They assert that the Seventh day of the week having been
expressly set apart as the Sabbath, by God, immediately
after the Creation, and it being expressly enjoined by the
fourth commandment, some very clear injunction of Scripture is requisite to justify the change to the first day of
the week; and that no such injunction exists. On the
contrary, Christ directly taught that "the Sabbath was
made for man," meaning thereby the Sabbath which was
then in use by the Jews, to whom he spoke. He also told
his disciples to pray that "their flight be not in the winter, neither on the Sabbath day," which necessarily meant
the Seventh day. And the Psalmist declares: "All his
commandments are sure; they stand fast for ever." In
regard to the argument that Christ rose from the dead on
the first day of the week, they answer, that he *died* on
Friday, thus effecting the atonement on that day; and
that, if such an argument should have any weight, it
would give Friday a greater claim to being observed as

the Sabbath than the Monday. It is true, Paul says, in his First Epistle to the Corinthians: "On the first day of the week let every one lay by him in store," &c.; but, say they, this injunction did not require the early Christians to *meet* on that day for public worship, and says nothing about the change of the Sabbath day. The Holy Spirit descended, as is supposed, on the first day of the week; but there is no *proof* that Pentecost *was* on that day of the week. Paul preached to Lydia and her household on the Seventh day. At Ephesus, he went into the synagogue and preached and reasoned with the Jews on the Seventh day; and he did the same thing at Thessalonica, three Sabbath days in succession. Certainly the Jews were not observing the *first* day of the week as their Sabbath.

ANTINOMIANS.

THESE derive their name from Greek words, meaning *against the law*. In the sixteenth century, while Luther was eagerly employed in censuring and refuting the Popish doctors, who mixed the law and gospel together, and represented eternal happiness as the fruit of legal obedience, a new teacher arose whose name was John Agricola, a native of Aisteben, and an eminent doctor in the Lutheran church. His fame began to spread in the year 1538, when from the doctrine of Luther, now mentioned, he took occasion to advance sentiments which were interpreted in such a manner, that his followers were distinguished by the title of Antinomians.

The principal doctrines which bear this appellation, together with a short specimen of the arguments made use of in their defence, are comprehended in the following summary:

I. That the law ought not to be proposed to the people as a rule of manners, nor useful in the church as a means of instruction; and that the gospel alone was to be inculcated and explained, both in the churches and in the schools of learning.

For the scriptures declare, that Christ is not the law-giver, as it is said, "The law was given by Moses; but grace and truth came by Jesus Christ." Therefore the ministers of the gospel ought not to teach the law. Christians are not ruled by the law, but by the spirit of regeneration, according as it is said, "Ye are not under the law, but under grace." Therefore the law ought not to be taught in the church of Christ.

II. That the justification of sinners, is an immanent and eternal act of God, not only preceding all acts of sin, but the existence of the sinner himself.

For nothing new can arise in God, on which account he calls things that are not as though they were; and the apostle saith, "Who hath blessed us with all spiritual blessings in heavenly places in Christ Jesus, before the foundation of the world." Besides, Christ was set up from everlasting, not only as the head of the church, but as the surety of his people; by virtue of which engagement the Father decreed never to impute unto them their sins. See 2d of Cor. iv. 19.

III. That justification by faith is no more than a manifestation to us of what was done before we had a being.

For it is thus expressed in Hebrews xi. 1. "Now faith is the substance of things hoped for, the evidence of things not seen." We are justified only by Christ; but by faith we perceive it, and by faith rejoice in it, as we apprehend it to be our own.

IV. That men ought not to doubt of their faith, nor question whether they believe in Christ.

For, we are commanded to "draw near in full assurance of faith." Heb. x. 22. "He that believeth on the Son of God hath the witness in himself." 2d of John v. 10, *i. e.*, he has as much evidence as can be desired.

V. That God sees no sin in believers, and they are not bound to confess sin, mourn for it, or pray that it may be forgiven.

For God has declared, Heb. x. 17. "Their sins and iniquities I will remember no more:" and in Jer. l. 20, "In those days, and in that time, saith the Lord, the iniquity of Israel shall be sought for, and there shall be none; and the sins of Judah, and they shall not be found: for I pardon them whom I reserve."

VI. That God is not angry with the elect, nor doth he punish them for their sins.

For Christ has made ample satisfaction for their sins. See Isaiah liii. 5. "He was wounded for our transgressions, he was bruised for our iniquities," &c. And to inflict punishment once upon the Surety, and again upon the believer, is contrary to the justice of God, as well as derogatory to the satisfaction of Christ.

VII. That by God's laying our iniquities upon Christ, he became as completely sinful as we, and we as completely righteous as Christ.

For Christ represents our persons to the Father; and we represent the person of Christ to him. The loveliness of Christ is transferred to us; on the other hand, all that is hateful in our nature is put upon Christ, who was forsaken by the Father for a time. See 2d of Cor. v. 21. "He was made sin for us, who knew no sin; that we might be made the righteousness of God in him."

VIII. That believers need not fear either their own sins or the sins of others, since neither can do them any injury.

See Rom. viii. 33, 34. "Who shall lay any thing to the charge of God's elect?" &c. The apostle does not say that they never transgress; but triumphs in the thought that no curse can be executed against them.

IX. That the new covenant is not made properly with us, but with Christ for us; and that this covenant is all of it a promise, having no conditions for us to perform; for faith, repentance, and obedience, are not conditions on our part, but Christ's; and he repented, believed, and obeyed for us.

For the covenant is so expressed, that the performance

lies upon the Deity himself, "For this is the covenant that I will make with the house of Israel after those days, saith the Lord; I will put my laws into their mind, and write them in their hearts; and I will be to them a God, and they shall be to me a people."

X. That sanctification is not a proper evidence of justification.

For those who endeavor to evidence their justification by their sanctification, are looking to their own attainments and not to Christ's righteousness for hopes of salvation.

OLD SCHOOL PRESBYTERIAN CHURCH.

BOTH branches of the Presbyterian Church in the United States derive their origin historically from the Reformed Church of Scotland, whose chief founder and most eminent leader was John Knox. It is usual to attribute the first preaching of the Protestant doctrines in Scotland to Knox; but this is an error. The person who, prior to all others, proclaimed the new system of belief in that country, was Patric Hamilton, a friend and pupil of Luther, who, after his return from Wittemberg, preached the opinions which he had learned in Germany, to his countrymen, and was rewarded for his zeal by martyrdom, in 1528. Among the few followers whom he had acquired was Wishart, who pursued the same career and met the same end. After him came John Knox, who carried on the work of Reformation with greater ability and zeal than any of his predecessors, and eventually succeeded in converting or perverting a very large majority of the Scottish people from the Church of Rome to the new faith.

Knox was born in Haddington, in 1505. His family, though not belonging to the nobility, was wealthy and respectable. He was educated at the University of Glasgow, and distinguished himself by his superior attainments and abilities. He soon after entered the priesthood of the Catholic Church, and being of a pious turn of mind, he endeavored to discharge the duties of his office faithfully, and to accomplish some good.

At that time a priest who displayed such a temper in Scotland was a phenomenon of rare occurrence. The bold and earnest preaching of Wishart converted Knox to the Protestant doctrine in the thirty-seventh year of his age, and he withdrew from the priesthood and all his ecclesiastical relations. But at first he seemed to have no aspirations after the career of fame of a Reformer, for he settled himself down into the quiet and obscure situation of tutor to the sons of a nobleman. He was drawn from this retirement by the eloquence of Wishart, who appreciated the great qualities of Knox at their real value, and labored to call them forth into active service in the Protestant cause. Knox first accompanied Wishart, in his preaching tours through the country, and at length undertook to preach the doctrine which he had espoused.

The most active and dangerous enemy of the Reformation at that time in Scotland was Cardinal Beaton. He succeeded in destroying Wishart, but was himself shortly afterward assassinated by a band of young men who were attached to the new faith. Persecution thickened around Knox and his associates. They took refuge in a castle near the city of St. Andrews, in which they were besieged for many months, and finally captured. Knox was punished by imprisonment in the galleys, and this degraded and revolting penalty he endured for the period of three years and a half. On his release he fled to England, over which country the pious Edward then reigned. The young King properly appreciated the merits of the Reformer, and appointed him one of the preachers to the Court. A still higher preferment in the English Church was offered him, but he declined it. From London he removed to Berwick, and there he preached and labored actively during two years. At the death of Edward, however, he was compelled to flee. Scotland was governed by French influence; a female monarch, devotedly attached to the Catholic Church, ruled in England; and Knox could find no safe retreat except at Geneva, on the free soil, and amid the mountain solitudes of Switzerland.

Several years were spent by Knox in this retreat, which he employed industriously in receiving instruction from Calvin, both as to the true doctrines of the Christian faith and in regard to the proper form and model of the government of the church. As is well known, Calvin had established a church at Geneva, which he believed to be arranged and governed precisely as were the churches of the apostolic era. Knox approved of Calvin's views in every respect, and when he returned to Scotland he was not only a thorough convert to all of Calvin's doctrinal opinions, but an earnest defender of the Presbyterial form of church government, in opposition to the Episcopal or Prelatical form.

Knox returned to Scotland in 1555. During his absence the Reformation had made some progress, and he found the state of affairs favorable to the continuance of the work. He immediately commenced to preach and labor with great zeal. He first proposed that all those who were opposed to the Romish Church should take an oath never again to attend the celebration of mass. This was a bold measure, and Knox was cited to appear before the Bishop's Court, at Edinburgh, to answer for his conduct. Ten years before, Wishart had been burnt in person for a similar offence. On this occasion, so different had the state of affairs become, that Knox was condemned merely to be burnt in effigy. Undismayed by this penalty, Knox drew up his celebrated " *Petition to the Queen Regent*," desiring to be heard in the defence of himself, and assailing the Church of Rome with great boldness and severity. The effect of this measure eventually was that Knox was compelled once more to flee for his life, and once more he took refuge in the welcome haven of Geneva.

He remained there till May, 1559, when he returned for the last time to Scotland, and resumed his work with greater boldness and resolution than ever. He was then fifty-four years of age, small in person, wearing a long beard, which reached nearly to his waist. His massive brow and large, piercing eye, indicated his superior mental capacity. His preaching is represented as having been effective and powerful, and as making a prodigious impression upon the minds of his hearers. He held forth at Perth and at various other places in the kingdom, and soon all Scotland was in a blaze of religious excitement and enthusiasm.

The worst enemy with whom Knox had to contend was Mary, the beautiful and unfortunate Queen of Scotland. It is said that in his interviews with her he spoke with such severity and rudeness as to cause her to shed tears. He was no respecter of persons, and proclaimed his message with the same spirit in the palace and the hovel. Thus he continued to preach and labor till 1572, when his life ended; but he had lived long enough to secure the prevalence of the Protestant religion throughout Scotland, and the final and total overthrow of the Church of Rome. He left the Presbyterian Church as it now exists, both in doctrine and government, the dominant, religious, or ecclesiastical power in his native land.

An attempt was made by James VI., afterward James I. of England, to overthrow the Presbyterian influence in Scotland, by substituting in its place the Episcopal Church. He procured the appointment of bishops, and the introduction of the rites and ceremonies of the Church of England, and the abolition of the General Assembly of the Scotch Kirk. Charles I., acting under the advice of Archbishop Laud, endeavored to complete the work which his father had begun, by enacting other measures of violence and usurpation. But the Scottish people resisted his measures, and in 1638, they abolished the modified form of Episcopacy which had been introduced; the General Assembly again convened, and Presbyterian doctrine and discipline once more became the recognized religion of the nation. This continued till 1660, when, during the reign and after the restoration of Charles II., his profligate government endeavored again to subvert Presbyterianism. It was not,

however, till 1688, when the Revolution placed William
of Orange and Mary on the throne of England, that perfect religious liberty was granted to the Scotch people.
From that period Presbyterianism became the religion of
the great masses of the people, and that also which was
established by law. It has remained the same till this
day; and although during the last century-and-a-half
there have been many ecclesiastical conflicts and disturbances in Scotland, they have been always between the
members of the Scotch Church themselves.

These conflicts, which have been numerous, have often
resulted in the forming of new sects, all of whom claim to
be the true and pure Presbyterian Church—such as the
Seceders, the Covenanters, the Burghers, and the anti-
Burghers, the Old and New Light Burghers, the Reformed
Presbyterian, and the Free Church of Scotland. In all
these divisions and subdivisions the inherent weakness of
the Scotch people to contend furiously for the most trifling
and insignificant differences of doctrine, displayed itself;
and the same peculiarity has been exhibited in the history
of the Presbyterians in this country, who have here been
the most litigious of all sects, and have consequently
experienced the greatest number of separations and
schisms.

The founders of Presbyterianism in the United States
were immigrants from Scotland and the North of Ireland.
The first Presbyterian Church which ever existed in this
country, was organized in Philadelphia about the close of
the seventeenth century. Other churches soon sprang up
around it; and in 1706 the Presbytery of Philadelphia
was formed, consisting of seven clergymen. Francis Mc-
Kemie was the first Presbyterian preacher who ever held
forth in the Colonies. The first pastor of the first Presbyterian Church in this city was Jedediah Andrews, a
native of New England. In 1710, there were also one
Presbyterian congregation in Virginia, four in Maryland,
five in Pennsylvania, in Jersey two, with a few scattered
members in New York. From this time the denomination

rapidly increased, by the growth of their native population, and by constant immigration from Scotland, and the
north of Ireland. Certain influential members wrote to
the Synod of Glasgow, to the Presbytery of Dublin, and
to the Independents of London, for a supply of ministers.
This appeal resulted in obtaining what was desired. So
much did the denomination increase in a short time, that
in 1716, the Presbytery of Philadelphia found it desirable
to divide itself into four subordinate presbyteries, and to
assume the name and the functions of a Synod. It was
composed at this period of thirteen ministers and six
elders. In 1718, the celebrated William Tennent left the
Protestant Episcopal Church and joined the Presbyterian.
He afterward became one of the most distinguished and
eloquent preachers who have ever flourished in this country. He set forth his reasons for his change in a clear
and condensed manner; and the Synod of Philadelphia,
of which he became a member, ordered the document to
be filed. As it is a production of some interest, we here
insert it :

"The reasons of William Tennent for his dissenting
from the Established Church in Ireland, delivered by him
to the Synod held at Philadelphia, September 17, 1718:
1. Their government by bishops, archbishops, deans, chancellors, and vicars, is wholly unscriptural. 2. Their discipline by surrogates and chancellors in their courts ecclesiastic, is without a foundation in the word of God. 3. Their
abuse of that supposed discipline by commutation. 4. A
diocesan bishop cannot be founded, *jure divino*, upon
Paul's epistles to Timothy or Titus, nor anywhere else in
the word of God, and so is a mere human invention.
5. The usurped power of the bishops at their yearly visi-
tations, acting all of themselves, without consent of the
brethren. 6. Pluralities of benefices. 7. The churches
conniving at the practice of Arminian doctrines inconsistent with the eternal purpose of God, and an encourage-
ment to vice. Besides, I could not be satisfied with their
ceremonial way of worship. Those have so affected my

conscience, that I could no longer abide in a Church where the same are practised.

WILLIAM TENNENT."

Prior to the Revolution, the Presbyterian churches continued to increase by a gradual process, throughout many of the original thirteen States; and with the formation of new churches, presbyteries and synods were established, which held ecclesiastical jurisdiction over them. In Virginia, they were much persecuted by the Episcopalians, who went so far, in 1618, as to enact by their House of Burgesses, that if any person came within the colony, and claimed to be a clergyman, and attempted to preach or perform any other clerical duty, without being able to show a testimonial that he had been ordained by an English diocesan bishop, he was to be expelled from the limits of the colony. By the operation of this law the Presbyterian clergy were entirely excluded from Virginia for a long series of years.

When the Revolution broke out, many of the most eminent patriots of the era were Presbyterians. Among these were John Witherspoon, who took a prominent part in securing the passage of the Declaration of Independence; and George Duffield, who was a chaplain in the Continental army. As a body, the Presbyterians contended for the validity of "a Church without a bishop, and a State without a king;" and their Church government is eminently a democratic or a republican one, by which the laity, through their representatives, the Ruling Elders, are admitted to an equal share of authority in the various ecclesiastical tribunals of the Church. Previous to the Revolution, a friendly correspondence was carried on between this sect and the Dutch Reformed, and Associate Reformed Synods; but the most important era in the consolidation and prosperity of the Presbyterian Church in this country, was at the time of the first convention of the General Assembly of the whole Church, which met in 1789.

By the establishment of the General Assembly, all the

Presbyterians in the various States were combined into one ecclesiastical congregation; a uniformity of discipline and of doctrine was introduced among them; and greater system was attained in carrying on their benevolent enterprises, as well as in enforcing discipline. Among the several institutions which the Church established at successive periods, were the Theological Seminary at Princeton, N. J., at a later day, the Western Seminary at Allegheny City, near Pittsburgh, and the Union Seminary in Prince Edward County, Virginia; while among the colleges which are exclusively or chiefly under their control, are Nassau Hall at Princeton, Jefferson College at Cannonsburg, La Fayette College at Easton, the University of Nashville in Tennessee, and Centre College at Danville, Kentucky. Besides these, there are a Board of Education for preparing young clergymen for the ministry; a Board of Publication, which has already issued nearly a hundred and fifty standard religious works; a Board of Missions, both domestic and foreign. The latter has sent forth many missionaries to various portions of the earth. Thus in Northern India, there is a Synod of American missionaries who are in connection with the Old School General Assembly. This Synod is composed of several Presbyteries which bear eastern names, as the Presbytery of Allahabad, having six ministers; the Presbytery of Ferrukabad, having four ministers; and the Presbytery of Lodiana, with five ministers, besides the usual number of elders.

In the year 1830, the great schism began which resulted in the division of the Presbyterian body in this country into two parts, of nearly equal numbers and importance. We will proceed to state the chief doctrines which the Old School entertain. As the opinions taught by this sect are those of extreme and unmitigated Calvinism, and are peculiarly obnoxious to every other class of Christians, both Orthodox and Liberal, we will state them at some length.

I. In regard to the Divine nature, Presbyterians hold the views which are universally termed Orthodox, such as that God is a spirit, infinite in glory and perfection, in power and wisdom, eternal, unchangeable, incomprehensible, everywhere present, just, merciful, and gracious; that there is but one true God, though there are three persons in the Godhead—that these three are one, the same in substance, equal in power and glory, though distinguished by their personal properties. In defining what the different properties of these three Persons are, they answer that it is the function of the Father to beget the Son, and of the Son to be begotten of the Father, and of the Holy Spirit to proceed from the Father and the Son from all eternity. Yet these three are perfectly equal in power; all three are equally eternal, without beginning, and un-created.

II. They believe and teach that Adam was created perfectly pure and holy; but that he fell from that estate (being left to the full freedom of his own will) by eating of the forbidden fruit. That when Adam fell, all his future posterity fell with him; that their nature became totally corrupted and sinful, wholly inclined to evil, and incapable of doing or thinking a particle of good. That by this fall Adam and all his posterity incurred the wrath and vengeance of Almighty God, his displeasure and his curse; that they became justly liable to eternal misery hereafter; and that, if left to themselves, they would inevitably suffer such a fate.

III. In regard to God's decrees and purposes, they hold that He foreordains from all eternity whatever comes to pass; and that, being Omnipotent, his decrees cannot be resisted. That He determined from all eternity that a few members of the human family should be made heirs of salvation, while all the rest should become the recipients of the eternal misery which their original and actual sins had deserved. That he has chosen an elect few to enjoy eternal life; and that, as none can enter Heaven without being holy and pure, the repentance and regeneration of the elect are necessarily as certainly foreordained by God, as is their final salvation. Hence men will repent or not repent, be lost or saved, precisely as God has decreed from all eternity.

This doctrine is the great bone of contention between Calvinists and Arminians; and to the vast majority of mankind it seems to be a most abominable sentiment, inasmuch as it appears to teach that God creates millions of his creatures, knowing that he has decreed beforehand that they shall be forever and supremely miserable— thereby making him cruel, partial, inexorable, and revengeful. And yet, there are passages of Scripture which seem to teach this doctrine as plainly as words could express it. Thus, for instance, Ephesians, i. 4, 5: "According as he hath chosen us in him [Christ] before the foundation of the world, that we should be holy—having *predestinated us* unto the adoption of children, by Jesus Christ, to himself." Verse 11 of the same chapter reads as follows: "In whom also we have obtained an inheritance, being *predestinated* according to the purpose of him who worketh all things after the counsel of his own will." So also Romans, ix. 18: "Therefore hath he mercy on whom he will have mercy, and whom he will he hardeneth." And stronger still in Romans, viii. 30: "Whom he did predestinate, them he also called; and whom he called, them he also justified; and whom he justified, them he also glorified." Scripture proofs, which are apparently so unanswerable as these seem to be, induce the members of this denomination to adhere tenaciously and with great earnestness to a doctrine which Orthodox churches generally condemn, and which liberal Christians abominate as disgraceful to God, and ruinous to human happiness.

IV. According to the Presbyterian doctrine, God has made two *covenants* with the human race: one with Adam, which Adam broke and forfeited; another with Christ, and in him with all the elect as his seed. The latter covenant is called the covenant of grace, by which a Mediator is provided for those whom God has ordained to eternal life. The covenant of grace was administered under the Old Testament by promises, prophecies, sacrifices, circumcision, and other types and ordinances; all of which were intended to represent the subsequent coming and sufferings of Christ. Under the New Testament this covenant is administered by the sacraments of Baptism and the Lord's Supper, the preaching of the word, and the other ordinances of Christianity. That the redemption procured by Christ might be efficacious, it was necessary that he should be both God and man. The divine nature in him was necessary to sustain and keep the human nature from sinking under the infinite wrath of God and the power of death; although his human nature *did* finally sink under that exorbitant wrath; and it was requisite that the Mediator should be human in order that he might perform perfect obedience to the law, suffer, and make intercession for men in their own nature, and have a fellow-feeling of sympathy with mankind.

V. Another prominent doctrine of the Presbyterian system is "the final perseverance of the saints," by which is meant that it is impossible for those who have once repented and become Christians to relapse, fall from grace, and go to hell. This opinion results from their theory of "effectual calling," which is the work of God's power and purpose, whereby, out of his free and especial love to his elect, he draws them in his own time and way to repentance and faith, by the *resistless* influence of the Holy Spirit; and that being thus called in accordance with God's purpose to redeem them, there can be no possibility of his intention being defeated, and they lost by a return to a sinful life. They admit that true believers may, in consequence of temptation and the inherent weakness of human nature, commit some sins, and that their best works are, after all, imperfect in the sight of God. But Christ continually makes intercession for them; they are meanwhile inseparably united to him; and they may at all times rest assured that they are in a state of grace, and that they will infallibly be saved in the end. This confidence is based upon the promises of God to his elect, and on the omnipotence and the truthfulness of his nature.

VI. Presbyterians believe in but two sacraments, Baptism and the Lord's Supper. The former is administered on all occasions by sprinkling, and to infants as well as adults. Their view of the Lord's Supper is, that the bread and wine are merely commemorative symbols intended to remind the communicant of the events of Christ's sufferings and death, and thus give rise to devout reflections. They do not in general receive the mysterious doctrine which John Calvin teaches in his Institutes, which asserts that the worthy communicant eats the flesh and bones of Christ, and drinks his blood, but that though he does this really, it is *spiritually* only; which is about as reasonable a doctrine as to assert that human beings are composed of body and spirit, yet that the corporeal part merely exists *spiritually*. Genuine Presbyterians in this country deny this doctrine, and adhere to the simply symbolical nature of the Supper.

VII. As to the final destination of the good and the wicked, the Presbyterian system, while it asserts that the elect few shall be saved, yet *barely* saved, teaches the extremest degree of horror and hell-fire in reference to the vast majority of mankind, who, not being among the elect, cannot, and never could by any possibility, enter heaven. The preaching of Presbyterian clergymen usually exhibits a larger proportion of gloom, and is generally pervaded by a greater degree of brimstone and teeth-gnashing, than the preaching of any other denomination of Christians.

Such are the main outlines of the doctrinal system held by the Old School Presbyterian Church. Many men of great eminence and distinction have belonged to the sect in this country, such as Dr. Archibald Alexander, Hodge, the two Breckenridges, Ashbel Green, and others. Since the separation between the Old and the New Schools, the former have increased more rapidly than the latter, and at the present time are more numerous and flourishing. They now have, under the jurisdiction of the General Assembly, some twenty-five synods, about one hundred and thirty presbyteries, fifteen hundred ministers, twenty-two hundred churches, and two hundred and fifty thousand regular communicants.

UNITARIANS.

THE controversy which took place in Boston between Dr. Channing and Dr. Samuel Worcester, in 1815, first attracted the attention of the *whole* community to the existence and to the doctrines of Unitarianism. The polemic storm raged during several years, many publications appearing on both sides of the question. After the tempest passed away, the unscathed and imposing form of Unitarian Christianity appeared through the gloom, towering toward heaven in attractive beauty, symmetry, and solidity, holding a recognized place among the religious denominations of the country. The principle which lies at the foundation of this church is that of the *unrestricted* right of private judgment in matters of religion. The advocates of Unitarianism hold that each individual is *responsible* to God for the opinions which he entertains, and that where there is responsibility there must of necessity be perfect freedom of thinking and acting. Neither primitive Fathers, nor ecclesiastical councils, nor synods, nor established creeds, possess any absolute authority for them. In the conscientious exercise of this right the founders, or rather revivers, of Unitarianism in this country, arrived at a system of belief something like the following: They hold to the absolute Unity of the Supreme Being; thus necessarily denying the doctrine of the Trinity, or three persons in one God. They teach that Christ was the first and greatest of all created beings; that he was the wisest and best personage who ever existed on earth; that his mission was divine, being what he himself declared it to be, sent by God "to bear witness to the truth;" that the Holy Spirit is not a separate personal entity, but an *influence* which the Creator exercises upon the minds of men under such circumstances as may comport with his will and purposes; that the Scriptures are for the most part the product of a divine influence exerted upon the minds of those who wrote them, and that they contain doctrines and precepts, the belief and observance of which will make men wise unto salvation. The Unitarians further believe that the death of Christ was not vicarious, but simply the necessary and natural result of his labors and innovations as a great and wise teacher; that by dying on the cross he gave the strongest possible evidence of his own sincerity, disinterestedness, and obedience to the will of Him who sent him; that he was raised from the dead "by the power of God;" that such miracles as he did perform, he performed by that same power, which was delegated to him; that inasmuch as he left no very specific and minute directions to his apostles in reference to the external religious organization of those who then were, and who would afterward become, his followers, he regarded that outward form as a matter of little consequence; that in proportion as mankind in every age believe and obey what they find recorded in the Scriptures, interpreted by their own enlightened consciousness of what they suppose to be taught therein, they will be happy here and hereafter. They hold that charity, and not ecclesiastical ferocity—love to God and man, and not implacable religious bigotry and spite—constitute the great fundamental essence of Christianity. They believe that every sinful act will be punished precisely *in proportion* to its deserts; and that the ultimate consequence of that punishment will be curative and remedial, which they regard as the only fit purpose of punishment when inflicted by an infinitely wise and benevolent Creator. Finally, they contend that, at the "consummation of all things," a result will be produced which will prove that the chief object of God in the creation of the world was *not* to construct an almost universal pandemonium, in which ninety-nine hundredths of his rational creatures should after death be eternally and hopelessly miserable, thus making a general hell in fact the *chef d'œuvre* of his moral government, and the most prominent and all-absorbing object in it; but that, on the contrary, the final destiny of the world will be the prevalence of universal holiness, such as God's pure law demands; of universal happiness, such as his merciful nature rejoices in; a whole race redeemed from sin and misery by obedience to the truth, such as Jesus taught it; and a universe exulting throughout its vast and illimitable domains in that unbroken harmony, purity, and felicity, which would alone confer glory upon the attributes and providence of the Creator and Father of all.

UNIVERSALISTS.

Of the *real* doctrines of Universalism, very great ignorance prevails in this country. As an organized denomination it is of comparatively recent date; being scarcely known anterior to the opening of the present century. Yet though the career of the organization is not very ancient, it is a circumstance worthy of note that the chief central doctrine of Universalism has been held by some few Christian teachers in all ages since the Apostolic era. Several of the early Fathers taught it. Origen and Arius believed it. Several of the divines of the Church of England have held it, such as Tillotson; as well as some eminent "Dissenters," such as John Foster; to say nothing of vast numbers of what are termed the Neological or Rationalistic theologians of Germany. It cannot be denied that important changes have taken place in the doctrinal system held by Universalists in this country, since it was originally preached by Hosea Ballou, the first. According to him and his immediate successors, the theory of Universalism was, that all penalty or punishment for sin was inflicted in the present life; and that in consequence of the universal and all-atoning power of Christ's sufferings and atonement, all men entered on the enjoyment of the felicities of heaven immediately after their departure from the earth. This theory entirely ignored the existence of hellfire; of a personal, living and tormenting Devil; of a literal judgment-day, in which a separation should be made between the good and the bad, the sheep and the goats; and it contended that though every man should be adequately and sufficiently punished for his unforgiven sins, that punishment would be inflicted only during the period and the progress of the present existence.

Subsequently the main doctrine of the denomination became altered, in consequence, probably, of future investigation, and also, doubtless, from the experience which had been felt of the difficulty of maintaining, by argument, the position originally and previously contended for. The opinion substituted for the old one by the general consent, or at least by the general use and concurrence of the denomination, was, that while denying the *eternity* of hell-fire, they admitted that *some* punishment for sin did take place in a future state, accurately proportioned by Infinite Wisdom and Justice to the precise deserts of the sinner. Universalists now hold to the existence of a future purgatory, not unlike, in some respects, to the Roman Catholic doctrine. They are at present, in fact and substance, Rationalists, teaching the final restoration of all mankind to holiness, and, as a necessary consequence, to happiness. Other important changes have taken place gradually in the doctrinal system held by them. Originally they taught the absolute divinity of Christ, with the vicarious nature and the universally efficacious power of his atonement. They held that, so great was the benefit produced by his sufferings and death for fallen, degraded and ruined humanity, that all men were saved thereby from future and eternal punishment : the disciplinary and punitive portion of human existence being confined to the present life. Now, however, they generally deny the divinity of Christ. Some are *Arians*, regarding him as a member of the Godhead, but greatly inferior in nature, power, and glory, to the Father. The majority of them are *Socinians*, believing Christ to have been only a man, but the greatest, best, and wisest of men and of teachers who ever existed and labored on earth. They deny the vicarious nature of the atonement, or, rather, they do not believe in any atonement at all, for the logical reason that, if Christ were a mere man, his sufferings, death, and obedience, would not be any more efficacious in propitiating the wrath of the offended Deity, and fulfilling the requirements of an all-perfect law, than would the sufferings, death, and obedience of any other great and good man. In fact, they go behind the theory of the atonement entirely, and hold that no atonement is necessary, because Adam and his descendants have never fallen. In other words, they deny original sin and native depravity. They do not regard human nature as the degraded, miserable, and detestable thing which the Orthodox system represents it as being. They contend that if Adam fell and thus threw a black mantle of misfortune and guilt over the moral uni verse immediately after his creation, such an event was a failure and a baulk at the very commencement of God's moral government, which would be by no means complimentary to the providence, foresight, and power of the Creator; who, originally creating the world and the human race for purity, holiness, and happiness alone, at once beheld the whole business spoiled, his handiwork defaced, his glory marred, his enemy the Devil triumphant, and his own benevolent purposes defeated at the very start of the experiment. Accordingly, Universalists do not believe that any such fearful catastrophe ever occurred; and while they admit that sin exists in the world, they do not believe in the same excess of it, nor in the necessity of the same remedy for its powers and its ravages which the Orthodox do; but they hold that by suffering the inevitable consequences of sin both here, and temporarily and sufficiently hereafter, it will be wiped out eventually from every spirit, and a holy and happy race will be the winding up of the world's history and experience.

MAHOMMEDANS.

THE Mohammedans, or Mahommedans, derive their name and doctrine from Mahomet, who was born in Arabia, in

the sixth century.   He was endowed with a subtle genius,
and possessed an enterprise and ambition peculiar to himself.   He pretended to receive revelations; and declared
that God sent him into the world, not only to teach his
will, but to compel mankind to embrace it.   The magistrates of Mecca were alarmed at the progress of his doctrines, and Mohammed being apprized of their design to
destroy him, fled to Medina: from this flight, which happened in the 622d year of Christ, his followers compute
their time.   This era is called in Arabic, Hegira.

The book in which the Mahometan religion is contained,
is called the Koran, or Alcoran, by way of eminence, as
we say the Bible, which means the Book.*   Its doctrines
made a most rapid progress over Arabia, Syria, Egypt, and
Persia; and Mohammed became the most powerful monarch in his time.   His successors spread their religion and
conquests over the greatest part of Asia, Africa, and
Europe; and they still give law to a very considerable
part of mankind.

The great doctrine of the Koran is the unity of God: to
restore which point, Mohammed pretended was the chief
end of his mission; it being laid down by him as a fundamental truth, that there never was, nor ever can be, more
than one true orthodox religion.   For though the particular laws or ceremonies are only temporary, and subject to
alteration according to the divine direction, yet the substance of it being eternal truth, is not liable to change,
but continues immutably the same.   And he taught, that
whenever this religion became neglected, or corrupted in
essentials, God had the goodness to re-inform and re-ad-
monish mankind thereof by several prophets, of whom
Moses and Jesus were the most distinguished, till the ap-

* The generality of the Mohammedans believe, that the first manuscript of the Koran has been from everlasting by God's throne, written
on a table of vast bigness called the Preserved Table, in which are recorded the divine decrees : that a copy from this table, in one volume
on paper, was, by the ministry of the angel Gabriel, sent down to the
lowest heaven, in the month of Ramadan.

pearance of Mohammed. The Koran asserts Jesus to be the true Messias, the word and breath of God, worker of miracles, healer of diseases, preacher of heavenly doctrine, and exemplary pattern of a perfect life; denying that he was crucified, but affirming that he ascended into Paradise; and that his religion was mended by Mohammed, who was the seal of the prophets, and was sent from God to restore the true religion, which was corrupted in his time, to its primitive simplicity; with the addition, however, of peculiar laws and ceremonies, some of which have been used in former times, and others were now first instituted.

The Mohammedans divide their religion into two general parts—faith or theory, and religion or practice. Faith or theory is contained in this confession of faith,—There is but one God, and Mohammed is his prophet. Under these two propositions are comprehended six distinct branches:

1. Belief in God.—2. In his angels.—3. In his scriptures.—4. In his prophets.—5. In the resurrection and judgment.—6. In God's absolute decrees.

They reckon four points relating to practice, viz:

1. Prayer, with washings.—2. Alms.—3. Fasting.—4. Pilgrimage to Mecca.

The idea which Mohammed taught his disciples to entertain of the Supreme Being, may be seen from a public address he made to his countrymen, which is as follows:

"Citizens of Mecca! The hour is now come, when you must give an account of your reason and your talents. In vain have you received them from an Almighty Master, liberal and beneficent—in case you use them negligently, or if you never reflect. In the name of this Master, I must tell you, he will not suffer you to abuse his inestimable gifts by wasting life away unprofitably, and employing them only in unworthy amusements. No more permit delusive pleasures to distract your hearts! Open your minds and receive the truth! Wo to you for the unworthy notion you have entertained of God! The heaven and the earth are his own! and there is nothing in all their copious furniture but what invariably obeys him! The sun and stars with all their glory, have never disdained his service! and no being can resist his will, and the exercise of his omnipotence! He will call men to an account, and require of them the reason for all those Gods they have invented in defiance of reason! There is no other God but God, and him only we must adore."*

The belief of the existence of angels is absolutely required in the Koran. The Mohammedans suppose they have pure and subtile bodies, created of fire; and that they have various forms and offices; some being employed in writing down the actions of men, others in carrying the throne of God, and other services. They reckon four angels superior to all the rest: These are, Gabriel, who is employed in writing down the divine decrees; Michael, the friend and protector of the Jews; Azrael, the angel of death; and Israsil, who will sound the trumpet at the resurrection. They likewise assign to each person two guardian angels.

The Devil, according to the Koran, was once one of the highest angels, but fell for refusing to pay homage to Adam at the command of God.

Besides angels and devils, the Mohammedans are taught by the Koran to believe an intermediate order of creatures, which they call Jin, or Genii, created also of fire, but of a grosser fabric than angels; and are subject to death. Some of these are supposed to be good, and others bad, and capable of future salvation or damnation as men are; whence Mohammed pretended to be sent for the conversion of Genii as well as men.

As to the Scriptures, the Mohammedans are taught by the Koran, that God, in divers ages of the world, gave revelations of his will in writing to several prophets. The number of these sacred books, according to them, are one hundred and four; of which ten were given to Adam, fifty to Seth, thirty to Enoch, ten to Abraham; and the other

* Boulanviller's Life of Mahomet.

four, being the Pentateuch, the Psalms, the Gospels, and the Koran, were successively delivered to Moses, David, Jesus, and Mohammed; which last, being the seal of the prophets, these revelations are now closed. All these divine books, excepting the four last, they agree to be entirely lost, and their contents unknown. And of these four, the Pentateuch, Psalms, and Gospels, they say, have undergone so many alterations and corruptions, that very little credit is to be given to the present copies in the hands of the Jews and Christians.

The number of prophets, who have been from time to time sent into the world, amounts to two hundred and twenty-four thousand; among whom three hundred and thirteen were apostles, sent with special commissions to reclaim mankind from infidelity and superstition; and six of them brought new laws or dispensations, which successively abrogated the preceding. These were Adam, Noah, Abraham, Moses, Jesus, and Mohammed.*

The next article of faith required by the Koran, is the belief of a general resurrection and a future judgment. But before these, they believe there is an intermediate state, both of the soul and of the body after death. When a corpse is laid in the grave, two angels come and examine it concerning the unity of God, and the mission of Mohammed. If the body answers rightly, it is suffered to rest in peace, and is refreshed by the air of Paradise: if not, they beat it about the temples with iron maces; then press the earth on the corpse, which is gnawed and stung by ninety-nine dragons, with seven heads each.

As to the souls of the faithful, when they are separated from the body by the angel of death, they teach, that those of the prophets are admitted into Paradise immediately. Some suppose, the souls of believers are with Adam in the lowest heaven; and there are various other opinions concerning their state. Those who are called the most orthodox, hold that the souls of the wicked are con-

* Sale's Koran, vol. i. p. 94, 95.

fined in a dungeon under a green rock, to be there tormented till their re-union with the body at the general resurrection.

That the resurrection will be general, and extend to all creatures, both angels, genii, men, and animals, is the received opinion of the Mohammedans, which they support by the authority of the Koran.

Mankind, at the resurrection, will be distinguished into three classes; the first, of those who go on foot; the second, of those who ride; and the third, of those who creep groveling with their faces to the ground. The first class will consist of those believers whose good works have been few; the second, of those who are more acceptable to God; whence Ali affirmed that the pious, when they come forth from their sepulchres, shall find ready prepared for them, white-winged camels, with saddles of gold. The third class will be composed of the infidels, whom God will cause to make their appearance with their faces on the ground. When all are assembled together, they will wait, in their ranks and orders, for the judgment; some say forty years, others seventy, others three hundred, and some no less than fifty thousand years. During which time they will suffer great inconveniences, the good as well as the bad, from their thronging and pressing upon each other, and the unusual approach of the sun, which will be no farther off them, than the distance of a mile; so that the skulls of the wicked will boil like a pot, and they will be all bathed with sweat. At length, God will come in the clouds surrounded by the angels, and will produce the books wherein every man's actions are written. Some (explaining those words so frequently used in the Koran, God will be swift in taking an account,) say, that he will judge all creatures in the space of half a day; and others, that it will be done in less time than the twinkling of an eye. At this tribunal, every action, thought, word, &c. will be weighed in a balance held by the angel Gabriel, of so vast a size, that its two scales are capacious enough to contain both heaven and earth.

The trials being over, and the assembly dissolved, those who are to be admitted into Paradise, will take the right hand way ; and those who are destined to hell-fire, the left; but both of them must first pass the bridge called in Arabic, *Al Sirat*, which is laid over the middle of hell, and is described to be finer than a hair, and sharper than the edge of a sword. The wicked will miss their footing and fall headlong into hell.*

In the Koran it is said that hell has seven gates ; the first for the Musselmen, the second for the Christians, the third for the Jews, the fourth for the Sabians, the fifth for the Magicians, the sixth for the Pagans, the seventh and worst of all, for the Hypocrites of all religions. The inhabitants of hell will suffer a variety of torments, which shall be of eternal duration, except with those who have embraced the true religion, who will be delivered thence, after they have expiated their crimes by their sufferings.†

The righteous, after having surmounted the difficulties in their passage, will enter Paradise, which they describe to be a most delicious place, whose earth is the finest wheat, or musk ; and the stones pearls, or jacinths. It is also adorned with flowery fields, beautiful with trees of gold, enlivened with the most ravishing music, inhabited by exquisite beauties, abounding with rivers of milk, wine, and honey, and watered by lesser springs, whose pebbles are rubies, emeralds, &c. Here the faithful enjoy the most exquisite sensual delights, free from the least alloy.‡

The sixth great point of faith which the Mohammedans are taught to believe, is, God's absolute decrees, and predetermination, both of good and evil. The doctrine which

---

* Sale's Koran, p. 90, 100, 112.

† Between Paradise and hell, they imagine there is a wall or partition, in which, some suppose, those were placed whose good and evil works exactly counterpoised each other. These will be admitted to Paradise at the last day, after they have performed an act of adoration, which will make the scale of their good works to over-balance.

‡ Some of the most refined Mohammedans understand their prophet's description of Paradise in an allegorical sense.

12

they call orthodox, is, that whatever doth or shall come to pass in the world, whether it be good or bad, proceedeth entirely from the divine will, and is irrevocably fixed and recorded from all eternity in the preserved table; and that God hath secretly predetermined not only the adverse and prosperous fortune of every person in the world, in the most minute particulars, but also his obedience or disobedience, and consequently his everlasting happiness or misery after death; which fate or predestination it is impossible by any foresight or wisdom to avoid.

Of the four practical duties required by the Koran, prayer is the first. Mohammed used to call prayer the pillar of religion and the key of Paradise. Hence he obliged his followers to pray five times every twenty-four hours, and always wash before prayers.

Circumcision is held by the Mohammedans to be of divine institution.

The giving of alms is frequently commanded in the Koran, and often recommended therein jointly with prayer; the former being held of great efficacy in causing the latter to be heard with God.

Fasting is a duty enjoined by Mohammed as of the utmost importance. His followers are obliged by the express command of the Koran, to fast the whole month of Ramadan; during which time, they are obliged to fast from daylight to sunset. The reason the month of Ramadan is pitched upon for that purpose, is, because they suppose that at that time the Koran was sent down from heaven.

The pilgrimage to Mecca is so necessary a point of practice, that, according to a tradition of Mohammed, he who dies without performing it, may as well die a Jew or a Christian; and the same is expressly commanded in the Koran.

The negative precepts of the Koran are, to abstain from usury, gaming, drinking of wine, eating of blood, and swine's flesh.

The Mohammedans are divided and subdivided into an

endless variety of sects.   As it is said there is as great a diversity in their opinions as among the Christians, it is impossible to give a particular account of their divisions in the compass of this work ; which will admit only of noticing a few of their principal denominations.

The divinity of the Mohammedans may be divided into scholastic and practical.   Their scholastic divinity consists of logical, metaphysical, theological, and philosophical disquisitions ; and is built on principles and methods of reasoning very different from what are used by those who pass among the Mohammedans themselves for the sounder divines, or more able philosophers.   This art of handling religious disputes was not known in the infancy of Mohammedism, but was brought in when sects sprang up, and articles of religion began to be called in question.

As to their practical divinity, or jurisprudence, it consists in the knowledge of the decisions of the law, which regard practice gathered from distinct proofs.   The principal points of faith subject to the examination and discussion of the school-men, are, the unity and attributes of God ; the divine decrees, or predestination ; the promises and threats contained in the law ; and matters of history and reason.

The sects among the Mohammedans who are esteemed orthodox, are called by the general name of Sonnites, or Traditionarists, because they acknowledge the authority of the Sonna, or collection of moral traditions of the sayings and actions of their prophet.

The Sonnites are subdivided into four chief sects, viz., 1st. The Hanisites.—2d. The Malekites.—3d. The Shafeits.—4th. The Hanbalites.

The difference between these sects consists only in a few indifferent ceremonies.

The sects whom the generality of the Mohammedans suppose entertain erroneous opinions are numerous ; the following are selected from a large number, in order to

give some ideas of the disputes among Mohammedan divines.*

I. The Montazalites, the followers of Wasel Ebn Ata.
As to their chief and general tenets: 1st. They entirely
rejected all eternal attributes of God, to avoid the distinction of persons made by the Christians. 2d. They
believed the word of God to have been created *in subjecto*,
as the school-men term it, and to consist of letters and
sounds; copies thereof being written in books to express
and imitate the original. They also affirmed, that whatever is created *in subjecto* is also an accident, and liable
to perish. 3d. They denied absolute predestination; maintaining, that God was not the author of evil, but of good
only; and that man was a free agent. 4th. They held,
that if a professor of the true religion is guilty of a grievous sin, and dies without repentance, he will be eternally
damned, though his punishment will be lighter than that
of the infidels. 5th. They denied all vision of God in Paradise by the corporeal eye, and rejected all comparisons
or similitudes applied to God.

This sect are said to have been the first inventors of
scholastic divinity, and are subdivided, as some reckon,
into twenty different sects.

II. The Hashbemians; who were so named from their
master Aba Hasham Abel al Salem. His followers were
so much afraid of making God the author of evil, that they
would not allow him to be said to create an infidel, because
an infidel is a compound of infidelity and man, and God is
not the creator of infidelity.

III. The Nohamians, or followers of Ibrahim al Ned-
ham, who imagining he could not sufficiently remove God
from being the author of evil, without divesting him of his
power in respect thereto, taught that no power ought to be
ascribed to God concerning evil and rebellious actions:
but this he affirmed against the opinion of his own disci-

---

* Sale's Koran, p. 142, 146, 148, 150, 152.

ples, who allowed that God could do evil, but did not, because of its turpitude.

IV. The Jabedhians, or followers of Amru Ebn Bahr, a great doctor of the Montazalites, who differed from his brethren, in that he imagined the damned would not be eternally tormented in hell, but would be changed into the nature of brutes, and the vilest classes of the animal creation.

ATHANASIANS.

Those who profess similar sentiments to those taught by Athanasius, bishop of Alexandria, who flourished in the fourth century. He was bishop during forty-six years; and his long administration was spent in a perpetual combat against the powers of Arianism. He is said to have consecrated every moment, and every faculty of his being, to the defence of the doctrine of the Trinity. The scheme of Athanasius made the Supreme Deity to consist of three persons, the same in substance, equal in power and glory. The first of those three persons and fountain of divinity to the other two, it makes to be the Father. The second person is called the Son, and is said to be descended from the Father, by an eternal generation of an ineffable and incomprehensible nature in the essence of the Godhead. The third person is the Holy Ghost, derived from the Father and the Son, but not by generation, as the Son is derived from the Father, but by an eternal and incomprehensible procession. Each of these persons are very and eternal God, as much as the Father himself; and yet though distinguished in this manner, they do not make three Gods, but one God.

This system also includes in it the belief of two natures in Jesus Christ, viz., the divine and human, forming one person.

To prove the divinity of Christ, and his co-equality with the Father, this denomination argue thus :

In John i. 1, it is said expressly, " In the beginning

was the Word, and the Word was with God, and the Word was God." Which implies, that the Word existed from all eternity, not as a distinct, separate power, but the Word was with God, and the Word was God, not another God, but only another person, of the same nature, substance, and Godhead.

It is evident, that St. John intended the word "God" in this strict sense, from the time of which he is speaking. In the beginning the Word was God, before the creation. It is not said, that he was appointed God over the things which should be afterwards created. He was God before any dominion over the creatures commenced.

It is said, that all things absolutely were made by him; therefore he who created all things, cannot be a created being. Since nothing was made but by and through him, it follows that the Son, as Creator, must be eternal and strictly divine.

Christ's divinity and co-equality with the Father, are plainly taught in Phil. ii. 5, 6, 7, &c. "Let this mind be in you, which was also in Christ Jesus, who being in the form of God, thought it not robbery to be equal with God, but made himself of no reputation, and took upon him the form of a servant."

Our Saviour says of himself, "I and my Father are one." John v. 19. "He that has seen me, has seen the Father." John x. 30. "All that the Father hath are mine." John xvi. 15. Those high and strong expressions are supposed to teach, that he is the supreme God.

The prophets describe the true God as the only Saviour of sinners. For thus it is written, "I, even I, am Jehovah, and besides me there is no Saviour. Jesus Christ not only professes to save sinners, but he calls himself the Saviour, by way of eminence. Hence it is evident, that he assumes a character in the most emphatical way, which the God of Israel had challenged and appropriated to himself.

The divine titles, which are ascribed to the Son in Scriptures are: "The true God." 1 John v. 28. "The mighty God." Isa. ix. 6. "The Alpha and Omega, the first and the last." Rev. i. 8. "The God over all blessed forever more." Rom. ix. 5. And Thomas calls Christ, after his resurrection, his Lord and God.

The titles given to Christ in the New Testament, are the same with those which are given to God in the Jewish Scriptures. The name Jehovah,* which is appropriated to God, Psalm lxxxiii. 18. Isa. xiv. 5, is given to Christ. See Isa. xiv. 23, 25, compared with Rom. xiv. 12. Isa. xi. 3, compared with Luke i. 76. Jesus is the person spoken of by St. John, whose glory Esaias is declared to have seen, when he affirms he saw the Lord of hosts. Therefore Jesus is the Lord of hosts.

The attributes, which are sometimes appropriated to God, are applied to Christ.

Omniscience is ascribed to Christ. John xvi. 10. "Now we are sure that thou knowest all things." To be the searcher of the heart, is the peculiar and distinguishing characteristic of the one true God, as appears from Jer. xvii. 10. Yet our blessed Lord claims this perfection to himself. "I am he," saith he, "that searcheth the reins and the heart." Rev. ii. 23.

Omnipresence, another divine attribute, is ascribed to Christ. Matt. xviii. 20. "Where two or three are gathered together in my name, there am I, in the midst of them."

Immutability is ascribed to Christ. Heb. i. 10, 11, 12. "Thou art the same, and thy years shall not fail." This is the very description which the Psalmist gives of the immutability of the only true God. See also Heb. xiii. 8.

Eternity is ascribed to Christ. Rev. i. 8. The Son's being Jehovah, is another proof of his eternity, that name expressing necessary existence.

---

* It has been observed by critics on the word Jehovah, that the first syllable *Jah* means the divine essence, and that by *hovah* may be understood, calamity, grief, destruction. Hence some have supposed, the design of that venerable name was to convey unto us the ideas of a divine essence in a human frame, and a suffering and crucified Messiah.

Christ is also said to have almighty power. Heb. i. 3.
See also Phil. iii. 21.

The truth and faithfulness of God are ascribed to Christ.
" I am," says he, " the truth," &c.

Divine works are also ascribed to Christ, viz., creation,
preservation, and forgiveness of sins.

There are numerous texts of Scripture, which assert
that Christ is the Creator of all things. See Heb. i. 10.
" Thou, Lord, in the beginning hast laid the foundation of
the earth, and the heavens are the work of thy hands.
See also Rev. iii. 14. 1 Cor. viii. 6, and various other
passages.

The work of creation is everywhere, in Scripture, represented as the mark and characteristic of the true God.
See 2 Kings xix. 15.   Job xxii. 7.   Psalm xix. 1.   Hence
it is evident that Christ, the Creator, is the true God.

Preservation is ascribed to Christ.   Heb. i. 3.   " Up-
holding all things by the word of his power."

Christ himself says, in Matt. ix. 6, " The Son of man
hath power on earth to forgive sins.

Christ's being appointed the supreme Judge of the
world, is an evidence that he is the true God.   The God
of Israel is emphatically styled, the Judge of all.

Religious worship, though appropriated to God, was by
divine approbation and command given to Christ.   Heb.
i. 6.   The apostle speaking of Christ, says, " Let the angels of God worship him."   See also Luke xxiv. 25.   John
v. 23.   Rev. i. 5, 6 ; v. 13, &c.

The Scripture everywhere asserts that God alone is to
be worshiped.   The same Scripture asserts that our
blessed Saviour is to be worshiped.   Thus St. Stephen
adores him with direct worship : " Lord Jesus, receive my
Spirit."   The obvious consequence of which is, our blessed
Saviour is God.

This denomination allege, that divine titles, attributes,
works, and worship, are also ascribed to the Holy Ghost.

Many plead that the Holy Spirit is called Jehovah in
the Old Testament, by comparing Acts xxviii. 23, with

Isa. vi. 9. And he also appears to be called God. Acts v. 4.

Eternity is clearly the property of the Holy Ghost, who is styled by the author of the epistle to the Hebrews, "the eternal Spirit." Heb. ix. 14.

Omnipresence is a necessary proof of divinity. This attribute belongs to the Holy Spirit; for thus saith the inspired poet, "Whither shall I go from thy Spirit?" Psalm cxxxix. 7.

Omniscience is ascribed to the Spirit. 1 Cor. ii. 10. "For the Spirit searcheth all things, even the deep things of God."

St. Paul declares, that his ability to work all manner of astonishing miracles, for the confirmation of his ministry, was imparted to him by the Spirit. Rom. xv. 19. The same act of divine grace, viz., our spiritual birth, is ascribed without the change of a single letter to God and the Spirit. John ii. 1. 1 John v. 4.

The chief texts produced to prove that divine worship is given to the Spirit are, Matt. xxiii. 19. Isa. vi. 3, compared with verse 9. Acts xxviii. 25,—&c. Rom. ix. 1. Rev. i. 4. 2 Cor. xiii. 14.

There are various texts of Scripture, in which, Father, Son, and Spirit, are mentioned together, and represented under distinct personal characters.

At the baptism of Christ, the Father speaks with an audible voice, the Son in human nature is baptized by John, and the Holy Ghost appears in the shape of a dove. Matt. iii. 16, 17.

The Trinity of persons in the Godhead appears from our baptism, because it is dispensed in the name of the Father, of the Son, and of the Holy Ghost.

The Trinity of persons also appears from the apostolic benediction, "The grace of the Lord Jesus, the love of God, and the communion of the Holy Ghost be with you all, Amen." 1 Cor. xiii. 14. And also from the testimony of the three in heaven, contained in 1 John v. 7. The Trinity in Unity is one Supreme Being, distinguished from all others by the name Jehovah.   Deut. vi. 4.   "The Lord our God is one Jehovah."   Yet Christ is Jehovah. Jer. xxiii. 6.   So is the Spirit.   Ezek. viii. i. 3.   Therefore Father, Son, and Holy Ghost, are one Jehovah. They are three persons, but have one name, and one nature.

ARIANS.

A denomination of the fourth century, which owed its origin to Arius, a man of subtle mind, and remarkable for his eloquence.   He maintained that the Son was totally and essentially distinct from the Father.   That he was the first and noblest of all those beings whom God the Father had created out of nothing, and the instrument by whose subordinate operation the Almighty Father formed the universe, and therefore inferior to the Father both in nature and in dignity.*   He added that the Holy Spirit was of a different nature from that of the Father, and of the Son; and that he had been created by the Son. However, during the life of Arius, the disputes turned principally on the divinity of Christ.

Such is the representation which is given of the opinion of Arius, and his immediate followers.   The modern defenders of this system, to prove the subordination and inferiority of Christ to God the Father, argue thus:

There are various passages of Scripture, where the Father is styled the one or only God.   Matt. xix. 17. "Why callest thou me good? there is none good but one, that is God."

The Father is styled God with peculiarly high titles and attributes.   See Matt. xv. 32.   Mark v. 7, &c.   It is said in Eph. iv. 6.   "There is one God and Father of all, who is above all."

---

* His followers deny that Christ had anything which could properly be called a *divine nature*, any otherwise than as anything very excellent may by a figure be called divine, or his delegated dominion over the system of nature might entitle him to the name of God.

Our Lord Jesus Christ expressly speaks of another God distinct from himself. Matt. xxvii. 46. John xx. 17.

Our Lord Jesus Christ not only owns another than himself to be God; but also that he is above, and over himself. He declares, that "his Father is greater than he." John xiv. 28. He says he came not in his own, but his Father's name and authority. That he sought not his own, but God's glory, nor made his own will but God's his rule; and in such a posture of subjection he came down from heaven into this earth, that it should seem that nature which did pre-exist, did not possess the supreme will even before it was incarnate.

Christ's saying, that he is of the Father must mean that he is derived from him; and this necessarily implies, that he is neither self-existent nor eternal; as the being derived from, must exist before another being can be derived from him.

Christ professes his knowledge to be limited and inferior to the Father's. Mark xiii. 32. " Of that day knows no man, no not the angels in heaven, nor the Son, but the Father only."

In like manner the apostle declares his subjection to another; not only as his Father, but his God, which is emphatically expressed, in calling the most blessed God the God "of our Lord Jesus Christ," after his humiliation was over. Eph. i. 17. And the head of Christ is God. See also 1 Cor. xi. 3.

It is said in 1 Cor. xv. 24, that " Christ will deliver up the kingdom to God, even the Father," therefore he will be subjected to him, and consequently inferior.

There are various passages of Scripture in which it is declared, that all prayers and praises ought primarily to be offered to the Father. See Matt. iv. 10. John iv. 23. Acts iv. 24. 1 Cor. i. 4. Phil. i. 3, 4.

The ancient Arians were divided among themselves, and torn into factions which regarded each other with the bitterest aversion. Of these the ancient writers make mention under the names of Semi-Arians, Eusebians, Aetians,

Eunomians, Acacians, Psatyrians, and others. But they may all be included with the utmost propriety in three classes ; the first of these were the primitive and genuine Arians, who rejected all those forms and modes of expression, which the moderns had invented to render their opinions less shocking to the Nicenians. They taught simply, that the Son was not begotten of the Father, *i. e.* produced out of his substance, but only created out of nothing. This class was opposed by the Semi-Arians, who in their turn were abandoned by the Eunomians, or Anomæans, the disciples of Aetias and Eunomius. The Semi-Arians held, that the Son was *similar* to the Father in his essence, not by nature, but by a peculiar privilege. The Eunomians, who were also called Aetians and Exucontians, and may be counted in the number of pure Arians, maintained that Christ was *unlike* the Father in his essence, as well as in other respects :

Under this general division were comprehended many subordinate sects, whose subtleties and refinements have been but obscurely developed by ancient writers.

The opinion of the Arians concerning Christ differs from the Gnostics chiefly in two respects.

First, the Gnostics supposed the *pre-existent* spirit which was in Jesus, to have been an emanation from the Supreme Being, according to the principles of the philosophy of that age, which made creation out of nothing to be an impossibility. But the Arians supposed the pre-existent spirit to have been properly created ; and to have animated the body of Christ, instead of the human soul.

Secondly, the Gnostics supposed that the pre-existent spirit was not the Maker of the world, but was sent to rectify the evils which had been introduced by the being who made it. But the Arians supposed, that their Logos was the being, whom God had employed in making the universe, as well as in all his communications with mankind.

Those who hold the doctrine, which is usually called *low Arianism* say, that Christ pre-existed, but not as the eternal Logos of the Father, or as the being by whom he made the worlds, and had intercourse with the patriarchs; or as having any certain rank or employment whatever in the divine dispensation. As this doctrine had not any existence till late years, and the author of it is unknown, it has not got any specific name among writers.

ARMINIANS.

THEY derive their name from James Arminius, who was born in Holland in the year 1560. He was the first pastor at Amsterdam; afterwards Professor of Divinity at Leyden, and attracted the esteem and applause of his very enemies, by his acknowledged candor, penetration, and piety. They received also the denomination of Remonstrants, from an humble petition entitled their remonstrances, which they addressed in the year 1610, to the States of Holland.

The principal tenets of the Arminians are comprehended in five articles, to which are added a few of the arguments they make use of in defence of their sentiments.

I. That the Deity has not fixed the future state of mankind, by an absolute unconditional decree; but determined, from all eternity, to bestow salvation on those whom he foresaw would persevere unto the end in their faith in Jesus Christ; and to inflict everlasting punishment on those who should continue in their unbelief, and resist unto the end his divine succors.

For as the Deity is *just*, *holy*, and *merciful*, wise in all his counsels, and true in all his declarations to the sons of men, it is inconsistent with his *attributes*, by an antecedent *decree*, to fix our commission of so many sins, in such a manner, that there is no possibility for us to avoid them. And he represents God dishonorably, who believes, that by his *revealed will*, he hath declared he would have *all men* to be saved; and yet, by an antecedent *secret* will, he would have the *greatest part* of them to perish. That he hath imposed a *law* upon them, which he requires them to obey, on penalty of his eternal displeasure, though he knows they cannot do it without his irresistible grace; and yet is absolutely determined to withhold this grace from them, and then punish them eternally for what they could not do without his divine assistance.

II. That Jesus Christ, by his death and sufferings, made an atonement for the sins of *all mankind* in general, and of every individual in particular: that, however, none but those who believe in him, can be partakers of their divine benefit.

That is, the death of Christ put all men in a capacity of being justified and pardoned, upon condition of their faith, repentance, and sincere obedience to the laws of the new covenant.

For the Scriptures declare, in a variety of places,—that Christ died for the whole world. John iii. 16, 17. "God so loved the world, that he gave his only begotten Son, that whosoever believeth on him, might not perish, but have everlasting life, &c." 1 John ii. 2. "He is the propitiation not only for our sins, but for the sins of the whole world." And the apostle expresses the same idea in Heb. ii. 9, when he says, "Christ tasted death for every man." Here is no limitation of that comprehensive phrase.

If Christ died for those who perish, and for those who do not perish, he died for *all*. That he died for those who do not perish, is confessed by all; and if he died for any who may or shall perish, there is the same reason to affirm that he died for all who perish. Now that he died for such, the Scripture says expressly, in 1 Cor. viii. 11. "And through thy knowledge shall the weak brother perish for whom Christ died." Hence it is evident Christ died for those who perish, and for those who do not perish; therefore he died for *all men*.

III. That mankind are not totally depraved, and that depravity does not come upon them by virtue of Adam's being their public head; but that mortality and natural evil only are the direct consequences of his sin to his posterity.

For, if all men are utterly disabled to all good, and continually inclined to all manner of wickedness, it follows, that they are not moral agents. For how are we capable of performing duty, or of regulating our actions by a law commanding good and forbidding evil, if our minds are bent to nothing but what is evil ? Then sin must be natural to us; and if natural, then necessary, with regard to us; and if necessary, then no sin. For what is natural to us, as hunger, thirst, &c., we can by no means hinder; and what we can by no means hinder, is not our sin. Therefore mankind are not totally depraved.

That the sin of our first parents is not imputed to us, is evident ; because, as the evil action they committed was personal, so must their real guilt be personal and belong only to themselves. And we cannot, in the eye of justice and equity, be punishable for their transgression.

IV. That there is no such thing as irresistible grace, in the conversion of sinners.

For, if conversion be wrought only by the unfrustrable operation of God, and man is purely passive in it, vain are all the commands and exhortations to wicked men " to turn from their evil ways :" Isa. i. 16. " To cease to do evil, and learn to do well :" Deut. x. 16. " To put off . the old man, and put on the new :" Eph. iv. 22. And divers other texts to the same purpose. Were an irresistible power necessary to the conversion of sinners, no man could be converted sooner than he is ; because, before this irresistible action came upon him, he could not be converted, and when it came upon him, he could not resist its operations. And therefore no man could reasonably be blamed, that he lived so long in an unconverted state : and it could not be praiseworthy in any person who was converted, since no man can resist an unfrustrable operation.

V. That those who are united to Christ by faith, may fall from their faith, and forfeit finally their state of grace.

For the doctrine of a possibility of the final departure of true believers from the faith, is expressed in Heb. vi. 4, 5, 6. " It is impossible for them who were once enlightened, &c.—if they shall fall away, to renew them again to repentance; seeing they crucify to themselves the Son of God afresh, and put him to open shame." See also 2 Peter, ii. 18, 20, 21, 22, and divers other passages of Scripture to the same purpose.

All commands to persevere and stand fast in the faith, show that there is a possibility that believers may not stand fast and persevere unto the end. All cautions to Christians not to fall from grace, are evidences and suppositions that they may fall. For what we have just reason to caution any person against, must be something which may come to pass and be hurtful to him. Now such caution Christ gives his disciples; Luke xxi. 34, 36. To them who had like precious faith with the apostles, St. Peter saith, "Beware lest being led away by the error of the wicked, you fall from your own steadfastness." 2 Pet. iii. 17. Therefore he did not look upon this as a thing impossible: and the doctrine of perseverance renders those exhortations and motives insignificant, which are so often to be found in Scripture.

In these five points, which are considered as fundamental articles in the Arminian system, the doctrine of the will's having a self-determining power is included. Perhaps some may wish to see a sketch of the arguments adduced to support this opinion.

Dr. Clarke defines liberty to be a power of self-motion, or self-determination. This definition is embraced by all this denomination, and implies, that in our volitions we are not acted upon. Activity and being acted upon are incompatible with one another. In whatever instances, therefore, it is truly. said of us, that we act, in those instances we cannot be acted upon. A being in receiving a change of its state from the exertion of an adequate force, is not an agent. Man therefore could not be an agent, were all his volitions derived from any force; or the effects of any mechanical causes. In this case, it would be no more true that he ever acts, than it is true of a ball that it acts, when struck by another ball.

CALIXTINS.

A BRANCH of the Hussites in Bohemia and Moravia in the fifteenth century. The principal point in which they differed from the church of Rome, was the use of the Chalice, (Calix,) or communicating in both kinds.

Calixtins was also a name given to those among the Lutherans, who followed the opinions of George Calixtus, a celebrated divine in the seventeenth century; who endeavoured to unite the Romish, Lutheran, and Calvinistic churches, in the bonds of charity and mutual benevolence.

He maintained,

I. That the fundamental doctrines of Christianity, by which he meant those elementary principles whence all its truths flow, were preserved pure in all three communions, and were contained in that ancient form of doctrine, that is vulgarly known by the name of the Apostles' Creed.

II. That the tenets and opinions which had been constantly received by the ancient doctors, during the first five centuries, were to be considered as of equal truth and authority with the express declarations and doctrines of Scripture.

CALVINISTS.

THESE derive their name from John Calvin, who was born at Nogen, in Picardy, in the year 1509. He first studied the civil law, and was afterwards made professor of divinity at Geneva, in the year 1536. His genius, learning, and eloquence, rendered him respectable even in the eyes of his very enemies.

The principal tenets of the Calvinists are comprehended in five articles, to which are added a few of the arguments they employ in defence of their sentiments.

I. That God has chosen a certain number in Christ unto everlasting glory, before the foundation of the world, according to his immutable purpose, and of his free grace

13

and love, without the least foresight of faith, good works, or any conditions performed by the creature ; and that the rest of mankind he was pleased to pass by, and ordain them to dishonor and wrath for their sins, to the praise of his vindictive justice.

For, as the Deity is infinitely perfect and independent in all his acts, the manifestation of his essential perfections must be the supreme end of the divine counsels and designs. Prov. xvi. 4. "The Lord hath made all things for himself, &c." Since God is omniscient, it is evident that he foresaw from everlasting whatever should come to pass : but there can be no prescience of future contingents ; for what is certainly foreseen, must infallibly come to pass ; consequently the prescience of the Deity cannot be antecedent to his decrees.

The sacred Scriptures assert the doctrine of the divine sovereignty in the clearest terms. Rom. ix. 21. "Has not the potter power over the clay of the same lump, to make one vessel unto honor, and another unto dishonor ?" See from verse 11 to the end of the chapter. The same divine author presents us with a golden chain of salvation in Rom. viii. 30. To the same purport see Eph. i. 4. Acts xiii. 48, and a variety of other passages in the sacred oracles.

II. That Jesus Christ, by his death and sufferings, made an atonement for the sins of the elect only.

That is, that redemption is commensurate with the divine decree. Christ has absolutely purchased grace, holiness, and all spiritual blessings for his people.

For, if God really intended the salvation of all men, then no man can perish. "For the counsel of the Lord standeth forever." Psalms xxxiii. 11. There are express texts of Scripture which testify that Christ did not die for all men. John v 37. "All that the Father giveth me, shall come to me, &c." and in John x. 11, Christ styles himself, "The good Shepherd, who lays down his life for his sheep." This is also implied in our Saviour s limitation of his intercession. John xvii. 9.

To suppose that the death of Christ procured only a possibility of salvation, which depends upon our performance of certain conditions, is contradictory to those scriptures which assert that salvation is wholly owing to free sovereign grace. If Christ died for all, and all are not saved, the purposes of his death are in many instances frustrated, and he shed his precious blood in vain. To suppose this would be derogatory to the infinite perfections of the great Redeemer. Therefore he did not die for all, and all for whom he died will certainly be saved.

III. That mankind are totally depraved in consequence of the fall; and by virtue of Adam's being their public head, the guilt of his sin was imputed, and a corrupt nature conveyed to all his posterity, from which proceed all actual transgressions. And that by sin we are made subject to death, and all miseries, temporal, spiritual, and eternal.

For the inspired pages assert the original depravity of mankind, in the most emphatical terms. Gen. viii. 21. "The imagination of man's heart is evil from his youth." Psalm xiv. 2, 3. "The Lord looked down from heaven upon the children of men, to see if there were any that did understand, and seek after God. They are all gone aside, they are altogether become filthy; there is none that doeth good, no, not one." To the same purport see Rom. iii. 10, 11, 12, &c. And it is evident, that Adam's sin was imputed to his posterity, from Rom. v. 19. "By one man's disobedience many were made sinners," &c., The Scriptures also teach, that all sin exposes us to everlasting destruction. See Gal. iii. 10. 2 Cor. iii. 6, 7, and Rom. iv. 14.

The total depravity of human nature is also evident from the universal reign of death over persons of all ages. From the propensity to evil which appears in mankind, and impels them to transgress God's law. From the necessity of regeneration. The nature of redemption. And the remains of corruption in the saints.

IV. That all whom God has predestinated unto life, he

is pleased, in his appointed time, effectually to call by his word and spirit, out of that estate of sin and death, in which they are by nature, to grace and salvation by Jesus Christ.

For an irresistible operation is evident from those passages in Scripture, which express the efficacious virtue of divine grace in the conversion of sinners. Eph. i. 19. "And what is the exceeding greatness of his power towards us who believe," &c. Eph. ii. 1, 5. Phil. ii. 13, and divers other passages. If there was any thing in us which renders the grace of God effectual, we should have cause for boasting; but the sacred pages declaim against this in the most emphatical terms. Rom. v. 27. "Where is boasting then? It is excluded," &c. See Titus iii. 5. 1 Cor. i. 31, and a variety of other texts to the same purport.

If the free will of man renders grace effectual, it may be made ineffectual by the same power, and so the creature frustrate the designs of his Creator; which is derogatory to the infinite perfections of that omnipotent Being, who worketh all things according to the counsel of his will.

V. That those whom God has effectually called and sanctified by his spirit, shall never finally fall from a state of grace.

For this doctrine is evident from the promises of persevering grace in the sacred Scriptures. Isa. liv. 10. "For the mountains shall depart, and the hills be removed, but my kindness shall not depart from thee, neither shall the covenant of my peace be removed, saith the Lord, that hath mercy on thee." See also Jer. xxxii. 38, 40. John iv. 14; vi. 39; x. 28; xi. 26. And the apostle exclaims with triumphant rapture, "I am persuaded that neither life, nor death, &c., shall be able to separate us from the love of God, which is in Christ Jesus, our Lord." Rom. viii. 38, 39.

The perseverance of the saints is also evident from the immutability of the Deity; his purposes and the reasons on which he founds them are invariable as himself. With him there is no variableness or shadow of turning. James i. 17. The faithfulness of the Deity is ever displayed in performing his promises; but the doctrine of falling from grace frustrates the design of the promises. For if one saint may fall, why not another, and a third, till no sincere Christians are left? But the doctrine of the believer's perseverance remains firm, as it is supported by the express tenor of Scripture, the immutability of the Deity, and his faithfulness in performing his promises.

These are the five points which distinguish this denomination from the Arminians. The Calvinistic system also includes in it, the doctrine of three co-ordinate persons in the Godhead forming one nature, and of two natures in Jesus Christ forming one person. Justification by faith alone and the imputed righteousness of Christ form an essential part of this system. They suppose, that on the one hand, our sins are imputed to Christ, and on the other, that we are justified by the imputation of Christ's righteousness to us; i. e. we the guilty are treated by God as righteous persons, out of regard to what Christ has done and suffered; who, though perfectly innocent, was appointed to suffer by the imputation of our sins to him. The Calvinists suppose that the doctrine of Christ's suffering in the place of sinners is strongly expressed in a variety of passages in Scripture. As Isa. liii. 4, 5, 6. "He has borne our griefs, and carried our sorrows. He was wounded for our transgressions, he was bruised for our iniquities, the chastisement of our peace was upon him, and with his stripes we are healed." 1 Pet. ii. 25. "Who himself bare our sins in his own body on the tree, that we, being dead unto sin should live unto righteousness." There are also a number of other texts to the same import.

COCCEIANS.

A DENOMINATION which arose in the seventeenth century, so called from John Cocceius, Professor of Divinity in the University of Leyden. He represented the whole history of the Old Testament as a mirror, which held forth an accurate view of the transactions and events, that were to happen in the church under the dispensation of the New Testament, and unto the end of the world. He maintained that by far the greatest part of the ancient prophecies foretold Christ's ministry and mediation, and the rise, progress, and revolutions of the church, not only under the figure of persons and transactions, but in a literal manner, and by the very sense of the words used in these predictions. And laid it down as a fundamental rule of interpretation, that the words and phrases of Scripture are to be understood in every sense of which they are susceptible. Or, in other words, that they signify in effect every thing that they can possibly signify.

Cocceius also taught that the covenant made between God and the Jewish nation, by the ministry of Moses, was of the same nature of the new covenant, obtained by the mediation of Jesus Christ.

In consequence of this general principle, he maintained: That the ten commandments were promulgated by Moses, not as a rule of obedience, but as a representation of the covenant of grace. That when the Jews had provoked the Deity by their various transgressions, particularly by the worship of the golden calf, the severe and servile yoke of the ceremonial law was added to the decalogue, as a punishment inflicted on them by the Supreme Being in his righteous displeasure. That this yoke which was painful in itself, became doubly so on account of its typical signification, since it admonished the Israelites, from day to day, of the imperfection and uncertainty of their state, filled them with anxiety, and was a perpetual proof that they had merited the righteous displeasure of God, and could not expect, before the coming of the Messiah, the entire remission of their iniquities.   That indeed good men, even under the Mosaic dispensation, were immediately after death made partakers of everlasting glory.   But, that they were nevertheless, during the whole course of their lives, far removed from that firm hope and assurance of salvation, which rejoices the faithful under the dispensation of the gospel.   And that their anxiety flowed naturally from this consideration, that their sins, though they remain unpunished, were not pardoned; because Christ had not, as yet, offered himself up a sacrifice to the Father to make an entire atonement for them.

GNOSTICS.

THIS denomination sprang up in the first century. Several of the disciples of Simon Magus held the principles of his philosophy, together with the profession of Christianity, and were distinguished by the appellation of Gnostics, from their boasting of being able to restore mankind to the *knowledge* of the Supreme Being, which had been lost in the world.   This party was not conspicuous for its numbers or reputation before the time of Adrian.*   It derives its origin from the Oriental philosophy.   The doctrine of a soul, distinct from the body, which had pre-existed in an angelic state, and was, for some offence committed in that state, degraded, and confined to the body as a punishment, had been the great doctrine of the eastern sages from time immemorial.   Not being able to conceive how evil in so great an extent, could be subservient to good, they supposed that good and evil have different origins.   So mixed a system as this is, they therefore thought to be unworthy of infinite wisdom and goodness. They looked upon matter as the source of all evil, and

---

* Under the general appellation of Gnostics, are comprehended all those, who, in the first ages of Christianity, blended the Oriental philosophy with the doctrines of the gospel.

argued in this manner: There are many evils in this world, and men seem impelled, by a natural instinct, to the practice of those things which reason condemns; but that eternal Mind, from which all spirits derive their existence, must be inaccessible to all kinds of evil, and also of a most perfect and beneficent nature. Therefore the origin of those evils, with which the universe abounds, must be sought somewhere else than in the Deity. It cannot reside in him who is all perfection; therefore, it must be without him. Now there is nothing without or beyond the Deity but matter; therefore matter is the centre and source of all evil and of all vice. Having taken for granted these principles, they proceed further, and affirmed that matter was eternal, and derived its present form, not from the will of the supreme God, but from the creating power of some inferior intelligence, to whom the world and its inhabitants owed their existence. As a proof of their assertion, they alleged that it was incredible the supreme Deity, perfectly good, and infinitely removed from all evil, should either create, or modify matter, which is essentially malignant and corrupt; or bestow upon it, in any degree, the riches of his wisdom and liberality.

In their system it was generally supposed that all intelligences had only one source, viz., the divine Mind. And to help out the doctrine concerning the origin of evil, it was imagined, that though the divine Being himself was essentially and perfectly good, those intelligences, or spirits, who were derived from him, and especially those who were derived from them, were capable of depravation. It was further imagined, that the derivation of those inferior intelligent beings from the' Supreme, was by a kind of efflux or emanation, a part of the substance being detached from the rest, but capable of being absorbed into it again.*

* The great boast of the Gnostics was their doctrine concerning the derivation of various intelligences from the Supreme Mind, which they thought to be done by emanation or efflux. And as those were equally capable of producing other intelligences in the same manner

To those intelligences derived mediately or immediately from the divine Mind, the author of this system did not scruple to give the name of gods, thinking some of them capable of a power of modifying matter.

The oriental sages expected the arrival of an extraordinary messenger of the Most High upon earth; a messenger invested with a divine authority; endowed with the most eminent sanctity and wisdom; and peculiarly appointed to enlighten with the knowledge of the Supreme Being, the darkened minds of miserable mortals, and to deliver them from the chains of the tyrants and usurpers of this world. When therefore some of these philosophers perceived that Christ and his followers wrought miracles of the most amazing kind, and also of the most salutary nature to mankind, they were easily induced to connect their fundamental doctrines with Christianity, by supposing him the great messenger expected from above, to deliver men from the power of the malignant genii, or spirits, to whom, according to their doctrine, the world was subjected, and to free their souls from the dominion of corrupt matter. But though they considered him as the Son of the Supreme God, sent from the *pleroma*, or habitation of the everlasting Father, they denied his divinity, looking upon him as inferior to the Father. They rejected his humanity, upon the supposition that every thing concrete and corporeal is in itself essentially and intrinsically evil. Hence the greatest part of the Gnostics denied that Christ was clothed with a real body, or that he suffered really for the sake of mankind, the pains and sorrows which he is said to have endured in the sacred history. They maintained, that he came to mortals with no other view, than to deprive the tyrants of this world of their influence upon virtuous and heaven born souls, and destroy-

and some of them were male, and others female, there was room for endless combinations of them. It is supposed, that the apostle Paul, when he censures endless genealogies and fables, has reference to the philosophy of the Gnostics.

ing the empire of these wicked spirits, to teach mankind how they might separate the divine mind from the impure body, and render the former worthy of being united to the Father of spirits.

Their persuasion, that evil resided in matter, rendered them unfavorable to wedlock; and led them to hold the doctrine of the resurrection of the body in great contempt. They considered it as a mere clog to the immortal soul; and supposed, that nothing was meant by it, but either a moral change in the minds of men, which took place before they died; or that it signified the ascent of the soul to its proper abode in the superior regions, when it was disengaged from its earthly encumbrance. The notion, which this denomination entertained, that the malevolent genii presided in nature, and that from them proceed all diseases and calamities, wars and desolations, induced them to apply themselves to the study of magic, to weaken the powers, or suspend the influences of these malignant agents.

The Gnostic doctrine concerning the creation of the world by one or more inferior beings of an evil, or at least of an imperfect nature, led them to deny the divine authority of the books of the Old Testament; and when they were challenged to produce authorities for their doctrines, some referred to writings of Abraham, Zoroaster, Christ, and his apostles. Others boasted of their having drawn their opinions from secret doctrines of Christ. Others, that they had arrived to these degrees of wisdom by an innate vigor of mind. Others, that they were introduced by Theudas, a disciple of St. Paul, and by Matthias, one of the friends of our Lord.

As the Gnostics were philosophic and speculative people, and affected refinement, they did not make much account of public worship, or of positive institutions of any kind. They are said, not to have had any order in their churches.

As many of this denomination thought that Christ had not any real body, and therefore had not any proper flesh and blood, it seems on this account, when they used to celebrate the Eucharist, they did not make any use of wine, which represents the blood of Christ, but of water only.

We have fewer accounts of what they thought or did with respect to baptism, but it seems that some of them at least disused it. And it is said, that some abstained from the Eucharist, and from prayer.

The greatest part of this denomination adopted rules of life, which were full of austerity, recommending a strict and rigorous abstinence, and prescribed the most severe bodily mortifications, from a notion, that they had a happy influence in purifying and enlarging the mind, and in disposing it for the contemplation of celestial things. That some of the Gnostics, in consequence of making no account of the body, might think, that there was neither good nor evil in any thing relating to it, and therefore supposed themselves at liberty to indulge in any sensual excesses, is not impossible; though it is more probable, that every thing of this nature would be greatly exaggerated by the enemies of this denomination.

The Egyptian Gnostics are distinguished from the Asiatic, by the following difference in their religious system:

I. That besides the existence of a Deity, they maintained that also of an eternal matter, endued with life and motion, yet they did not acknowledge an eternal principle of darkness, or the evil principle of the Persians.

II. They supposed that our blessed Saviour was a compound of two persons, of the man Jesus, and of Christ the Son of God; that the divine nature entered into the man Jesus, when he was baptized by John in the river Jordan, and departed from him, when he was seized by the Jews.

III. They attributed to Christ a real, not an imaginary body.

IV. Their discipline, with respect to life and manners, was much less severe than that of the Asiatic sect.

SOCINIANS.

A DENOMINATION which appeared in the sixteenth century, and embraced the opinions of Lelius Socinus, a man of uncommon genius and learning; and of Faustus Socinus, his nephew, who propagated his uncle's sentiments in a public manner after his death.

The principal tenets maintained by this denomination are as follow: to which are added a few of the arguments they use in defence of their sentiments.

That the Holy Scriptures are to be understood and explained in such a manner, as to render them conformable to the dictates of reason.

In consequence of this leading point in their theology, they maintain, that God, who is infinitely more perfect than man, though of a similar nature in some respects, exerted an act of that power by which he governs all things; in consequence of which, an extraordinary person was born of the Virgin Mary. That person was Jesus Christ, whom God first translated to heaven by that portion of his divine power which is called the Holy Ghost;* and having instructed him fully in the knowledge of his counsels and designs, sent him again into this sublunary world, to promulgate to mankind a new rule of life, more excellent than that under which they had formerly lived, to propagate divine truth by his ministry, and to confirm it by his death.

---

* Socinus and some of his followers entertained a notion, of Christ's having been in some unknown time of his life, taken up personally into heaven, and sent down again to the earth, which was the way in which they solved these expressions concerning him : John iii. 13. " No man has ascended to heaven, but he that came down from heaven, even the Son of man, which is in heaven." Thus Moses who was the type of Christ, before the promulgation of the law, ascended to God upon Mount Sinai. So Christ, before he entered on the office assigned him by the Father, was, in consequence of the divine counsel and agency, translated into heaven, that he might see the things he had to announce to the world in the name of God himself.

That those who obey the voice of this *divine teacher* (and this obedience is in the power of every one whose will and inclination leads that way) shall, one day, be clothed with new bodies, and inhabit, eternally, those blessed regions, where God himself immediately resides. Such, on the contrary, as are disobedient and rebellious, shall undergo most terrible and exquisite torments, which shall be succeeded by annihilation, or the total extinction of their being.

The above is an account of the religious tenets of Socinus, and his immediate followers. Those at the present day, who maintain the *mere humanity of Christ*, differ from Socinus in many things; particularly in not paying religious worship to Jesus Christ, which was a point that Faustus Socinus vehemently insisted on, though he considered Christ as a man only, with divine powers conferred upon him. He supposed, that in condescension to human weakness, in order that mankind might have one of their own brethren more upon a level with them, to whom they might have resource in their straits and necessities, Almighty God, for his eminent virtues, had conferred upon Jesus Christ, the son of Mary, some years after he was born, a high divine power, lordship, and dominion, for the government of the Christian world only; and had qualified him to hear and answer the prayers of his followers, in such matters as related to the cause of the gospel. The chief foundation on which Socinus founded the opinion of Christ's being an object of religious worship, was: the declarations in the Scriptures concerning the kingdom and power bestowed upon Christ; the interpretation which he put on those passages which speak of angels and heavenly powers being put under him and worshiping him; his having a knowledge of the secret thoughts of men imparted to him, and the like, which with some presumed instances of the fact, of prayer being actually made to him, he maintained to be a sufficient, though indirect, signification of the divine will, that men should invoke Christ by prayer. But he constantly acknowledged, that there was no express precept for making him an object of religious worship.

Socinus allowed that the title of true God might be given to Christ; though all he meant by it was, that he had a real divine power and dominion bestowed upon him, to qualify him to take care of the concerns of Christians, and to hear and answer their prayers, though he was originally nothing more than a human creature.

There were some among the early Socinians, who disapproved and rejected the worship paid to Christ, as being without any foundation in the Holy Scriptures, the only rule of a Christian's faith and worship.

At present it is agreed, both by Arians and Socinians, that the Supreme God in one person is the only object of prayer.

Socinus was a strict Pelagian, in his sentiments respecting human nature.

This denomination differs from the Arians, in the following particulars:

The Socinians assert, that Christ was *simply a man*, and consequently, had no existence before his birth and appearance in this world.

The Arians maintain, that Christ was a *super-angelic being*, united to a human body. That though he was himself created, he was the creator of all other things under God, and the instrument of all the divine communications to the patriarchs.

The Socinians say, that the Holy Ghost is the power and wisdom of God, which is God.

The Arians suppose, that the Holy Spirit is the creature of the Son, and subservient to him in the work of redemption.

SERVETIANS.

A NAME which, in the 16th century, distinguished the followers of Michael Servetus, a Spaniard by birth. He taught that the Deity, before the creation of the world, had produced within himself two personal representations, or manners of existence, which were to be the medium of intercourse between him and mortals, and by whom, consequently, he was to reveal his will, and to display his mercy and beneficence to the children of men. That these two representatives were the Word and the Holy Ghost— that the former was united to the man Christ, who was born of the Virgin Mary, by an omnipotent act of the divine will; and that, on this account, Christ might be properly called God—that the Holy Spirit directed the course, and animated the whole system of nature; and more especially produced in the minds of men, wise counsels, virtuous propensities, and divine feelings. And finally, that these two representations were to cease after the destruction of this terrestrial globe, and to be absorbed into the substance of the Deity, whence they had been formed.

NECESSARIANS.

LEIBNITZ, a celebrated German philosopher, who was born in the year 1646, is a distinguished writer on this subject. He attempted to give Calvinism a more pleasing and philosophical aspect. He considered the multiplicity of worlds, which compose the universe, as one system or whole, whose greatest possible perfection is the ultimate end of creating goodness, and the sovereign purpose of governing wisdom. As the Leibnians laid down this great end, as the supreme object of God's universal dominion, and the scope to which all his dispensations were directed, they concluded, that if this end was proposed, it must be accomplished. Hence the doctrine of necessity, to fulfill the purposes of predestination founded on wisdom and goodness; a necessity physical and mechanical in the motions of material and inanimate things; but a necessity moral and spiritual in the voluntary determinations of intelligent beings, in consequence of prepollent motives, which produce their effects with certainty, though those effects are contingent, and by no means the offspring of an absolute and essentially immutable fatality.*

Mr. Leibnitz observes, that, if it be said, that the world might have been without sin and misery, such a world would not have been the best. For all things are linked together in each possible world. The universe, whatever it may be, is all of a piece, like an ocean; the least motion produces its effect to any distance, though the effect becomes less sensible in proportion to the distance. God having settled every thing beforehand, once for all, having foreseen good and evil actions, &c., every thing did ideally contribute, before its existence, to his creating plan; so that no alteration can be made in the universe, any more than in a number, without destroying its essence, or its numerical individuality. And therefore if the least evil which happens in the world was wanting, it would not be the world, which all things duly considered, the all-wise Creator has chosen and accounted the best.

Colors are heightened by shadows, and a dissonance, well placed, renders harmony more beautiful. We desire to be frightened by rope-dancers who are ready to fall; and to shed tears at the representation of a tragedy. Does any one sufficiently relish the happiness of good health, that has never been sick? Is it not most times necessary, that a little evil should render a good more sensible, and consequently greater?

The Edwardean scheme of moral necessity is as follows:

That the will is, in every case, necessarily determined by the strongest motives; and that this moral necessity may be as absolute as natural necessity; i. e. a moral effect may be as perfectly connected with its moral cause, as a naturally necessary effect is with its natural cause.

President Edwards rejects the notion of liberty, as im-

---

* Augustine, Leibnitz, and a considerable number of modern philosophers who maintain the doctrine of necessity, consider this necessity in moral actions as consistent with spontaneity and choice. According to them, constraint alone, and external force, destroy merit and imputation.

plying any self-determining power in the will, any indifference or contingency; and defines liberty to be the power, opportunity, and advantage, which any one has to do as he pleases. This liberty is supposed to be consistent with moral certainty, or necessity.

He supports his scheme by the connection between cause and effect—by God's certain foreknowledge of the volitions of moral agents, which is supposed to be inconsistent with such a contingence of those volitions, as excludes all necessity. He shows that God's moral excellence is necessary, yet virtuous and praise-worthy—that the acts of the will of the human soul of Christ are necessarily holy, yet virtuous, praise-worthy, and rewardable—and that the moral inability of sinners, consisting in depravity of heart, instead of excusing, constitutes their guilt.

Lord Kames has the following idea of necessity:

That, comparing together the moral and material world, every thing is as much the result of established laws in the one as in the other. There is nothing in the whole universe, which can properly be called contingent; but every motion in the material, and every determination and action in the moral world, are directed by immutable laws; so that while those laws remain in force, not the smallest link in the chain of causes and effects can be broken, nor any one thing be otherwise than it is.

That as man must act with consciousness and spontaneity, it is necessary that he should have some sense of things possible and contingent. Hence the Deity has wisely implanted a delusive sense of liberty in the mind of man; which fits him to fulfill the ends of action to better advantage, than he could do, if he knew the necessity which really attends him.

Lord Kames observes, that in the material world, it is found, that the representations of external objects, and their qualities, conveyed by the senses, differ sometimes from what philosophy discovers these objects and their qualities to be. Were man endowed with a microscopic eye, the bodies which surround him would appear as differ-

14

ent from what they do at present, as if he was transported into another world. His ideas, upon that supposition, would be more agreeable to strict truth, but they would be far less serviceable in common life.

Analogous to this, in the moral world, the Deity has implanted in mankind the delusive notion of liberty or indifference, that they may be led to the proper exercise of that activity, for which they were designed.

The Baron de Montesquieu, in his Persian Letters, observes, that as God makes his creatures act just according to his own will, he knows every thing he thinks fit to know. But though it is in his power to see every thing, yet he does not always make use of that power. He generally leaves his creatures at liberty to act, or not act, that they may have room to be guilty or innocent. In this view he renounces his right of acting upon his creatures, and directing their resolutions. But when he chooses to know any thing, he always does know it; because he need only will that it shall happen as he sees it; and direct the resolutions of his creatures according to his will. Thus he fetches the things, which shall happen, from among those which are merely possible, by fixing by his decrees the future determinations of the minds of his creatures; and depriving them of the power of acting, or not acting, which he has bestowed upon them.

If we may presume to make comparison of a thing, which is above all comparison, a monarch does not know what his ambassador will do in an affair of importance. If he thinks fit to know it, he need only give him directions to behave so and so; and he may be assured he will follow his directions.

President Edwards makes the following distinction between his, and Lord Kame's ideas of necessity:

I. Lord Kames supposes, that such a necessity takes place with respect to all men's actions, as is inconsistent with liberty. Edwards maintains, that the moral necessity, which universally takes place, is not inconsistent with the utmost liberty, which can be defined, or conceived.

II. Kames seems every where to suppose, that necessity, properly so called, attends all men's actions; and that the terms "unavoidable," "impossible," &c., are equally applicable to the case of moral and natural necessity.

Edwards maintains, that such a necessity as attends the acts of men's wills, can with more propriety be called certainty; it being no other, than the certain connection between the subject and predicate of the proposition, which affirms their existence.

III. Kames supposes, that if mankind could clearly see the real necessity of their actions, they would not appear to themselves, or others, praiseworthy, culpable, or accountable for their actions.

Edwards maintains, that moral necessity, or certainty, is perfectly consistent with praise and blame, rewards and punishments.

Lord Kames agrees with president Edwards, in supposing, that praise or blame rests ultimately on the disposition, or frame of mind.

The Rev. Mr. Dawson in a late pamphlet entitled, The Necessarian, or the Question concerning Liberty and Necessity stated and discussed, endeavors to prove, that the will is determined by motives. He accounts, however, every act, which proceeds not from mechanical force, a voluntary act. Every voluntary act he calls a free act, because it proceeds from the will, from the man himself. But calls that voluntary act necessary, in conformity to their idea of necessity, who, on supposition of the will's being determined by motives, will not allow it to be free, though voluntary. Having established this species of necessity, he endeavors to show that free will leaves no foundation for attributing merit, or demerit, to the agent. And, that on the contrary, the doctrine of necessity does that, which the doctrine of free will does not. By leaving the foundation of morality secure, it leaves a foundation for merit and demerit, viz., the moral nature of actions.

The morality of an action is its motive. That, which gives the action its moral quality, gives it at the same time its worth, or merit. But on the doctrine of free will there can be no foundation for attributing merit, or demerit, to the agent, because it destroys all distinctions between actions; good and bad being terms without a meaning, when applied to actions without a moral motive.

As in the account of Dr. Priestley's sentiments, the manner in which that celebrated author distinguishes his scheme of philosophical necessity from the Calvinistic doctrine of predestination is inserted, perhaps those, who are fond of speculating on this subject, will be gratified, by being presented, on the other hand, with the following distinction, which the Rev. Mr. Emmons of Franklin has made between the Calvinistic idea of necessity, and Dr. Priestley's.

It has long been a subject of controversy among Arminians and Calvinists, whether moral agents can act of necessity. Upon this subject, Dr. Priestley takes the Calvinistic side, and labors to prove the doctrine of necessity upon the general principle, that no effect can exist without a cause. His train of reasoning runs very much in this form: Every volition must be an effect; every effect must have a cause; every cause must necessarily produce its effect; therefore every volition, as well as every other effect, must be necessary. But though he agrees with Calvinists in their first principle, and general mode of reasoning; yet, in one very capital point, he differs from them totally. For he maintains, that motives, which are the cause of volitions, must operate mechanically, which, they suppose, totally destroys the freedom of the will. He is obliged to maintain the mechanical operation of motives, by his maintaining the materiality of the soul. If the soul is material, the natural conclusion is, that motives must act upon it, by a mechanical operation. This conclusion, he owns, he means to draw from the doctrine of materialism. In the preface to his illustrations of philosophical necessity, he says, "Every thing belonging to the doctrine of materialism is, in fact, an argument for the doctrine of necessity; and, consequently, the doctrine of necessity is a direct inference from materialism."

JANSENISTS.

A DENOMINATION of Roman Catholics in France, which was formed in the year 1640. They follow the opinions of Jansenius, bishop of Ypres, from whose writings the following propositions are said to have been extracted:

I. That there are divine precepts, which good men, notwithstanding their desire to observe them, are, nevertheless, absolutely unable to obey; nor has God given them that measure of grace, which is essentially necessary to render them capable of such obedience.

II. That no person, in this corrupt state of nature, can resist the influence of divine grace, when it operates upon the mind.

III. That in order to render human actions meritorious, it is not requisite that they be exempt from necessity, but that they be free from constraint.

IV. That the Semi-Pelagians err greatly in maintaining that the human will is endowed with the power of either receiving, or resisting the aids and influences of preventing grace.

V. That whoever affirms, that Jesus Christ made expiation, by his sufferings and death, for the sins of all mankind, is a Semi-Pelagian.

This denomination was also distinguished from many of the Roman Catholics, by their maintaining that the Holy Scriptures and public Liturgies should be offered to the perusal of the people in their mother tongue. And they look upon it as a matter of the highest moment to persuade all Christians, that true piety does not consist in the performance of external acts of devotion, but in inward holiness and divine love.

JESUITS.

A FAMOUS religious order in the Romish church, established in the year 1540, under the name of the company of Jesus.

Ignio, or Ignatius Loyola, a Spanish gentleman of illustrious rank, was the founder of this order, which has made a most rapid and astonishing progress through the world.

The doctrinal points which are ascribed to the Jesuits, in distinction from many others of the Roman communion, are as follows :

I. This order maintain, that the pope is infallible—that he is the only visible source of that universal and unlimited power which Christ has granted to the church—that all bishops and subordinate rulers derive from him alone the authority and jurisdiction with which they are invested ; and that he alone is the supreme law-giver of that sacred community ; a law-giver whose edicts and commands it is, in the highest degree, criminal to oppose, or disobey.

II. They comprehend within the limits of the church, not only many who live separate from the communion of Rome, but even extend the inheritance of eternal salvation to nations that have not the least knowledge of the christian religion, or of its divine author; and consider as true members of the church, open transgressors who profess its doctrines.

III. The Jesuits maintain, that human nature is far from being deprived of all power of doing good—that the succors of grace are administered to all mankind in a measure sufficient to lead them to eternal life and salvation—that the operations of grace offer no violence to the faculties and powers of nature, and therefore may be resisted—and that God from all eternity has appointed everlasting rewards and punishments, as the portion of men in a future world, not by an absolute, arbitrary, and unconditional decree, but in consequence of that divine and unlimited prescience by which he foresaw the actions, merits, and characters of every individual.

IV. They represent it as a matter of perfect indifference from what motives men obey the laws of God, provided these laws are really obeyed. And maintain, that the service of those who obey from the fear of punishment, is as agreeable to the Deity, as those actions which proceed from a principle of love to him and his laws.

V. They maintain, that the sacraments have in themselves an instrumental and efficient power, by virtue of which they work in the soul (independently of its previous preparation or propensities) a disposition to receive the divine grace.

VI. The Jesuits recommend a devout ignorance to such as submit to their direction, and think a Christian sufficiently instructed, when he has learned to yield a blind and unlimited obedience to the orders of the Church.

The following maxims are said to be extracted from the moral writings of this order:

I. That persons truly wicked, and void of the love of God, may expect to obtain eternal life in heaven, provided that they be impressed with a fear of the divine anger, and avoid all heinous and enormous crimes, through the dread of future punishment.

II. That those persons may transgress with safety, who have a probable reason for transgressing, *i. e.* any plausible argument or authority in favor of the sin they are inclined to commit.

III. That actions intrinsically evil, and directly contrary to the divine law, may be innocently performed by those who have so much power over their own minds as to join, even ideally, a good end to this wicked action.

IV. That philosophical sin is of a very light and trivial nature, and does not deserve the pains of hell.

V. That the transgressions committed by a person blinded by the seductions of tumultuous passions, and destitute of all sense and impression of religion, however detestable and heinous they may be in themselves, are not imputable to the transgressor before the tribunal of God; and that such transgressions may be often, as involuntary as the actions of a madman.

VI. That the person who takes an oath, or enters into a contract, may, to elude the force of the one and obligation of the other, add to the form of the words that express them certain mental additions and tacit reservations.

This entire society is composed of four sorts of members, viz. Novices, Scholars, spiritual and temporal Coadjutors, and professed Members. Beside the three ordinary vows of poverty, chastity, and obedience, which are common to all the monastic tribes, the professed Members are obliged to take a fourth, by which they solemnly bind themselves to go, without deliberation or delay, wherever the Pope shall think fit to send them. They are governed by a General, who has four Assistants.

SHAKERS.

THE first persons who acquired this epithet were Europeans; a part of whom came from England to New York, in the year 1774, and being joined by others, they settled at Niskyuna, above Albany; whence they have spread their doctrines, and increased to a considerable number.

Anne Lee, whom they styled the Elect Lady, was the head of this party. They assert, that she was the woman spoken of in the twelfth chapter of Revelation; and that she spoke seventy-two tongues: and though those tongues are unintelligible to the living, she conversed with the dead, who understood her language. They add further, that she was the mother of all the elect; that she travailed for the whole world; and that no blessing can descend to any person, but only by and through her, and that in the way of her being possessed of their sins, by their confessing and repenting of them, one by one, according to her direction.

The tenets which are peculiarly distinguishing to this denomination, are comprised in seven articles. To which is added a short specimen of their manner of defending their religious sentiments:

I. That the first resurrection is already come, and now is the time to judge themselves.

II. That they have power to heal the sick, to raise the dead, and to cast out devils.

This, they say, is performed by the preaching of the word of God, when it is attended with the divine power, the wonderful energy and operation of the Holy Spirit; which performs those things, by healing the broken-hearted, by raising up those, who are dead in trespasses and sins, to a life of holiness and righteousness, which causes the devils to be cast out. Matt. x. 8.

III. That they have a correspondence with angels, the spirits of the saints, and their departed friends.

This they attempt to prove, from 1 Cor. xii. 8, 10. "There are diversities of gifts, but the same spirit. To some is given the word of wisdom, to some prophecy, to some the discerning of Spirits."

IV. That they speak with divers kind of tongues in their public assemblies.

This, they think, is done by the divine power and influence of the Holy Spirit.

V. That it is lawful to practice vocal music with dancing, in the Christian churches, if it be practiced in praising the Lord.

VI. That their Church is come out of the order of natural generation, to be as Christ was; and that those who have wives be as though they had none. That by these means heaven begins upon earth, and they hereby lose their earthly and sensual relation to Adam the first, and come to be transparent in their ideas in the bright and heavenly visions of God.

They suppose, that some of their people are of the number "of the one hundred and forty-four thousand who were redeemed from the earth, that were not defiled with women."

VII. That the word "everlasting," when applied to the

punishment of the wicked, refers only to a limited space of time, excepting in the case of those who fall from their Church; but for such "there is no forgiveness, neither in this world, nor in that which is to come."

They quote Matt. xii. 32, to prove this doctrine.

This denomination maintain, that it is unlawful to swear, game, or use compliments to each other; and that water-baptism and the Lord's Supper are abolished.

They deny the imputation of Adam's sin to his posterity, and the doctrine of election, and reprobation.

The discipline of this denomination is founded on the supposed perfection of their leaders. The mother, it is said, obeys God through Christ. European elders obey her. American laborers, and the common people obey them, while confession is made of every secret in nature, from the oldest to the youngest. The people are made to believe that they are seen through and through in the gospel glass of perfection, by their teachers, who behold the state of the dead, and innumerable worlds of spirits good and bad.

From the shaking of their bodies in religious exercises, they were called Shakers, and some gave them the name of Shaking Quakers. This name, though used in derision, they acknowledge to be proper, because they are both the subjects and instruments of the work of God in this latter day.

"Thus the Lord promised, that he would shake the earth with terror:" Lowth's translation of Isaiah ii. 19, 21. "That, in that day, there should be a great shaking in the land of Israel:" Ezek. xxxviii. 19, 20. "That he would shake the heavens and the earth:" Isaiah xiii. 13; Joel iii. 16; Hag. ii. 6, 7, 21. "That he would shake all nations, and that the desire of all nations should come." And according to the apostle: "That yet once more, he would shake not the earth only, but also heaven:" Heb. xii. 26. Signifying the removing of things that are shaken, as of things that are made, that those things which cannot be shaken may remain. All which particularly alluded to the latter day, and now in reality began to be fulfilled; of which the name itself was a striking evidence, and much more the nature and operations of the work.

This work went on under Wardley, till the year 1770, when the present Testimony of Salutation and Eternal Life was fully opened according to the special gift and revelation of God through Anne Lee. She was born about the year 1736; her father, John Lee, lived in Toad Lane, Manchester, and was a blacksmith; with him she lived till she embarked for America. She herself was a cutter of hatter's fur, and had five brothers and two sisters. She was married to Abraham Standley, a blacksmith, and had four children, who died in their infancy.

In 1758, this singular woman joined the society under Wardley, and became a distinguished leader amongst them.

When therefore Anne, who, by her perfect obedience, had attained to all that was made manifest in the leading characters of the society, still, however, found in herself the seed or remains of human depravity and a lack of the divine nature, which is eternal life abiding in the soul, she did not rest satisfied in that state, but labored in continual watchings and fastings, and in tears and incessant cries to God, day and night, for deliverance. And under the most severe tribulation, and violent temptations, as great as she was able to resist and endure, such was, frequently, her extreme agony of soul, that she would clinch her hands together, till the blood would flow through the pores of her skin!

By such deep mortification and suffering, her flesh wasted away, and she became like a skeleton, wholly incapable of helping herself, and was fed and nourished like an infant, although naturally free from bodily infirmities, and a person of strong and sound constitution, and invincible fortitude of mind.

And from the light and power of God, which attended her ministry, and the certain power of salvation transmitted to those who received her testimony, she was received and acknowledged as the *first Mother*, or spiritual parent in the line of the female, and the second heir in the covenant of life, according to the present display of the gospel. Hence among believers, she hath been distinguished by no other name or title than that of *Mother*, from that period to the present day. To such as addressed her with the customary titles used by the world, she would reply,—'I am *Anne* the *Word*;' signifying that in her dwelt the *Word*."

In 1774, Anne Lee, with some of her followers, having been thought mad, and sorely persecuted, settled their temporal affairs in England, and set sail from Liverpool for New York. James Wardley and his wife, remaining behind, were removed into an almshouse, and there died.

The others, we are told, "being without lead or protection, lost their power, and fell into the common course and practice of the world!" Anne Lee and their brethren reached New York, after working a kind of miracle, for the ship sprang a leak on the voyage, and it is more than hinted that had it not been for their exertions at the pump, the vessel would have gone down to the bottom of the ocean. They fixed their residence at Niskyuna, now Watervliet, near the city of Albany. In this retired spot, they greatly multiplied, but Anne was not without bitter reproaches and manifold persecutions. She and the elders would delight in missionary journeys—being out for two or three years, and returning with wonderful accounts of their success.

The decease of Elder William served as a particular means of preparing the minds of believers for a still heavier trial, in being deprived of the visible presence and protection of Anne—the thought of which seemed almost insupportable to many. But having finished the work which was given her to do, she was taken out of their sight in the ordinary way of all living, at Watervliet, on the 8th day of the ninth month, 1784.

Thus in the early dawn of the American Revolution, when the rights of conscience began to be established,

the morning star of Christ's second coming, disappeared
from the view of the world, to be succeeded by the increasing brightness of the Sun of righteousness and all
the promised glory of the latter day.

And thus the full revelation of Christ, in its first degree, was completed; which was according to that remarkable prophecy of Christopher Love, who was beheaded under Cromwell—"Out of thee, O England! shall
a bright star arise, whose light and voice shall make the
heavens to quake, and knock under with submission to the
blessed Jesus."

The most remarkable tenet of the Shakers is the abolition of marriage and indeed the total separation of the
sexes.   The essence of their argument is, that the Resurrection spoken of in the New Testament means nothing
more than conversion; our Saviour declares that in the
resurrection they neither marry nor are given in marriage, therefore on conversion, or the resurrection of the
individual, marriage ceases.   To speak more plainly, the
single must continue single and the married must separate.   Every passage in the Gospel and in the epistles is
interpreted according to this hypothesis.

Whatever degree of indulgence, say they, was extended to some among the gentile nations, who professed
faith in Christ, because they were not able to bear the
whole truth ; yet the truth did not conceal the pointed
distinction which Christ made between his own true followers, and the children of this world.

"But I would have you without carefulness," saith the
apostle ; "He that is unmarried careth for the things that
belong to the Lord, how he may please the Lord: (his
noblest and principal affections are there.)   But he that is
married careth for the things that are of the world, how
he may please his wife."   The wife is put in the place of
the Lord, as the first object of his affections.

The unmarried woman careth for the things of the
Lord, (upon whom she places her affections,) that she may
be holy both in body and spirit ; but she that is married

careth for the things of the world, how she may please her
husband, instead of the Lord.

The same pointed distinction is made by Christ; not
only when he says of his disciples, "They are not of the
world, even as I am not of the world," but when in answer-
ing the Sadducees, who denied and knew not that he was
the Resurrection, he says, "The children of this world
marry, and are given in marriage; but they which shall
be accounted worthy to obtain that world, and the resurrection from the dead, neither marry nor are given in
marriage." Neither can they die any more (spiritually),
for they are equal unto the angels, and are the children
of God, being the children of the resurrection.

An idea of the notions of the Shakers in regard to their
founder may be formed from the following passages: In
the fulness of time, according to the unchangeable purpose
of God, that same Spirit and word of power, which created
man at the beginning—which spake by the prophets—
which dwelt in the man Jesus—which was given to the
apostles and true witnesses, as the Holy Spirit and Word
of promise, which groaned in them waiting for the day of
redemption—and which was spoken of in the language of
prophecy as a woman travailing with child, and pained to
be delivered, was revealed in a woman.

And that woman, in whom was manifested the Spirit
and Word of power, who was anointed and chosen of God,
to reveal the mystery of iniquity, to stand as the first in
order, to accomplish the purpose of God, in the restoration
of that which was lost by the transgression of the first woman, and to finish the work of man's final redemption,
was Anne Lee.

As the chosen vessel, appointed by divine Wisdom,
she, by her faithful obedience to that same anointing,
became the temple of the Holy Ghost, and the second heir
with Jesus, her Lord and Head, in the covenant and promise of eternal life. And by her sufferings and travail for
a lost world, and her union and subjection to Christ Jesus,
her Lord and Head, she became the first-born of many

sisters, and the true Mother of all living in the new creation.

Thus the perfection of the translation of God in this latter day, excels particularly, in that which respects the most glorious part in the creation of man, namely, the woman. And herein is the most condescending goodness and mercy of God displayed, not only in redeeming that most amiable part of creation from the curse, and all the sorrows of the fall, but also in condescending to the lowest estate of the loss of mankind.

The four leading peculiarities of the Shakers are: first, community of property; secondly, the celibacy of the entire body, in both sexes; thirdly, the non-existence of any priesthood; and, fourthly, the use of the dance in their religious worship. All these they defend on Scriptural authority, and quote very largely from the writings of the Old and New Testaments in confirmation of their views. The following are their rules for the admission of members:

1. All persons who unite with the society must do it voluntarily and of their own free will.

2. No one is permitted to do so without a full and clear understanding of all its obligations.

3. No considerations of property are ever made use of to induce persons to join or to leave the society; because it is a principle of the sect, that no act of devotion or service that does not flow from the free and voluntary emotions of the heart, can be acceptable to God as an act of true religion.

4. No believing husband or wife is allowed, by the principles of this society, to separate from an unbelieving partner, except by mutual agreement, unless the conduct of the unbeliever be such as to warrant a separation by the laws of God and man. Nor can any husband or wife, who has otherwise abandoned his or her partner, be received into communion with the society.

5. Any person becoming a member must rectify all his wrongs, and, as fast and as far as it is in his power,

discharge all just and legal claims, whether of creditors or filial heirs. Nor can any person, not conforming to this rule, long remain in union with the society. But the society is not responsible for the debts of any individual, except by agreement; because such responsibility would involve a principle ruinous to the institution.

6. No difference is to be made in the distribution of parental estate among the heirs, whether they belong to the society or not; but an equal partition must be made, as far as may be practicable and consistent with reason and justice.

7. If an unbelieving wife separate from a believing husband by agreement, the husband must give her a just and reasonable share of the property; and if they have children who have arrived at years of understanding sufficient to judge for themselves, and who choose to go with their mother, they are not to be disinherited on that account. Though the character of this institution has been much censured on this ground, yet we boldly assert that the rule above stated has never, to our knowledge, been violated by this society.

8. Industry, temperance, and frugality, are prominent features of this institution. No member who is able to labor, can be permitted to live idly upon the labors of others. All are required to be employed in some manual occupation, according to their several abilities, when not engaged in other necessary duties.

As all persons enter this society voluntarily, so they may voluntarily withdraw; but, while they remain members, they are required to obey the regulations of the society.

The leading authority of the society is vested in a ministry, generally consisting of four persons, including both sexes. These, together with the elders and trustees, constitute the general government of the society in all its branches.

No creed is framed to restrain the progress of improvement. It is the faith of the society that the operations of

Divine light are unlimited. All are at liberty to improve their talents and exercise their gifts, the younger being subject to the elder.

In the beginning of the year 1780 the society consisted of but about ten or twelve persons, all of whom came from England. From this time there was a gradual and extensive increase in their numbers until the year 1787, when they began to collect at New-Lebanon. Here the Church was established, as a common centre of union for all who belonged to the society in various parts of the country. This still remains as the mother church, being the first that was established; all the societies in various parts of the country are considered branches of this; and there are now twenty separate communities, numbering about 4000 members.

In Ohio there are two societies, one at Union Village, in the county of Warren, 30 miles northeast from Cincinnati, which contains nearly 600 members; and one at Beaver Creek, in the county of Montgomery, six miles southeast from Dayton, which contains 100 members. In Kentucky there are also two societies, one at Pleasant Hill, in Mercer county, 21 miles southwest of Lexington, containing nearly 500 members; the other at South Union, Jasper Springs, in Logan county, 15 miles northeast from Russellville, which contains nearly 400 members. In Indiana there is one society, at West Union, Knox county, 16 miles above Vincennes, which contains more than 200 members.

"The Shakers," says one of their visitors, "are, in their religious notions, a compound of almost all the other sects. They are a kind of religious eclectics, with this commendable trait, that they are enemies to every sort of coercion in matters of religion. They have chosen what appeared to them to be good out of every denomination. The Shakers unite with the Quakers in an entire submission to the Spirit, and in the rejection of baptism and the Lord's Supper—with the Calvinists and Methodists in laying great stress on conversion—with the Arminians in rejecting election and reprobation, as well as the imputation of Adam's guilt to his posterity—with the Unitarians in exploding a Trinity of three persons in one God, together with the satisfaction of Christ—with the Roman Catholics in contending for the continuation of miracles in the church—with the Sandemanians in practicing a sort of community of goods, and having no person regularly educated for the ministry—with the followers of Joanna Southcott, in believing that a woman is the instrument to bring on the glory of the latter day—with the Moravians and Methodists in encouraging missionary undertakings—with the Swedenborgians in denying the resurrection of the body, and asserting that the day of judgment is past—with the Jumpers in dancing and shouting during divine worship ; and lastly, with the Universalists in renouncing the eternity of hell torments. To all this, they have added a tenet hitherto unthought of by any body of Christians. The Catholics indeed led the way in enjoining the celibacy of the clergy, and in the institution of monachism. It was left to the Shakers to enjoin celibacy as one of their religious exercises."

As far as the history of the Shakers can establish the fact, it has certainly shown that, where property is held in community, and not individually, the disposition to bestow it in works of charity and benevolence to others is greatly increased. And that the property itself is better managed for accumulation and preservation, no one can doubt who has watched the progressive advancement which this society has made in the augmentation, as well as improvement, of its possessions, and in the neatness, order, and perfection by which everything they do or make is characterized : this is so much the case, that over all the United States, the seeds, plants, fruits, grain, cattle, and manufactures furnished by any settlement of Shakers, bear a premium in the market above the ordinary price of similar articles from other establishments. There being no idleness among them, all are productive. There being no intemperance among them, none are destructive. There being no misers among them, nothing is hoarded, or made to perish for want of use; so that while production and improvement are at their maximum, and waste and destruction at their minimum, the society must go on increasing the extent and value of its temporal possessions, and thus increase its means of doing good, first within, and then beyond its own circle.

The most remarkable religious ceremony among the Shakers is that of dancing. The following account, from Buckingham's Travels in America, appears to be a wholly unprejudiced one:

"The males were first arranged in pairs, following each other like troops in a line of march; and when their number was completed, the females followed after, two and two, in the same manner. In this way they formed a complete circle round the open space of the room. In the centre of the whole was a small band of about half a dozen males and half a dozen females, who were there stationed to sing the tunes and mark the time; and these began to sing with a loud voice and in quick time, like the allegro of a sonata, or the vivace of a canzonet, the following verse:

> ' Perpetual blessings to demand,
> Perpetual praise on every hand;
> Then leap for joy, with dance and song,
> To praise the Lord forever.'

"The motion of the double line of worshippers, as they filed off before us, was something between a march and a dance. Their bodies were inclined forward like those of persons in the act of running; they kept the most perfect time with their feet, and beat the air with their hands to the same measure. Some of the more robust and enthusiastic literally 'leaped' so high as to shake the room by the weight with which they fell to their feet on the floor; and others, though taking the matter more moderately, bore evident signs of the effects of the exercise and heat united on their persons. The first dance lasted about five minutes, and was performed to the air of 'Scots wha ha'e wi' Wallace bled,' sung with great rapidity. The second dance was of still quicker measure, and to the much less respectable old English tune of 'Nancy Dawson,' and to this lively and merry tune the whole body, now formed into three abreast instead of two, literally scampered round the room in a quick gallopade, every individual of both the choir and the dancers singing with all their might these words:

' Press on, press on, ye chosen band,
        The angels go before ye ;
     We're marching through Immanuel's land,
        Where saints shall sing in glory.'

" This exercise was continued for at least double the time of the former, and by it the worshipers were wrought up to such a pitch of fervor, that they were evidently on the point of some violent outbreak or paroxysm. Accordingly, the whole assembly soon got into the 'most admired disorder,' each dancing to his own tune and his own measure, and the females became perfectly ungovernable. About half a dozen of these whirled themselves round in what opera dancers call a *pirouette*, performing at least fifty revolutions each, with their arms extended horizontally, their clothes being blown out like an air-balloon all round their persons, their heads sometimes falling on one side, and sometimes hanging forward on the bosom, till they would at length faint away in hysterical convulsions, and be caught in the arms of the surrounding dancers.

"This, too, like the singing and dancing which preceded it, was accompanied by clapping of hands to mark the time, while the same verse was constantly repeated, and at every repetition with increased rapidity. Altogether the scene was one of the most extraordinary I had ever witnessed, and, except among the howling dervishes of Bagdad, and the whirling dervishes of Damascus, I remember nothing in the remotest degree resembling it."

The Shakers vindicate this singular ceremony by quotations from the Bible. "The exercise of dancing, in the worship of God," say they, "was brought to light not as an exercise of human invention, instituted by human authority, but as a manifestation of the will of God, through the special operations of his Divine power. No reader of the Scriptures can doubt but that dancing was acceptable to God as an exercise of religious worship in times past, and will be in time to come, according to the prediction of the prophet :

"'Again I will build thee, and thou shalt be built, O virgin of Israel! thou shalt again be adorned with thy tablets, and shalt go forth in the dances of them that make merry. Then shall the virgin rejoice in the dance, both young men and old together. Turn again, O virgin of Israel! turn again to these thy cities.'*

"God requires the faithful improvement of every created talent. 'O clap your hands, all ye people; shout unto God with the voice of triumph. Sing unto the Lord a new song; sing his praise in the congregation of the saints. Let the children of Zion be joyful in their King; let them praise his name in the dance.'

"These expressions of the inspired Psalmist are worthy of serious consideration. Do they not evidently imply that the Divine Spirit which dictated them requires the devotion of all our faculties in the service of God? How, then, can any people professing religion expect to find acceptance with God by the service of the tongue only?

"Since we are blessed with hands and feet, those active and useful members of the body on which we mostly depend in our own service, shall we not acknowledge our obligations to God who gave them by exercising them in our devotions to him? There is too powerful a connection between the body and the mind, and too strong an influence of the mind upon the body, to admit of much activity of mind·in the service of God without the co-operating exercises of the body. But where the heart is sin-

---

* Jeremiah, c. 31, v. 4, 13, 21.

cerely and fervently engaged in the service of God, it has a tendency to produce an active influence on the body."

"From every inquiry I could make," says Mr. Buckingham, "of those longest resident in the neighborhood of the Shakers, I could learn no authenticated case of evil practices among them. On the contrary, every one appeared ready to bear testimony to their honesty, punctuality, industry, sobriety, and chastity."

HOPKINSIANS.

THIS sect is called after the Rev. Samuel Hopkins, D. D., pastor of a Church at Newport; who in his sermons and tracts, has made several additions to the sentiments first advanced by the celebrated Jonathan Edwards, President of New Jersey College.*

The following is a summary of the distinguishing tenets of this denomination, together with a few of the reasons which they employ to support their sentiments:

I. That all true virtue, or real holiness, consists in disinterested benevolence.

The object of benevolence is universal Being, including God, and all intelligent creatures. It wishes and seeks the good of every individual, so far as is consistent with the greatest good of the whole, which is comprised in the glory of God, and the perfection and happiness of his kingdom.

The law of God is the standard of all moral rectitude, or holiness. This is reduced into love to God, and our neighbor as ourselves; and universal good-will comprehends all the love to God, our neighbor, and ourselves, required in the divine law; and therefore must be the whole of holy obedience. Let any serious person think

---

* This denomination supposes, that this eminent divine not only illustrated and confirmed the main doctrines of Calvinism, but brought the whole system to a greater degree of consistency and perfection, than any who had gone before him. They profess only to pursue the same design of still further perfecting the same system.

what are the particular branches of true piety; when he has viewed each one by itself, he will find, that disinterested, friendly affection is its distinguishing characteristic. For instance, all the holiness in pious fear, which distinguishes it from the fear of the wicked, consists in love. Again, holy gratitude is nothing but good will to God and our neighbour, in which we ourselves are included, and correspondent affection excited by a view of the good will and kindness of God.

Universal good will also implies the whole of the duty we owe to our neighbor. For justice, truth, and faithfulness, are comprised in universal benevolence. So are temperance and chastity. For an undue indulgence of our appetites and passions is contrary to benevolence, as tending to hurt ourselves or others; and so opposite to the general good, and the divine command, in which all the crime of such indulgence consists. In short, all virtue is nothing but benevolence acted out in its proper nature and perfection, or love to God and our neighbor made perfect in all its genuine exercises and expressions.

II. That all sin consists in selfishness.

By this is meant, an interested, selfish affection, by which a person sets himself up as supreme, and the only object of regard; and nothing is good or lovely, in his view, unless suited to promote his own private interest. This self-love is in its whole nature and every degree of it, enmity against God. It is not subject to the law of God; and is the only affection that can oppose it. It is the foundation of all spiritual blindness; and therefore the source of all the open idolatry in the heathen world, and false religion under the light of the gospel. All this is agreeable to that self-love which opposes God's true character. Under the influence of this principle, men depart from truth, it being itself the greatest practical lie in nature, as it sets up that which is comparatively nothing, above Universal Existence. Self-love is the source of all profaneness and impiety in the world; and of all pride and ambition among men, which is nothing but selfishness acted out in this particular way. This is the foundation of all covetousness and sensuality; as it blinds people's eyes, contracts their hearts, and sinks them down, so that they look upon earthly enjoyments as the greatest good. This is the source of all falsehood, injustice, and oppression, as it excites mankind by undue methods to invade the property of others. Self-love produces all the violent passions, envy, wrath, clamor, and evil speaking, and everything contrary to the divine law, is briefly comprehended in this fruitful source of all iniquity, self-love.

III. That there are no promises of regenerating grace made to the doings of the unregenerate.

For as far as men act from self-love, they act from a bad end. For those who have no true love to God, really do no duty, when they attend on the externals of religion. And as the unregenerate act from a selfish principle, they do nothing which is commanded. Their impenitent doings are wholly opposed to repentance and conversion, therefore not implied in the command, To repent, &c. So far from this, they are altogether disobedience to the command. Hence it appears, that there are no promises of salvation to the doings of the unregenerate.

IV. That the impotency of sinners, with respect to believing in Christ, is not natural but moral.

For it is a plain dictate of common sense, that natural impossibility excludes all blame. But an unwilling mind is universally considered as a crime, and not as an excuse, and is the very thing wherein our wickedness consists. That the impotence of the sinner is owing to a disaffection of heart, is evident from the promises of the gospel. When any object of good is proposed and promised to us upon asking, it clearly evinces that there can be no impotency in us with respect to obtaining it, beside the disapprobation of the will; and that inability, which consists in disinclination, never renders anything properly the subject of precept or command.

V. That in order to faith in Christ, a sinner must approve in his heart of the divine conduct, even though God should cast him off forever; which, however, neither implies love to misery, nor hatred of happiness.*

For if the law is good, death is due to those who have broken it. The Judge of all the earth cannot but do right. It would bring everlasting reproach upon his government to spare us, considered merely as in ourselves. When this is felt in our hearts, and not till then, we shall be prepared to look to the free grace of God through the redemption which is in Christ, and to exercise faith in his blood, "who is set forth to be a propitiation to declare God's righteousness, that he might be just, and yet be the justifier of him who believeth in Jesus."

VI. That the infinitely wise and holy God has exerted his omnipotent power in such a manner, as he purposed should be followed with the existence and entrance of moral evil in the system.

For it must be admitted on all hands, that God has a perfect knowledge, foresight, and view of all possible existences and events. If that system and sense of operation, in which moral evil should never have existence, was actually preferred in the divine mind, certainly the Deity is infinitely disappointed in the issue of his own operations. Nothing can be more dishonorable to God, than to imagine that the system, which is actually formed by the Divine

---

* As a particle of water is small in comparison with a generous stream, so the man of humility feels small before the great family of his fellow-creatures. He values his soul, but when he compares it to the great soul of mankind, he almost forgets and loses sight of it: for the governing principle of his heart is to estimate things according to their worth. When, therefore, he indulges a humble comparison with his Maker, he feels lost in the infinite fullness and brightness of divine love, as a ray of light is lost in the sun, and a particle of water in the ocean. It inspires him with the most grateful feelings of heart, that he has opportunity to be in the hand of God, as clay in the hand of the potter: and as he considers himself in this humble light, he submits the nature and size of his future vessel entirely to God. As his pride is lost in the dust, he looks up with pleasure towards the throne of God, and rejoices with all his heart in the rectitude of the divine administration.

hand, and which was made for his pleasure and glory, is yet not the fruit of wise contrivance and design.

VII. That the introduction of sin is, upon the whole, for the general good.

For the wisdom and power of the Deity are displayed in carrying on designs of the greatest good : and the existence of moral evil has undoubtedly occasioned a more full, perfect, and glorious discovery of the infinite perfections of the divine nature, that could otherwise have been made to the view of creatures.   If the extensive manifestations of the pure and holy nature of God, and his infinite aversion to sin, and all his inherent perfections in their genuine fruits and effects, is either itself the greatest good, or necessarily contains it ; it must necessarily follow, that the introduction of sin is for the greatest good.

VIII. That repentance is before faith in Christ.

By this is not intended, that repentance is before a speculative belief of the being and perfections of God, and of the person and character of Christ; but only, that true repentance is previous to a saving faith in Christ, in which the believer is united to Christ, and entitled to the benefits of his mediation and atonement.   That repentance is before faith in this sense, appears from several considerations :

1st. As repentance and faith respect different objects, so they are distinct exercises of the heart, and therefore one not only may, but must be prior to the other.

2d. There may be genuine repentance of sin without faith in Christ ; but there cannot be true faith in Christ without repentance of sin : and since repentance is necessary in order to faith in Christ, it must necessarily be prior to faith in Christ.

3d. John the Baptist, Christ, and his apostles, taught, that repentance is before faith.   John cried, "Repent, for the kingdom of heaven is at hand;" intending, that true repentance was necessary in order to embrace the gospel of the kingdom.   Christ commanded, "Repent ye, and believe the gospel."   And Paul preached "repentance toward God, and faith toward our Lord Jesus Christ."

IX. That though men became sinners by Adam according to a divine constitution, yet they have, and are accountable for no sins but personal.

1st. Adam's act in eating the forbidden fruit was not the act of his posterity, therefore, they did not sin at the same time he did.

2d. The sinfulness of that act could not be transferred to them afterwards ; because the sinfulness of an act can no more be transferred from one person to another, than an act itself. Therefore,

3d. Adam's act in eating the forbidden fruit was not the cause, but only the occasion of his posterity's being sinners. God was pleased to make a constitution, that, if Adam remained holy through his state of trial, his posterity should, in consequence of it, be holy too; but if he sinned, his posterity, in consequence of it, should be sinners too. Adam sinned, and now God brings posterity into the world sinners. By Adam's sin we are become sinners, not for it ; his sin being only the occasion, not the cause of our committing sins.

X. That though believers are justified through Christ's righteousness, yet his righteousness is not transferred to them.

1st. Personal righteousness can no more be transferred from one person to another than personal sin.

2d. If Christ's personal righteousness were transferred to believers, they would be as perfectly holy as Christ, and so stand in no need of forgiveness. But,

3d. Believers are not conscious of having Christ's personal righteousness, but feel and bewail much in-dwelling sin and corruption. And,

4th. The Scripture represents believers as receiving only the benefits of Christ's righteousness in justification, or their being pardoned and accepted for Christ's righteousness' sake. And this is the proper Scripture notion of imputation. Jonathan's righteousness was imputed to Mephibosheth, when David showed kindness to him for his father Jonathan's sake.

The Hopkinsians warmly advocate the doctrine of the divine decrees, the doctrine of particular election, the doctrine of total depravity, the doctrine of the special influences of the Spirit of God in regeneration, the doctrine of justification by faith alone, the final perseverance of the saints, and the consistency between entire freedom and absolute dependence. And therefore claim it as their just due, since the world will make distinctions, to be called Hopkinsian Calvinists.

COME-OUTERS.

THIS is a term which has been applied to a considerable number of persons in various parts of the Northern States, principally in New England, who have recently *come out* of the various religious denominations with which they were connected;—hence the name. They have not themselves assumed any distinctive name, not regarding themselves as a sect, as they have not formed, and do not contemplate forming, any religious organization. They have no creed, believing that every one should be left free to hold such opinions on religious subjects as he pleases, without being held accountable for the same to any human authority.

Hence, as might be expected, they hold a diversity of opinions on many points of belief upon which agreement is considered essential by the generality of professing Christians. Amongst other subjects upon which they differ is that of the authority of the Scriptures of the Old and the New Testaments, some among them holding the prevailing belief of their divine inspiration, whilst others regard them as mere human compositions, and subject them to the same rules of criticism as they do any other book, attaching to them no authority any further than they find evidence of their truth. They believe the commonly-received opinion of the plenary inspiration of the writers of those books to be unfounded, not claimed by the writers themselves, and therefore unscriptural, as well as unreasonable.

Whilst, then, they believe the authors of the Gospels to have been fallible men, liable to err both in relation to matters of fact and opinion, they believe they find in their writings abundant evidence of their honesty. Therefore they consider their testimony satisfactory as regards the main facts there stated of the life of Jesus Christ, at least so far, that there can be no difficulty in deducing therefrom the great principles of the religion which he taught. They all believe him to have been a divinely-inspired teacher, and his religion, therefore, to be a revelation of eternal truth. They regard him as the only authorized expositor of his own religion, and believe that to apply in practice its principles as promulgated by him, and as exemplified in his life, is all that is essential to constitute a Christian, according to his testimony, (Matt. vii. 24,) "Whosoever heareth these sayings of mine, and doeth them, I will liken him unto a wise man which built his house upon a rock," &c. Hence they believe, that to make it essential to Christianity to assent to all the opinions expressed by certain men, good men though they were, who wrote either before or after his time, involves a denial of the words of Christ. They believe that, according to his teachings, true religion consists in purity of heart, holiness of life, and not in opinions; that Christianity, as it existed in the mind of Christ, is a life rather than a belief.

This class of persons agree in the opinion that he only is a Christian who has the spirit of Christ; that all such as these are members of his church, and that it is composed of none others; therefore that membership in the Christian church is not, and cannot, in the nature of things, be determined by any human authority. Hence they deem all attempts to render the church identical with any outward organizations as utterly futile, not warranted by Christ himself, and incompatible with its spiritual character. Having no organized society, they have no stations of authority or superiority, which they believe to be inconsistent with the Christian idea, (Matt. xxiii. 8,) " But be not ye called Rabbi : for one is your Master, even Christ ; and all ye are brethren." (Matt. xx. 25, 26,) " Ye know that the princes of the Gentiles exercise dominion over them, and they that are great exercise authority upon them. But it shall not be so among you."

As might be inferred from the foregoing, they discard all outward ordinances as having no place in a spiritual religion, the design of which is to purify the heart, and the extent of whose influence is to be estimated by its legitimate effects in producing a life of practical righteousness, and not by any mere arbitrary sign, which cannot be regarded as a certain indication of the degree of spiritual life, and must consequently be inefficient and unnecessary.

Their views of worship correspond, as they believe, with the spiritual nature of the religion they profess. They believe that true Christian worship is independent of time and place ; that it has no connection with forms, and ceremonies, and external arrangements, any further than these are the exponents of a divine life ; that it spontaneously arises from the pure in heart at all times and in all places : in short, they regard the terms Christian worship and Christian obedience as synonymous, believing that he gives the highest and only conclusive evidence of worshiping the Creator, who exhibits in his life the most perfect obedience to his will. These views they consider in perfect harmony with the teachings of Jesus, particularly in his memorable conversation with the woman of Samaria.

They also agree in the belief that the religion of Christ asserts the equality of all men before God ; that it confers upon no man, or class of men, a monopoly of Heaven's favours ; neither does it give to a portion of his children any means of knowing his will not common to the race. They believe the laws of the soul are so plain, that they may be easily comprehended by all who sincerely seek to know them, without the intervention of any human teacher or expounder.   Hence they regard no teaching as authoritative but that of the Spirit of God, and reject all priesthoods but the universal priesthood which Christianity establishes.   They believe that every one whose soul is imbued with a knowledge of the truth, is qualified to be its minister, and it becomes his duty and his pleasure, by his every word and action, to preach it to the world.   It follows, then, that, as Christ prepares and appoints his own ministers, and as they receive their commissions only from him, they are accountable to him alone for their exercise, and not to any human authority whatsoever.   They therefore reject all human ordinations, appointments, or control, or any designation by man of an order of men to preach the gospel, as invasions of his rightful prerogative.

Amongst the prevailing sins, against which they feel bound to bear testimony, are slavery and war; and it is alleged as the main reason why many of them have disconnected themselves from the professedly Christian denominations to which they belonged, that those bodies gave their sanction to those anti-Christian practices. They believe slave-holding to be sinful under all circumstances, and that, therefore, it should be immediately abandoned.   They believe not only that national wars are forbidden by Christianity, but that the taking of human life for any purpose, by governments or individuals, is incompatible with its spirit.   A large proportion of them, also, consider all resort to punishment, as a penalty for crime, equally inconsistent with the law of love. Hence they deem it their duty to withhold their voluntary sanction or support from human governments, and all institutions which claim the right to exercise powers which they thus regard as unlawful.

In various places, these persons hold meetings on the first day of the week, which are conducted consistently with their views of Christian freedom and equality.   It is understood that the object of thus meeting together, is to promote their spiritual welfare.   For this purpose, they encourage a free interchange of sentiment on religious subjects, without any restraint or formality. They have no prescribed exercises, but every one is left free to utter his thoughts as he may feel inclined; and even those who differ from them in opinion are not only at liberty, but are invited, to give expression to their thoughts. They believe this to be the only mode of holding religious meetings consistent with the genius of their religion, and for an example of like gatherings they refer to those of the primitive Christians.

HUTCHINSONIANS.

HUTCHINSONIANS are the followers of John Hutchinson, born in Yorkshire, 1674, who in the early part of his life served the Duke of Somerset in the capacity of a steward. The Hebrew Scriptures, he says, comprise a perfect system of natural philosophy, theology, and religion. In opposition to Dr. Woodward's Natural History of the Earth, Mr. Hutchinson, in 1724, published the first part of his curious book called Moses Principia. Its second part was presented to the public in 1727, which contains, as he apprehends, the principles of the Scripture philosophy, which are a plenum and the air. So high an opinion did he entertain of the Hebrew language, that he thought the Almighty must have employed it to communicate every species of knowledge, and that accordingly every species of knowledge is to be found in the Old Testament. Of his mode of philosophising, the following specimen is brought forward to the reader's attention: "The air (he supposes) exists in three conditions, fire, light, and spirit: the two latter are the finer and grosser parts of the air in motion; from the earth to the sun, the air is finer and finer till it becomes pure light near the confines of the sun, and fire in the orb of the sun, or solar focus. From the earth towards the circumference of this system, in which he includes the fixed stars, the air becomes grosser and grosser till it becomes stagnant, in which condition it is at the utmost verge of this system, from whence (in his opinion) the expression of outer darkness, and blackness of darkness, used in the New Testament, seems to be taken."

NESTORIANS.

THIS denomination, which arose in the fifth century, is so called from Nestorius, a patriarch of Constantinople, who was born in Germanica, a city of Syria, in the latter part of the fourth century. He was educated and baptized at Antioch, and soon after his baptism, withdrew to a monastery in the vicinity of that city. His great reputation for eloquence, and the regularity of his life, induced the emperor Theodosius to select him for the see of Constantinople; and he was consecrated bishop of that Church A. D. 429. He became a violent persecutor of heretics; but, because he favored the doctrine of his friend Anastasius, that "the virgin Mary cannot with propriety be called the mother of God," he was anathematized by Cyril, bishop of Alexandria, who, in his turn, was anathematized by Nestorius. In the council of Ephesus, A. D. 431, (the third General Council of the Church,) at which Cyril presided, and at which Nestorius was not present, he was judged and condemned without being heard, and deprived of his see. He then retired to his monastery in Antioch, and was afterwards banished to Petra, in Arabia, and thence to Oasis, in Egypt, where he died about A. D. 435 or 439.

The decision of the council of Ephesus caused many difficulties in the Church; and the friends of Nestorius carried his doctrines through all the Oriental provinces, and established numerous congregations, professing an invincible opposition to the decrees of the Ephesian council. Nestorianism spread rapidly over the East, and was embraced by a large number of the oriental bishops. Barsumus, bishop of Nisibis, labored with great zeal and activity to procure for the Nestorians a solid and permanent footing in Persia; and his success was so remarkable that his fame extended throughout the East. He established a school at Nisibis, which became very famous, and from which issued those Nestorian doctors who, in that and the following centuries, spread abroad their tenets through Egypt, Syria, Arabia, India, Tartary, and China.

The Nestorian Church is Episcopal in its government, like all the Oriental churches. Its doctrines, also, are, in general, the same with those of those churches, and they receive and repeat, in their public worship, the Nicene creed. Their distinguishing doctrines appear to be, their believing that Mary was not the mother of Jesus Christ, as God, but only as man, and that there are, consequently, two persons, as well as two natures, in the Son of God. This notion was looked upon in the earlier ages of the Church as a most momentous error; but it has in latter times been considered more as an error of words than of doctrine; and that the error of Nestorius was in the words he employed to express his meaning, rather than in the doctrine itself. While the Nestorians believe that Christ had two natures and two persons, they say "that these natures and persons are so closely united that they have but one aspect." Now the word *barsopa*, by which they express this aspect, is precisely of the same signification with the Greek word *prosopon*, which signifies a *person;* and hence it is evident that they attached to the word *aspect* the same idea that we attach to the word *person*, and that they understood by the word *person*, precisely what we understand by the term *nature*.

The Nestorians, of all the Christian Churches of the East, have been the most careful and successful in avoiding a multitude of superstitious opinions and practices, which have infected the Romish and many of the Eastern churches.

Dr. Asahel Grant, an American, has published an interesting work, in which he adduces strong evidence to prove that the Nestorians and the "Lost Tribes" are one people. The London Times of a recent date contains the following letter, relating to the massacre of a large body of the Nestorians, and the success of the Circassians:

"The Kurds, who for a long period have entertained a ferocious hatred to this Christian republic, situated in the centre of the Mahometan states, committed, on their invasion, all kinds of atrocities. The villages were pillaged, women and young girls were violated, and, in fact, the massacres committed were worthy of a plundering tribe having in their power a detested enemy. In the districts adjoining Dzumalesk might be seen during several days the Christian villages on fire. Some of those villages were burned by the inhabitants themselves, who fled before the Pasha's hordes, destroying their property to prevent its falling into the hands of the Kurds. The result of this abominable outrage was, that the Nestorians, after much bloodshed, surrendered their territory to the Pasha of Mousul. This is a deplorable event, as the Nestorians of Dzumalesk formed a small state well worthy of liberty. They were brave, industrious, and peaceable. Dr. Grant, who has for a long time resided at Urmia, has left for Mousul, where he was about to take some steps in favor of those persecuted Christians."

PELAGIANS.

THIS denomination arose in the fifth century, and was so called from Pelagius, a monk who looked upon the doctrines which were commonly received, concerning the original corruption of human nature, and the necessity of divine grace to enlighten the understanding and purify the heart, as prejudicial to the progress of holiness and virtue, and tending to establish mankind in a presumptuous and fatal security. He maintained the following doctrines:

I. That the sins of our first parents were imputed to them only, and not to their posterity; and that we derive no corruption from their fall; but are born as pure and unspotted, as Adam came out of the forming hand of his Creator.

II. That mankind, therefore, are capable of repentance and amendment, and of arriving at the highest degrees of piety and virtue, by the use of their natural faculties and powers. That, indeed, external grace is necessary to excite their endeavours, but that they have no need of the internal succors of the Divine Spirit.

III. That Adam was, by nature, mortal; and, whether he had sinned or not, would certainly have died.

IV. That the grace of God is given in proportion to our merits.

V. That mankind may arrive at a state of perfection in this life.

VI. That the law qualified men for the kingdom of heaven, and was founded upon equal promises with the gospel.

ORIGENISTS.

ORIGEN was a presbyter of Alexandria, who lived in the third century. He was a man of vast and uncommon abilities, who interpreted the divine truths of religion according to the tenor of the Platonic philosophy. He alleged, that the source of many evils lies in adhering to the literal and external part of Scripture; and that the true meaning of the sacred writers was to be sought in a mysterious and hidden sense, arising from the nature of things themselves.

The principal tenets ascribed to Origen, together with a few of the reasons made use of in their defence, are comprehended in the following summary:

I. That there is a pre-existent state of human souls.

For the nature of the soul is such as makes her capable of existing eternally, backward, as well as forward. For her spiritual essence, as such, makes it impossible that she should, either through age or violence, be dissolved: so that nothing is wanting to her existence, but

His good pleasure, from whom all things proceed. And if, according to the Platonic scheme, we assign the production of all things to the exuberant fulness of life in the Deity, which, through the blessed necessity of his communicative nature, empties itself into all possibilities of being, as into so many capable receptacles, we must suppose her existence, in a sense necessary and in a degree, co-eternal with God.

II. That souls were condemned to animate mortal bodies, in order to expiate faults they had committed in a pre-existent state.

For we may be assured, from the infinite goodness of their Creator, that they were at first joined to the purest matter,* and placed in those regions of the universe which were most suitable to the purity of essence they then possessed; for that the souls of men are an order of essentially incorporate spirits, their deep immersion into terrestrial matter, the modification of all their operations by it, and the heavenly body, promised in the Gospel, as the highest perfection of our renewed nature, clearly evince. Therefore, if our souls existed before they appeared inhabitants of the earth, they were placed in a purer element, and enjoyed far greater degrees of happiness. And certainly, He whose overflowing goodness brought them into existence, would not deprive them of their felicity, until, by their mutability, they rendered themselves less pure in the whole extent of their powers, and became disposed for the susception of such a degree of corporeal life, as was exactly answerable to their present disposition of spirit. Hence it was necessary, that they should become terrestrial men.

III. That the soul of Christ was united to the Word before the incarnation.†

---

* Origen supposed that our souls, being incorporeal and invisible, always stand in need of bodies suitable to the nature of the places where they exist.

† See this subject more fully illustrated in Dr. Watts' Glory of Christ.

For the Scriptures teach us, that the soul of the Messiah was created before the beginning of the world. See Phil. ii. 5, 6, 7. This text must be understood of Christ's human soul, because it is unusual to propound the Deity as an example of humility, in scripture. Though the humanity of Christ was so God-like, he emptied himself of this fulness of life and glory, *to take upon him the form of a servant*. It was this Messiah, who conversed with the patriarchs under a human form: it was he, who appeared to Moses upon the Holy Mount: it was he, who spoke to the prophets under a visible appearance; and it is he, who will at last come in triumph upon the clouds, to restore the universe to its primitive splendor and felicity.

IV. That, at the resurrection, we shall be clothed with ethereal bodies.

For the elements of our terrestrial compositions are such, as almost fatally entangle us in vice, passion, and misery. The purer the vehicle the soul is united with, the more perfect is her life and operations. Besides, the Supreme Goodness, who made all things, assures us, he made all things best at first; and therefore, his recovery of us to our lost happiness (which is the design of the Gospel) must restore us to our better bodies and happier habitations; which is evident from 1 Cor. xv. 49, 2 Cor. v. 1, and other texts of Scripture.

V. That, after long periods of time, the damned shall be released from their torments, and restored to a new state of probation.

For the Deity has such reserves in his gracious providence as will vindicate his sovereign goodness and wisdom from all disparagement. Expiatory pains are a part of his adorable plan. For this sharper kind of favor has a righteous place in such creatures as are by nature mutable. Though sin has extinguished or silenced the divine life, yet it has not destroyed the faculties of reason and understanding, consideration and memory, which will serve the life, which is most powerful. If therefore, the vigorous attraction of the sensual nature be abated by a ceaseless pain, these powers may resume the seeds of a better life and nature.

As in the material system, there is a gravitation of the less bodies towards the greater, there must of necessity, be something analogous to this in the intellectual system : and since the spirits created by God are emanations and streams from his own abyss of being, and as self-existent power must needs subject all beings to itself, the Deity could not but impress upon her intimate natures and substances, a central tendency towards himself, an essential principle of reunion to their great original.

VI. That the earth, after its conflagration, shall become habitable again, and be the mansion of men and other animals, and *that* in eternal vicissitudes.

For it is thus expressed in Isaiah : "Behold, I make new heavens and a new earth;" and in Heb. i. 10–12 "Thou, Lord, in the beginning hast laid the foundations of the earth : As a vesture shalt thou change them, and they shall be changed." Where there is only a change, the substance is not destroyed; this change being only as that of a garment worn out and decaying. The fashion of the world passes away like a turning scene, to exhibit a fresh and new representation of things; and if only the present dress and appearance of things go off, the substance is supposed to remain entire.

QUIETISTS.

THIS name has been generally applied to a class of enthusiasts, who conceive the great object of religion to be the absorption of all human sentiments and passions into devout contemplation and love of God. This idea has found its admirers and encomiasts in all ages. A sect called by this name (in Greek *Hesychastœ*) existed among the religious of Mount Athos; and in the 17th century it was given in France to a peculiar class of devout persons with a tendency towards a higher spiritual devotion,

which seems to have arisen, in a great measure, out of a
natural oposition to the hierarchical coldness and positive
immorality of the Roman Catholic religion at that time,
especially under the influence of the Jesuits.

A Spanish priest, Molinos, published at Rome a work
entitled *The Spiritual Guide* (1657), of which the ardent
language attracted a multitude of partisans. Its leading
feature was the description of the happiness of a soul reposing in perfect quiet on God, so as to become conscious
of his presence only, and untroubled by external things.
He even advanced so far as to maintain that the soul, in
its highest state of perfection, is removed even beyond
the contemplation of God himself, and is solely occupied
in the passive reception of divine influences. The work
of Molinos was afterwards condemned on the application
of the Jesuits.

Akin to the ideas of Molinos seems to have been those
of the French Quietists, of whom Madame de la Motte
Guyon and Fenelon are the most celebrated names. The
former was at one time treated as insane, on account of
some strange delusions which led her to represent herself
(unless she was calumniated) as the mystical woman of
the Apocalypse; at another she was admitted to the inti-
macy of Madame de Maintenon, and high in court favor.
Fenelon praised her in his treatise *Sur la Vie Interieure*
(1691), in which many of the most dangerous tenets of
Quietism were contained. The writings of the latter upon
this subject were finally condemned by Innocent XII;
and the example of the Archbishop in submitting to the
decision, and declaring himself satisfied and convinced by
the opinion of the church, has been dwelt on by pious
writers as a signal triumph of a truly religious mind.

The dissolute conduct of some hypocritical priests, under the pretence of inculcating the tenets and practice of
Quietism, brought it eventually into disrepute more than
the repeated condemnations of the head of the Roman
Catholic church.

MANICHEISTS.

THESE were the followers of Manes, an Oriental heretic of the third century, who, having been ordained a Christian presbyter, attempted to effect a combination between the religion which he was appointed to preach, and the current philosophical systems of the East. He pursued herein the same course as the Valentinians, Basilidians, and many others, whose leading ideas may be denominated Gnostic. He maintained a dualism of principles governing the world, and a succession of dualisms generated from them, like the Gnostic æons.

All things were effected by the combination or repulsion of the good and the bad; men had a double soul, good and evil; even their bodies were supposed to be formed, the upper half by God, the lower by the devil. The Old Testament was referred to the inspiration of the evil principle, the New to that of the good. In the latter, however, Manes proposed many alterations, and maintained also the authenticity of various apocryphal Scriptures. A great part of his system related to cosmogony and psychology, in which fields of speculation he expatiated with the most arbitrary freedom. Like most other Oriental systems, the Manichean heresy was celebrated alike for the austerities which it enjoined, and for the scandalous excesses which were attributed to its most zealous votaries. The charge of Manicheism, which in latter times becomes scarcely intelligible, was frequently brought against the early reforming sects, such as the Albigenses, Waldenses, and Picards.

Manes commanded his followers to mortify and macerate the body, which he looked upon as essentially corrupt; to deprive it of all those objects which could contribute either to its convenience or delight; to extirpate all those desires which lead to the pursuit of external objects; and to divest themselves of all the passions and instincts of nature.

DISCIPLES OF CHRIST, OR CAMPBELLITES.

SEVERAL important movements of a reformatory nature have occurred in the American Church during its past history; one of the most influential and extensive of which was that effected by Thomas and Alexander Campbell, and which is now embodied in the denomination known by the title of "Disciples of Christ," or by the more popular epithet of "Campbellites." Shortly after the commencement of the present century, the Rev. Thomas Campbell, a prominent clergyman of the Seceder Church, emigrated from the North of Ireland to the United States, and located in Washington county, Pennsylvania. He was accompanied by his son Alexander, at that time a young man, and possessing superior talents, who had just completed his studies for the ministry. Both of these labored at first among the destitute Seceder Churches in the western part of Pennsylvania, and as they became more thoroughly acquainted with the state of sects and denominations in this country, and observed the vast variety and number of religious organizations which here existed, they conceived the idea of accomplishing an union between them. The restoration of the primitive unity of the Christian Church was the prominent purpose for which they determined to labor.

The Campbells began to preach among the Seceders with reference to this object, and to aid in the accomplishment of it, they resolved to discard all human creeds and confessions, and receive the Scriptures as the only source of instruction and authority in the development and determination of religious truth. They denied that confessions of faith were necessary, or even useful, to the success or purity of the Christian Church; and they contended that the impartial and enlightened interpretation of the Bible would infallibly lead mankind to a knowledge of the truth.

These views were of course very obnoxious to the rigorous sect of Seceders to which the Campbells belonged—a sect who had experienced innumerable splits and subsplits, divisions and subdivisions, in reference to the most minute and insignificant points of Christian doctrine and practice. The Campbells accordingly withdrew from them and established a congregation on Brush Run, in Washington county, in this State in 1810, which thus became the foundation of their future organization—the birthplace of one of the most numerous and influential denominations now existing in the southern and western States. The principle on which the new Church was founded was simply this: That nothing should be received as a doctrine of belief, or as a maxim of duty, for which there could not be produced the authority of Scripture, either directly expressed or indirectly implied by inference or example.

Guided by this principle, the Campbells proceeded in the free examination of the Bible, and arrived at the conclusion, as among the first fruits of their inquiries, that infant baptism was a usage not enjoined or approved by Scripture, and consequently improper. They also objected to sprinkling, and contended that immersion was the only legitimate and valid method of administering the ordinance of baptism. In consequence of this expression of views, the Campbells and their adherents were invited to become members of the Redstone Baptist Association. They did so in 1813, and Alexander Campbell was appointed the "Messenger" of the Brush Run Church to that association. Even among these people, however, Mr. Campbell's views were singular and extreme in consequence of their liberality; his talents were so commanding, and his influence soon became so great, that the utmost jealousy was excited. About this period he engaged in several public discussions on theological topics, which greatly extended his fame. One of these was with Rev. J. Walker, a Seceder minister; the other was with Mr. McCalla, of the Presbyterian Church. Both debates discussed the subject of baptism, and the result in both instances was to create many converts to Mr. Campbell's doctrine.

His adherents had become so numerous in 1828, that in

that year a convention of preachers took place, composed chiefly of members of the Redstone Association, whose object was to consider the ancient and apostolic order of the church, and see what could be done to restore it. After proper deliberation they determined to reject all human creeds, all ecclesiastical carpentry in the shape of confessions and formulas, and, receiving the Bible as the only source of authority, live and preach accordingly. This principle led them to the rejection of many usages which had been observed by the Baptists, with whom they had formerly been associated. Thus a new sect was organized, based on different principles and characterized by different practices from surrounding sects; but the purpose of the new society was to attain unity by the adoption of a free and catholic principle which could attract and ultimately embrace members of the various sects, and thus incorporate them into one. From this period the "Disciples" formed a separate organization, the professed object of which was to restore pure and primitive Christianity both in letter and spirit, in doctrine and in practice.

In accordance with this principle the establishment of the doctrinal belief of this denomination has been progressive in its nature, and the different leading theories which they entertain have been developed successively. The starting point was the essential nature and importance of *Christian unity* in the Christian church. Ten years afterwards the doctrine of the immersion of adults was accepted as the only proper mode of baptism, and as the only means by which men could obtain remission of sins, and could appropriate to themselves the blessings of the gospel. And thus all the other leading doctrines which they now entertain were successively approved and adopted.

Alexander Campbell, the chief founder of this denomination, was without question one of the ablest polemics and theologians in this country. He conducted many public debates, some of which have been with the most eminent men of the day—such as Bishop Purcell, of Cincinnati, on the subject of Romanism and Protestantism, and Mr. Robert Owen on Infidelity and Socialism. In both of these great logical tournaments Mr. Campbell was confessedly the victor. He has spent a long and active life in preaching the doctrines which he believes, and in establishing churches and institutions which are intended to diffuse education and theological knowledge among the community. His efforts have been highly successful. His followers at this time are very numerous in Virginia, Kentucky, Ohio, Indiana, Illinois, and Missouri; and the whole number of communicants belonging to the Disciples' churches is about two hundred and fifty thousand, while their ministers number between two and three thousand.

Among the leading peculiarities of this denomination are the following: they practice weekly communion, the Lord's Supper being administered in a simple manner on every Sunday. They are not in favor of close communion, but are very liberal and charitable in this respect, permitting persons of piety belonging to other sects to commune with them. They observe the first day of the week, not as a Jewish or Christian *Sabbath*, but as a day commemorative simply of Christ's resurrection, and useful as a season of religious worship. They condemn all written creeds and formulas of faith. Their church government is congregational, each society having exclusive control of its own affairs. They believe that the Scriptures are the means employed by the Spirit to lead men to repentance, and that the *contents of the Scriptures* are the direct source of that faith by which the Gospel is received savingly and effectually. They discard the use of all human terms and phraseology in speaking of religious truth, such as the "*trinity*," "*triune*," &c., confining themselves to the very words employed in Scripture. In consequence of this peculiarity, they have been charged with denying the doctrine of the Trinity; but the truth is, that they believe and receive every thing which the Scriptures affirm and teach in reference to the Father, the Son, and the Holy Spirit.

FLAGELLANTS.

This denomination sprang up in Italy in the year 1260, and was thence propagated through almost all the countries of Europe. They derive their name from the Latin *flagello*, to *whip*. The society that embraced this new discipline ran in multitudes, composed of persons of both sexes, and all ranks and ages, through the public streets, with whips in their hands, lashing their naked bodies with the most astonishing severity, with a view to obtain the divine mercy for themselves and others, by their voluntary mortification and penance. This sect made their appearance anew in the fourteenth century, and taught, among other things, that flagellation was of equal virtue with baptism and the other sacraments; that the forgiveness of all sins was to be obtained by it from God, without the merit of Jesus Christ; that the old law of Christ was soon to be abolished, and that a new law, enjoining the baptism of blood, to be administered by whipping, was to be substituted in its place.

A new denomination of Whippers arose in the fifteenth century, who rejected the sacraments and every branch of external worship, and placed their only hopes of salvation in *faith* and *flagellation*.

FRATRES ALBATI.

A NAME which distinguished a denomination in the fifteenth century. They owed their origin to a certain priest, who descended from the Alps, arrayed in a white garment, and accompanied with a prodigious number of both sexes, who, after the example of their chief, were also clothed in white linen. Hence they acquired the name Fratres Albati, *i. e.* White Brethren. They went in a kind of procession through several provinces, following a cross, which their leader held erected like a standard, and by the striking appearance of their sanctity and devotion, captivated to such a degree the minds of the people, that persons of all ranks and orders flocked in crowds to augment their number. The new chief exhorted his followers to appease the anger of an incensed Deity; emaciated his body by voluntary acts of mortification and penance, endeavored to persuade the European nations to renew war against the Turks in Palestine; and pretended, that he was favored with divine visions, which instructed him in the will and in the secrets of heaven.

FRENCH PROPHETS.

THESE first appeared in Dauphiny and Vivarais. In the year 1688, five or six hundred Protestants of both sexes gave themselves out to be Prophets, and inspired of the Holy Ghost. They soon became so numerous, that there were many thousands of them inspired. They had strange fits, which came upon them with tremblings and faintings as in a swoon, which made them stretch out their arms and legs, and stagger several times before they dropped down. They struck themselves with their hands; they fell on their backs; shut their eyes, and heaved with their breasts. They remained a while in trances, and coming out of them with twitchings, uttered all which came into their mouths. They said they saw the heavens open, the angels, paradise, and hell. Those who were just on the point of receiving the spirit of prophecy, dropped down, not only in the assemblies, crying out mercy, but in the fields, and in their own houses. The least of their assemblies made up four or five hundred, and some of them amounted to even three or four thousand persons. When the Prophets had for a while been under agitations of body, they began to prophesy. The burden of their prophecies was, "Amend your lives; repent ye; the end of all things draws nigh." The hills rebounded with their loud cries for mercy; and with imprecations against the Priests, the Church, the Pope, and against the Anti-Christian dominion; with predictions of the approaching

fall of Popery.   All they said at these times was heard
and received with reverence and awe.

In the year 1706, three or four of these Prophets came
over into England, and brought their prophetic spirit along
with them; which discovered itself in the same ways and
manners, by ecstasies, and agitations, and inspirations under them, as it had done in France.   And they propagated the like spirit to others, so that before the year was
out, there were two or three hundred of these Prophets in
and about London, of both sexes, of all ages, men, women,
and children; and they had delivered, under inspiration,
four or five hundred prophetic warnings.

The great thing they pretended by their spirit was, to
give warning of the near approach of the kingdom of God,
the happy times of the Church, the millennium state.
Their message was, (and they were to proclaim it as her-
alds to the Jews, and every nation under heaven, beginning first at England,) That the grand jubilee; the acceptable year of the Lord; the accomplishment of those numerous scriptures concerning the new heavens and the
new earth; the kingdom of the Messiah; the marriage of
the Lamb; the first resurrection; or the new Jerusalem
descending from above, were now even at the door.   That
this great operation was to be wrought, on the part of
man, by spiritual arms only, proceeding from the mouths
of those, who should, by inspiration, or the mighty gift of
the Spirit, be sent forth in great numbers to labor in the
vineyard.   That this mission of his servants should be
witnessed to, by signs and wonders from heaven, by a deluge of judgments on the wicked universally throughout
the world, as famine, pestilence, earthquakes, &c.   That
the exterminating angels shall root out the tares, and
there shall remain upon earth only good corn.   And the
works of men being thrown down, there shall be but one
Lord, one faith, one heart, and one voice, among mankind.
They declared, that all the great things they spoke of,
would be manifest over the whole earth, within the term
of three years.

These Prophets also pretended to the gift of languages; of discerning the secrets of the heart; the gift of ministration of the same spirit to others by the laying on of hands, and the gift of healing.

To prove they were really inspired by the Holy Ghost, they alleged the complete joy and satisfaction they experienced; the spirit of prayer which was poured forth upon them; and the answer of their prayers by God.

LABBADISTS.

A DENOMINATION which arose in the seventeenth century; so called from their founder John Labbadie, a native of France, a man of no mean genius, and remarkable for a natural and masculine eloquence. He maintained among other things:

I. That God might, and did, on certain occasions, deceive men.

II. That the Holy Scripture was not sufficient to lead men to salvation, without certain particular illuminations and revelations from the Holy Ghost.

III. That in reading the Scripture we ought to give less attention to the literal sense of the words, than to the inward suggestions of the Spirit: and that the efficacy of the word depended upon him that preached it.

IV. That the faithful ought to have all things in common.

V. That there is no subordination, or distinction in the true church of Christ.

VI. That Christ was to reign a thousand years upon earth.

VII. That the *contemplative life* is a state of grace and union with God, and the very height of perfection.

VIII. That the Christian, whose mind is contented and calm, sees all things in God, enjoys the Deity, and is perfectly indifferent about every thing that passes in the world.

IX. That the Christian arrives at that happy state by the exercise of a perfect self-denial, by mortifying the flesh and all sensual affections, and by mental prayer.

LATITUDINARIANS.

A name which distinguished those of the seventeentk century, who attempted to bring Episcopalians, Presbyterians, and Independents into one communion, by compromising the difference between them. The chief leaders of this denomination were Hales and Chillingworth, men of distinguished wisdom and piety. The respectable names of More, Cudworth, Gale, Whitchcot, and Tillotson, add a high degree of lustre to this eminent list.

They were zealously attached to the forms of ecclesiastical government and worship, which were established in the church of England; but they did not look upon Episcopacy as absolutely and indispensably necessary to the constitution of the Christian church. Hence they maintained, that those who followed other forms of government and worship, were not, on that account, to be excluded from the communion, or to forfeit the title of brethren. They reduced the fundamental doctrines of Christianity to a few points.

By this way of proceeding they showed, that neither the Episcopalians, who, generally speaking, were Arminians, nor the Presbyterians and Independents, who as generally adopted the doctrines of Calvin, had any reason to oppose each other with such animosity and bitterness; since the subjects of their debates were matters of an indifferent nature with respect to salvation, and might be variously explained and understood, without any prejudice to their eternal interests.

LIBERTINES.

This denomination arose in Flanders about the year 1525; the heads of this party were one Copin and one Quintin of Picardy.

The doctrines they taught, are comprised in the following propositions:

I. That the Deity was the sole *operating cause* in the mind of man, and the immediate *author* of all human actions.

II. That, consequently, the distinctions of good and evil, that had been established with respect to those actions, were false and groundless, and that man could not properly speaking, commit sin.

III. That religion consisted in the union of the spirit, or rational soul, with the Supreme Being.

IV. That all those who had attained this happy union, by sublime contemplation, and elevation of mind, were then allowed to indulge, without exception or restraint, their appetites and passions, as all their actions were then perfectly innocent.

V. That after the death of the body, they were to be united to the Deity.

MANICHEANS.

A DENOMINATION founded by one Manes or Manicheus, in the third century, and settled in many provinces. He was a Persian by birth, educated among the Magi, and himself one of the number, before he embraced Christianity. His genius was vigorous and sublime, but redundant and ungoverned. He attempted a coalition of the doctrine of the Magi with the Christian system, or rather the explication of the one by the other. And in order to succeed in the enterprise, affirmed that Christ had left the doctrine of salvation imperfect and unfinished; and that he was the Comforter whom the departing Saviour had promised to his disciples to lead them into all truth. The principles of Manes are comprehended in the following summary:

That there are two principles, from which all things proceed. The one, a most pure and subtle matter, called Light; and the other a gross and corrupt substance, called Darkness. Each of these are subject to the dominion of a superintending Being, whose existence is from all eternity. The Being who presides over the Light, is called

God; he that rules the land of Darkness, bears the title of Hyle, or Demon. The Ruler of the Light is supremely happy, and in consequence thereof benevolent and good. The Prince of Darkness is unhappy in himself, and desiring to render others partakers of his misery, is evil and malignant. These two beings have produced an immense multitude of creatures, resembling themselves, and distributed them through their respective provinces.

The Prince of Darkness knew not for a long series of ages, that Light existed in the universe; and no sooner perceived it by means of a war kindled in his dominions, than he bent his endeavors towards the subjecting of it to his empire. The Ruler of the Light opposed to his efforts an army, commanded by the first man, but not with the highest success; for the Generals of the Prince of Darkness, seized upon a considerable portion of the celestial elements, and of the light itself, and mingled them in the mass of corrupt matter. The second General of the Ruler of the Light, whose name was the Living Spirit, made war with more success against the Prince of Darkness, but could not entirely disengage the pure particles of the celestial matter, from the corrupt mass through which they had been dispersed. The Prince of Darkness, after his defeat, produced the first parents of the human race. The beings engendered from this original stock, consist of a body formed out of the corrupt matter of the kingdom of Darkness, and of two souls, one of which is sensitive and lustful, and owes its existence to the evil principle; the other rational and immortal, a particle of that divine Light which was carried away by the army of Darkness, and immersed into the mass of malignant matter.

Mankind being thus formed by the Prince of Darkness, and those minds that were the productions of the eternal Light being united to their mortal bodies, God created the earth out of the corrupt mass of matter, by that Living Spirit who had vanquished the Prince of Darkness. The design of this creation was to furnish a dwelling for the human race; to deliver by degrees the captive souls from the corporeal prisons; and to extract the celestial elements from the gross substance in which they were involved. In order to carry this design into execution, God produced two Beings of eminent dignity from his own substance, which were to lend their auspicious succors to imprisoned souls. One of these sublime entities was Christ, and the other the Holy Ghost. Christ is that glorious intelligence which the Persians called Mythras; he is a most splendid substance, consisting of the brightness of the eternal Light; subsisting in and by himself; endowed with life; enriched with infinite wisdom; and his residence is in the sun. The Holy Ghost is also a luminous animated body, diffused through every part of the atmosphere, which surrounds this terrestrial globe. This genial principle warms and illuminates the minds of men, renders also the earth fruitful, and draws forth gradually from its bosom, the latent particles of celestial fire, which it wafts up on high to their primitive station.

After that the Supreme Being had, for a long time, admonished and exhorted the captive souls, by the ministry of the angels and holy men raised up and appointed for that purpose, he ordered Christ to leave the solar regions, and to descend upon earth, in order to accelerate the return of those imprisoned spirits to their celestial country. In obedience to this divine command, Christ appeared among the Jews, clothed with the shadowy form of a human body, and not with the real substance. During his ministry, he taught mortals how to disengage the rational souls from the corrupt body, to conquer the violence of malignant matter; and he demonstrated his divine mission by stupendous miracles. On the other hand, the Prince of Darkness used every method to inflame the Jews against this divine messenger, and incited them at length to put him to death upon an ignominious cross; which punishment, however, he suffered not in reality, but only in appearance, and in the opinion of men. When Christ had fulfilled the purposes of his mission, he returned to his throne in the sun, and appointed a certain number of chosen apostles to propagate through the world, the religion he had taught during the course of his ministry.

But before his departure, he promised, that at a certain period of time, he would send an apostle superior to all others in eminence and dignity, whom he called the Paraclete, or Comforter, who should add many things to the precepts he had delivered, and dispel all the errors under which his servants labored with respect to divine things. This Comforter, thus expressly promised by Christ, is Manes the Persian, who, by the order of the Most High, declared to mortals the whole doctrine of salvation without exception, and without concealing any of its truths under the veil of metaphor, or any other covering.

Those souls who believe Jesus Christ to be the Son of God, renounce the worship of the God of the Jews, who is the Prince of Darkness, obey the laws delivered by Christ, as they are enlarged and illustrated by the Comforter, Manes, and combat with persevering fortitude, the lusts and appetite of a corrupt nature, derive from this faith and obedience the inestimable advantage of being gradually purified from the contagion of matter. The total purification of souls cannot indeed be accomplished during this mortal life. Hence it is, that the souls of men, after death, must pass through two states more of probation and trial, by water and fire, before they can ascend to the regions of Light. They mount therefore first into the moon, which consists of benign and salutary water; whence, after a lustration of fifteen days, they proceed to the sun, whose purifying fire removes entirely all their corruption, and effaces all their stains. The bodies, composed of malignant matter, which they have left behind them, return to their first state, and enter into their original mass.

On the other hand, those souls who have neglected the salutary work of their purification, pass, after death, into the bodies of animals or other natures, where they remain until they have expiated their guilt and accomplished their salvation.

Some, on account of their peculiar obstinacy and perverseness, pass through a severer course of trial, being delivered over, for a certain time, to the power of malignant aerial spirits, who torment them in 'various ways. When the greatest part of the captive souls are restored to liberty, and to the regions of light, then a devouring fire shall break forth, at the divine command, from the caverns in which it is at present confined, and shall destroy the frame of the world. After this tremendous event, the Prince and Powers of Darkness shall be forced to return to their primitive seats of anguish and misery, in which they shall dwell forever. For to prevent their ever renewing this war in the regions of Light, God shall surround the mansions of Darkness with an invincible guard, composed of those souls who have not finished their purifications, who, set in array like a military band, shall surround those gloomy seats of wo, and hinder any of their wretched inhabitants from coming forth again to the Light.*

To support their fundamental doctrine of two principles, the Manicheans argue in this manner: If we depend only on one almighty cause, infinitely good and infinitely free, who disposes universally of all beings, according to the pleasure of his will, we cannot account for the existence of natural and moral evil. If the Author of our being is supremely good, he will take continual pleasure in promoting the happiness of his creatures, and preventing every thing which can diminish or disturb their felicity. We cannot therefore explain the evils which we experience but by the hypothesis of two principles; for it is impossible to conceive that the first man could derive the faculty of doing ill from a good principle; since this faculty, and every thing which can produce evil is vicious, for evil can-

---

* The punishments, which God inflicts on human souls are corrective, and will produce reformation sooner or later. Yet those who are found in a state of imperfection at the last day, must be doomed to this situation, which they consider rather as a depravation of superior happiness and glory, than as actual misery.

not proceed but from a bad cause. Therefore the free-will of Adam was derived from two opposite principles. He depended upon the good principle for his power to persevere in innocence; but his power to deviate from virtue owed its rise to an evil principle. Hence it is evident there are two contrary principles; the one the source of good, the other the fountain of all misery and vice.*

Manes commanded his followers to mortify and macerate the body, which he looked upon as essentially corrupt; to deprive it of all those objects which could contribute either to its convenience or delight; to extirpate all those desires which lead to the pursuit of external objects; and to divest themselves of all the passions and instincts of nature. But he did not impose this severe manner of living, without distinction, upon his adherents. He divided his disciples into two classes; one of which comprehended the perfect Christians, under the name of the Elect; the other, the imperfect and feeble, under the title of Hearers. The Elect were obliged to an entire abstinence from flesh, eggs, milk, fish, wine, all intoxicating drink, wedlock, and all amorous gratifications; and to live in a state of the sharpest penury, nourishing their emaciated bodies with bread, herbs, pulse, and melons. The discipline appointed for the Hearers was of a milder nature. They were allowed to possess houses, lands, and wealth, to feed upon flesh, and to enter into the bonds of conjugal tenderness. But this liberty was granted them with many limitations, and under the strictest conditions of moderation and temperance.

The General Assembly of the Manicheans was headed by a President, who represented Jesus Christ. There were joined to him twelve rulers, or masters, who were designed to represent the twelve apostles; and these were

---

* To remove the strongest obstacles to this system, Manes rejected the Old Testament, the four Gospels, and the Acts of the Apostles, and said that the Epistles of St. Paul were falsified in a variety of places. He wrote a gospel which he pretended was dictated to him by God himself, and distinguished it by the name of Erteng.

followed by seventy-two bishops, the images of the seventy-two disciples of our Lord. These bishops had presbyters and deacons under them; and all the members of these religious orders were chosen out of the class of the Elect.

The Manicheans observed the Lord's day, but fasted upon it. They likewise celebrated Easter; and had a regular Church discipline and censures. They read the Scriptures; they baptized even infants in the name of the Father, Son, and Holy Ghost, and partook of the Lord's Supper.

The doctrine of the Manes differs from the Gnostics in this respect: instead of supposing evil to have originated ultimately from inferior and subordinate beings, he held the doctrine of two original independent principles; the one immaterial and supremely good, the other material and the source of all evil, but actuated by a soul, or something of the nature of intelligence.

MILLENARIANS.

A NAME given to those who believe that the saints will reign on earth with Jesus Christ a thousand years.

The Millenarians hold, that after the coming of Antichrist, and the destruction of all nations which shall follow, there shall be a first resurrection of the just alone. That all who shall be found upon earth, both good and bad, shall continue alive; the good to obey the just, who are risen as their princes; the bad to be conquered by the just, and to be subject to them. That Jesus Christ will then descend from heaven in his glory. That the city of Jerusalem will be rebuilt, enlarged, embellished, and its gates stand open night and day. They applied to this new Jerusalem, what is said in the Apoc. chap. xxi., and to the temple, all that is written in Ezek. xxxvi. Here they pretended Jesus Christ will fix the seat of his empire, and reign a thousand years, with the saints, patriarchs, and prophets, who will enjoy perfect and uninterrupted felicity.

The ancient Millenarians were divided in opinion: some pretended, that the saints should pass their time in corporeal delights; others that they should only exercise themselves in spiritual pleasures.

The opinions of some celebrated modern authors, con cerning the Millennium, are as follow:

Dr. Thomas Burnet and Mr. Whiston concur in asserting, that the earth will not be entirely consumed; but tha) the matter of which it consists, will be fixed, purified, and refined; which the action of fire upon it will naturally effect. They suppose, that from these materials thus refined, as from a second chaos, there will, by the will of God, arise a new creation; and that the face of the earth, and likewise the atmosphere, will then be so restored, as to resemble what it originally was in the paradisaical state; and consequently, to render it a more delightful abode for human creatures than it is at present. They urge for this purpose the following texts: 2 Pet. iii. 13. "Nevertheless we, according to his promise, look for new heavens and a new earth, wherein dwelleth righteousness." See also Matt. xiii. 29, 30. Luke xvii. 29, 30. Acts iii. 21.

They both suppose, that the earth, thus beautified and improved, shall be inhabited by those who shall inherit the first resurrection, and shall here enjoy a very considerable degree of happiness; though not equal to that, which is to succeed the general judgment; which judgment shall, according to them, open, when the thousand years are expired, mentioned in Rev. xx. 4.

Though Mr. Fleming does not entirely agree with the above mentioned scheme, he interprets Rev. xx. 6, as referring to a proper resurrection; of which he supposes that the event, which is recorded in Matt. xxvii. 32, was a pledge. He conjectures, that the most celebrated saints, of the Old Testament times, then arose, and ascended with Christ to heaven. Agreeable to this he apprehends, that the saints, who are to be subjects of the first resurrection, will appear to some of the inhabitants of this earth, which may be the means of reviving religion among them. Yet they will not have their abode here. But during the thousand years, in which the kingdom of Christ will have the highest triumph on earth, they shall be rejoicing with him in heaven, in a state of happiness far superior to that which they enjoyed in a separate state; yet not equal to that which is to be expected after the general judgment. To this peculiar privilege of the martyrs, and some other eminent saints, he supposed St. Paul to have referred. Phil. iii. 9, 11.

This author argues, that as there has been already a special resurrection of the more eminent saints of the Old Testament; it is rational to conclude, from the ideas we form of Christ, as a just and impartial judge, that the eminent saints of the New Testament, who lived and died under sufferings, shall be rewarded by a special resurrection to glory, when Christ shall give universal peace and prosperity to the Church.

Mr. Ray agrees that there will be a renovation of the earth; and though he does not grant, as some have supposed, the same animals which once lived, shall be raised again, yet he supposes that other like animals will be created anew, as well as similar vegetables, to adorn the earth, and to support the animals, only in higher degrees of beauty and perfection than they ever before possessed.

But he pretends not to determine, whether this new earth, thus beautified and adorned, after the general resurrection, shall be the seat of a new race of men, or only remain as the object of contemplation to some happy spirits who may behold it, though without any rational animals to inhabit it, as a curious plan of the most exquisite mechanism.

He argues, that the apostle, speaking of the heavens and earth says, "As a vesture thou shalt fold them up, and they shall be changed." Heb. i. 12. To be changed, is different from being annihilated and destroyed. The earth shall be transfigured, or its outward form changed, not its matter or substance destroyed.

Dr. Whitby supposes the Millennium to refer entirely to the prosperous state of the Christian Church, after the conversion of the Jews. That then shall begin a glorious and undisturbed reign of Christ over both Jew and Gentile, to continue a thousand years. And as John the Baptist was Elias, because he came in the spirit and power of Elias; so shall this be the Church of martyrs, and of those who have not received the mark of the beast, because the spirit and purity of the times of the primitive martyrs shall return.

He argues, that it would be a great detriment to the glorified saints, to be brought down to dwell upon earth, in the most pleasing form which it can be supposed to put on.

That it is contrary to the genius of the Christian religion, to suppose it built on temporal promises. For the Christian is represented as one, who is entirely dead to the world, and whose conversation is in heaven. Phil. iii. 19.

Mr. Worthington's scheme is, that the gospel, being intended to restore the ruins of the fall, will gradually meliorate the world, till by a train of natural consequences, under the influence of divine providence and grace, it is restored to a paradisaical state. He supposes this plan is already advanced through some important stages, of which he thinks the amendment of the earth's natural state at the deluge, which, with Dr. Sherlock, he maintains to have been a very considerable one. He considers all improvements in learning and arts, as well as the propagation of the gospel among the heathen nations, as the process of this scheme. But he apprehends much greater advances are to be made, about the year of Christ, 2000, when the Millennium will commence; which shall be, according to him, such a glorious state as Dr. Whitby supposes; but with this additional circumstance, that after some interruption from the last effects of wickedness by Gog and Magog, this shall terminate in the yet nobler state of the new heaven and the new earth, spoken of in Rev. xxi. xxii., which he supposes, will be absolutely paradise restored. And that all natural and moral evil shall be banished from the earth, and death itself shall have no further place. But good men shall continue in the highest rectitude of state, and in the greatest imaginable degree of terrestrial felicity, till the coming of Christ, and universal judgment, close this beautiful and delightful scene, perhaps several thousand years hence. Indeed he seems to intimate some apprehension, that the consummation of all things will happen about the year of the world 25,920 ; the end of the great year, as the Platonics called it, when the equinoxes shall have revolved. The reasoning by which those conjectures are supported is too diffuse to be represented.

Mr. Lowman agrees with Dr. Whitby, in supposing the Scripture description of the Millennium to be figurative ; representing the happy state of the church upon its deliverance from the persecution, and corruption of the third period.

He regarded the book of Revelation, after the fifth chapter, as a prophetic representation of the most remarkable events, which were to befal the Christian church, from that time to the consummation of all things.

He divides the remainder into seven periods. The first of which represented by seals, shews according to him, the state of the church under the heathen Roman emperors, from the year 95 to 323.

The second period, which is that of the trumpets, according to him, relates to what was to happen in the Christian church, A. D. 337 to 750, when the Mahometan conquests ceased in the west.

The third period, according to him, represents the state of the church and world, in the time of the last head of the Roman government, i. e. under the popes, for 1260 years, viz. from A. D. 756 to 2016. Each of the vials, which are poured out, he supposes to denote some great judgment upon the Papal kingdom.

The sixth and seventh vials he supposes are yet to

come; and that the seventh will complete the final destruction of Rome.

The fourth period is that of a thousand years, or the Millennium, in which the church will be in a most prosperous state, A. D. 2000 to 3000. So that the seventh chiliad is to be a kind of sabbath.

The fifth period is the renewed invasion of the enemies of the church, for a short time, not defined, but which is to end in their final extirpation and ruin. Chap. xx. 7, 10.

The sixth period is the general resurrection, and final judgment, Chap. xx. 11, 15, which terminate,

In the seventh grand period, in which the saints are represented as fixed in a state of everlasting triumph and happiness in the heavenly world. Chap. xxi. 1, 5.

Dr. Cotton Mather supposed that the conflagration would take place at Christ's second personal coming. That after this great event, God will create new heavens, and a new earth. The raised saints will inhabit the new heaven, attending on our Saviour there, and receiving inconceivable rewards for their services and sufferings for his sake. The new earth will be a paradise, and inhabited by those, who shall be caught up to meet the Lord, and be with him in safety, while they see the earth flaming under them. They shall return to the new earth, possess it, and people it with an offspring, who shall be sinless and deathless. The raised saints in the new heavens, who will neither marry, nor be given in marriage, but be equal to the angels, will be sent down from time to time, to the new earth, to be teachers and rulers, and have power over nations. And the will of God will be done on earth as it is in heaven. This dispensation will continue at least for a thousand years. There will be a translation from the new earth to the new heavens, either successively during the thousand years, or all at once, after the termination of that period.

Dr. Bellamy supposed that the Millennium will be a glorious scene of Christ's spiritual reign on earth, when universal peace shall prevail; wars, famines, and all desolating judgments be at an end; industry shall flourish, and all luxury, intemperance, and extravagance be banished. Then this globe will be able to sustain with food and raiment, a number of inhabitants immensely greater than ever dwelt upon it at a time. And if all those shall, as the Scripture asserts, "know the Lord from the least to the greatest, and the knowledge of the Lord fill the earth as the waters do the sea," for a thousand years to gether, it will naturally come to pass, that there will be more saved in those thousand years, than ever before dwelt upon the face of the earth from the foundation of the world.

Some understand the thousand years in the Revelation, agreeable to other prophetical numbers in that book, a day for a year. By that rule, as the Scripture year contains 360 days, the thousand years will amount to 360,000 years; in which there might be millions saved, to one which has been lost. But if this glorious period is to last only a thousand years literally, there may be many more saved than lost.

PRE-EXISTENTS.

A TERM which may not improperly be applied to those who hold the doctrine of Christ's pre-existence. This name comprehends two classes; the Arians, who defend Christ's pre-existence, but deny that he is a divine person; and others on the Calvinist system, who assert both his divinity, and that his intelligent created soul was produced into being, and united, by an ineffable union, to the second person of the Trinity, before the heavens and the earth were created.*

Under the article Arians, the reader has been presented with the view of the system of Arius and his immediate followers.

---

* This class of Pre-existents are not entirely agreed in their sentiments.

The sentiments of the celebrated Dr. Richard Price, are brought to view under the article Unitarians.   And, perhaps, some may be gratified with a short sketch of the plan, which was maintained by Dr. Samuel Clarke.

This learned man held that there is one supreme cause and original of all things; one simple, uncompounded, undivided, intelligent agent, or person.*   And that from the beginning, there existed with the first and supreme cause, or Father, a second person, called the Word, or Son. This Son, is our Lord Jesus Christ.   He derived his being, his attributes, and his powers from the Father; he is therefore called the Son of God, and the only begotten.†   For generation, when applied to God, is only a figurative word, signifying immediate derivation of being and life from him. This production or derivation of the Son is incomprehensible, and took place before the world began.   To prove, that Jesus Christ was generated, or produced into being before the world was created, the Dr. adduces the following considerations.

The Father made the world by the operation of the Son.   John i. 3, 10.   1 Cor. viii. 6.   Eph. iii. 9, &c.   The action of the Son, both in making the world, and in all his other operations, is only the exercise of the Father's power communicated to him, after a manner to us unknown.

That all Christ's authority, power, knowledge, and glory, are the Father's communicated to him, Dr. Clarke endeavors to prove by a variety of passages of scripture.

The Son before his incarnation with God, was in the

---

* This learned divine considers this doctrine as the foundation of piety, and the first principle of natural religion.   He supposes, that all the texts, which speak of the one God, the only God, the Father, the most High, are to be considered as establishing the personal unity of one only Supreme Being.

† Dr. Clarke avoids calling Christ a creature, as the ancient Arians did, and principally on that foundation disclaims the charge of Arianism.

form of God, and had glory with the Father. John i. 4; xvii. 5. Phil. ii. 5.

The Son, before his incarnation, made visible appearances, and spake, and acted in the name and authority of the invisible Father.

Dr. Clarke calls Christ a divine person, solely on acacount of the power and knowledge, which were communicated to him by the Father. He indeed owns, that Christ is an object of religious worship; but then he confines it to a limited sense. The worship paid to Christ terminates not in him, but in the supreme God and Lord of all. The doctrine of the pre-existence of Christ's human soul has been held by several divines, as Mr. Fleming and Dr. Goodwin. These gentlemen all profess to maintain the divinity of Christ. The following sketch of the plan of Dr. Watts, is selected from the rest. He maintained one supreme God, dwelling in the human nature of Christ, which he supposed to have existed the first of all creatures; and speaks of the divine Logos, as the wisdom of God, and the Holy Spirit as the divine power, or the influence and effect of it; which he says, is a scriptural person, i. e. spoken of figuratively in scripture, under personal characters.*

In order to prove, that Christ's human soul existed previous to his incarnation, the following arguments are adduced:

I. Christ is represented as his Father's messenger, or angel, being distinct from his Father, sent by his Father long before his incarnation, to perform actions, which seem to be too low for the dignity of pure Godhead. The appearances of Christ to the patriarchs are described like the appearances of an angel, or man, really distinct from God, yet such an one in whom God or Jehovah had a peculiar

---

* Dr. Watts says, in his preface to the Glory of Christ, that true and proper Deity is ascribed to the Father, Son, and Holy Spirit.

The expression, Son of God, he supposes is a title appropriated exclusively to the humanity of Christ.

in-dwelling, or with whom the divine nature had a personal union.

II. Christ, when he came into the world, is said, in several passages of scripture, to have divested himself of some glory, which he had before his incarnation. Now, if there had existed before this time nothing but his divine nature, this divine nature could not properly divest itself of any glory. "I have glorified thee on earth, I have finished the work which thou gavest me to do. And now, O Father, glorify thou me with thine own self, with the glory which I had with thee before the world was." See John xvii. 4, 5. "Ye know the grace of our Lord Jesus Christ, that though he was rich, yet for our sakes he became poor, that we, through his poverty, might be made rich." 2 Cor. viii. 9. It cannot be said of God, that he became poor. He is infinitely self-sufficient, He is necessarily and eternally rich in perfections and glories. Nor can it be said of Christ, as man, that he was rich, if he was never in a richer state before, than while he was on earth.

It seems needful that the soul of Christ should pre-exist, that it might have opportunity to give its previous actual consent to the great and painful undertaking of atonement for our sins. It was the human soul of Christ, that endured the weakness and pain of his infant state, all the labors and fatigues of life, the reproaches of men, and the sufferings of death. The divine nature is incapable of suffering. The covenant of redemption between the Father and Son is, therefore, represented in scripture as being made before the foundation of the world. To suppose, that simple Deity, or the divine essence, which is the same in all the three personalities, should make a covenant with itself, is inconsistent.

Christ is the angel to whom God was in a peculiar manner united, and who, in this union, made all the divine appearances related in the Old Testament.

God is often represented in scripture as appearing in a visible manner and assuming a human form. See Gen. iii.

8; xvii. 1; xxviii. 12; xxxii. 24. Exod. ii. 2, 3, and a variety of other passages.

The Lord Jehovah, when he came down to visit men, carried some ensign of divine majesty; he was surrounded with some splendid appearance. It was such a light appeared often at the door of the tabernacle, and fixed its abode on the ark between the cherubims. It was by the Jews, called the Shekinah, *i. e.* the habitation of God. Hence he is described as dwelling in light, and clothed with light as with a garment. In the midst of this brightness, there seems to have been sometimes a human shape and figure. It was probably of this heavenly light, that Christ divested himself, when he was made flesh. With this he was covered at his transfiguration in the mount, when his garments were white as the light. And at his ascension into heaven, when a bright cloud received or invested him, and when he appeared to John. Rev. i. 13. And it was with this, he prayed his Father would glorify him.

Sometimes the great and blessed God appeared in the form of a man or angel. It is evident, that the true God resided in this man or angel;* because, on account of this union to proper Deity, the angel calls himself God, the Lord God. He assumes the most exalted names and characters of Godhead. And the spectators, and the sacred historians, it is evident, considered him as true and proper God. They payed him the highest worship and obedience. He is properly styled the angel of God's presence. Isa. lxiii. The messenger or angel of the covenant. Mal. iii. 1.

This same angel of the Lord was the particular God and king of the Israelites. It was he who made a covenant

---

* God considered in the person of the Father, is always' represented as invisible, whom no man hath seen, nor can see. But Jesus Christ is described, as the image of the invisible God, the brightness of the Father's glory, and he in whom the Father dwells. Christ was therefore the person by whom God appeared to man under the Old Testament, by the name Jehovah.

with the patriarchs—who appeared to Moses in the burning bush—who redeemed the Israelites from Egypt—who conducted them through the wilderness—who gave the law at Sinai—and transacted the affairs of the ancient church.

The angels, who have appeared since our blessed Saviour became incarnate, have never assumed the names, titles, characters, or worship belonging to God. Hence we may infer, that the angel, who under the Old Testament, assumed divine titles, and accepted religious worship, was that peculiar angel of God's presence in whom God resided, or who was united to the Godhead in a peculiar manner, even the pre-existent soul of Christ, who afterwards took flesh and blood upon him, and was called Jesus Christ on earth.

Christ represents himself as one with the Father. I and the Father are one. John x. 30. See also John xiv. 10, 11. There is, we may hence infer, such a peculiar union between God and the man Christ Jesus, both in his pre-existent and incarnate state, that he may properly be called God-man in one complex person.

Among those expressions of scripture, which discover the pre-existence of Christ, there are several from which we may derive a certain proof of his divinity.

Such are those places in the Old Testament, where the angel who appeared to the ancients is called God, the almighty God, Jehovah, the Lord of hosts, I am that I am, &c.

Dr. Watts supposes, that the doctrine of the pre-existence of the soul of Christ, explains dark and difficult scriptures, and discovers many beauties and proprieties of expression in the word of God, which on any other plan lie unobserved. For instance, in Col. i. 15, &c. Christ is described as the image of the invisible God, the first-born of every creature. His being the image of the invisible God, cannot refer merely to his divine nature, for that is as invisible in the Son as in the Father; therefore it seems to refer to his pre-existent soul in union with the Godhead. Again, when man is said to be created in the image of God, Gen. i. 2, it may refer to the God-man, to Christ in his pre-existent state. God said, "Let us make man in our image, after our likeness." The word is redoubled, perhaps to intimate, that Adam was made in the likeness of the human soul of Christ; as well as that he bore something of the image and resemblance of the divine nature.

From this view of Dr. Watts' plan, and what is exhibited of the Arian scheme, the difference will be obvious. They are thus distinguished by Dr. Price: This system, says he, speaking of Dr. Watts' sentiments, differs from Arianism in asserting the doctrine of Christ's consisting of two beings, one the self-existent Creator, and the other a creature, made into one person by an ineffable union and in-dwelling, which renders the same attributes and honors equally applicable to both.

CUMBERLAND PRESBYTERIANS.

THIS denomination took its origin from the peculiar wants and circumstances which the Presbyterian Churches experienced in the early period of their existence in Kentucky and Tennessee. About the year 1800, preachers and congregations were very few in that vast country, which had then but recently been reclaimed from savage wildness by the emigration of the white adventurer. In the progress of time, a few Presbyterian clergymen, who gained a precarious livelihood by attending to the wants of widely extended or scattered churches, formed themselves into an association which was known as the "Transylvania Presbytery." In view of the great religious destitution which existed in that part of the country, they felt justified in admitting to the ministry some young men who had not received a classical education, and whose attainments were in other respects inferior to those which are uniformly required of the candidates for the clerical office in the Presbyterian Churches.

his irregular conduct on the part of the Presbytery was the cause of the origin of this new sect. In October, 1802, the Transylvania Presbytery was divided, by the order of the Synod of Kentucky, into two sections; to one portion of which the name of the Cumberland Presbytery was given. Several years elapsed before the peculiar policy of this Presbytery in regard to licensing ministers was made the subject of dispute; but in 1804 three of its preachers sent a remonstrance to the Synod of Kentucky, complaining of the matter and requesting the interposition of the higher court. Her Synod appointed commissioners to examine into the subject, and they cited the Cumberland Presbytery, including all its candidates and licentiates, to appear before them. This order the Presbytery refused to obey, and after an *ex parte* hearing they were called on to submit the persons whom they had licensed and ordained to be reëxamined as to their qualifications for the ministry.

This order, also, the Presbytery resisted; and the result was that eventually they were interdicted from continuing the exercise of their clerical functions. The Cumberland Presbytery then sent a petition to the General Assembly of the Presbyterian Church, requesting a redress of grievances; and in the meantime they resolved to lay aside the name of Presbytery and assume that of "Council." The result of this appeal to the General Assembly was that that body decided that they could not act in the matter, inasmuch as the appeal had not been regularly brought before them; at the same time the Synod of Kentucky was advised to review its proceedings. The latter body accordingly did so; but the result was, that it became more confirmed in its conclusion than before. In 1807 it dissolved the Cumberland Presbytery by a formal and official resolution on the subject.

In 1808 the "Council" again appealed to the General Assembly, and again the answer given was, that the latter body could not interfere in the matter. In 1809 the Synod of Kentucky sent a memorial to the General Assembly, setting forth their action in regard to the Cumberland Presbytery; and the result was, that the General Assembly approved the action of the Synod, and excluded the Cumberland Presbytery from the Presbyterian Church.

It now became necessary for the association to take action in regard to their future organization. Three ordained preachers, Revs. Finis Ewing, Samuel McAdam, and Samuel King, were the founders of the new denomination. In February, 1810, they organized themselves, assumed the title of the Cumberland Presbytery, and adopted a constitution setting forth their peculiar views. The chief feature of their doctrinal belief was, that they denounced the dogma of fatality, or the rigid Calvinistic theory of election and reprobation, as taught in the Confession of Faith and Discipline of the Presbyterian Church. They also confined the examination of candidates for the ministry to the branches of English grammar, geography, astronomy, natural and moral philosophy, and church history. Examinations in the several departments of theological science were not required. The object of the Presbytery was merely to admit those to the ministry whose practical abilities for preaching were of a commendable character. Immediately after the organization of the Presbytery a large number of persons were licensed to preach, and the work of organizing and establishing congregations on those popular principles was commenced with vigor and activity.

Very considerable success attended these labors. In a new country, preachers of this description are much more efficient and useful than in older and more cultivated communities. Accordingly the Cumberland Presbyterians soon became numerous in Kentucky and Tennessee, and not many years elapsed before their influence and numbers extended to the neighboring States. In 1813, a Synod was formed out of the various churches of the sect, which had three Presbyteries connected with it. At this time they so modified the Westminster Confession of Faith as to expunge the objectionable points, especially that having reference to absolute decrees, and adapt it for the use of the members of the church. The chief points of difference which were introduced into that Confession were as follows: They deny that the doctrines of Election or Reprobation, as taught in the Bible, are absolute, irrespective of faith or men's conduct; but that Christians are elected and chosen in consideration of their voluntary obedience, and that the wicked are reprobated in consideration of their voluntary disobedience. They teach that Christ tasted death for every man; that all persons who die in infancy are saved through the merits of Christ and the sanctifying influence of the Holy Spirit; thus condemning the good old rigidly Presbyterian doctrine, that "*there are infants in hell not a span long.*" They believe, also, that the Holy Spirit operates on all men in such a manner that they may be saved, and that the reason *why* the Spirit is effectual in one case and not in another, is because the dispositions of the persons subjected to its influence are different.

In the progress of time the Cumberland Presbyterians established a General Assembly, which convened for the first time at Princeton, Kentucky, in May, 1829. By this means they organized the Presbyterian form of church government among themselves to its full extent, including Pastor, Session, Presbytery, Synod, and General Assembly. About this period they founded a college at Princeton, Ky., of which the Rev. F. R. Cossit was elected the first president. The sect have also another college at Lebanon, Tennessee, of which Rev. Richard Beard was the first president. Subsequently several church papers were established at different places, such as the *Banner of Peace*, at Lebanon, Tennessee; the *Ark*, at Memphis; and the *Cumberland Presbyterian*, at Uniontown, Pennsylvania. The sect was introduced into Western Pennsylvania about the year 1831, and some churches still exist in that region of country. Not a few also are to be found in Texas, where a Synod has been organized. Several Presbyteries exist in connection with it, and a paper called the *Texas Presbyterian*. The denomination has a Board of Foreign and Domestic Missions, a Book Agency, established at Louisville, Kentucky, and several other useful institutions. Its members generally reside in the Southern States. There are twenty Synods in connection with the General Assembly, seventy Presbyteries, eight hundred congregations, seven hundred preachers, and about a hundred thousand communicants.

WESLEYAN METHODISTS.

THE sect of Wesleyan Methodists arose in this country in the year 1824, in consequence of the dissatisfaction entertained by many members of the Methodist Episcopal Church with the introduction of Bishops into the government of that Church. They contended that not only is such an order in the ministry unscriptural, but also in express violation of the wishes of John Wesley. They quote a declaration of that eminent man as contained in one of his letters to Mr. Ashbury, in which he speaks as follows: "One instance of this, your greatness, has given me great concern. How can you, how dare you, suffer yourself to be called a Bishop? I shudder at the very thought. Men may call me a man, or a fool, or a rascal, or a scoundrel, and I am content; but they shall never, with my consent, call me a Bishop. For my sake, for God's sake, for Christ's sake, put a full end to this."

But Episcopacy was introduced into the Methodist Episcopal Church in spite of Wesley's earnest protest against it; and those members who could not reconcile their consciences to this policy left the denomination, and formed the Wesleyan Methodist Church. They were also in favor of a more democratic and popular form of ecclesiastical government, by which the laity would be allowed to have some share in the control of the affairs of the churches. The reformers held their first conference in Baltimore, in November, 1828. Their second meeting was in November, 1830, at which time they matured and adopted definite articles of association, together with a constitution and dis-

cipline. They also declared their abhorrence of the institution of American slavery, and forbade any of their members to have any connection with it. A more complete
organization was subsequently made at Utica, N. Y., in
May, 1843. They then organized annual conferences,
enrolled three hundred itinerant preachers, holding regular appointments, and recognized about twenty thousand
members. They have congregations in the New England
States, in New York, Pennsylvania, Maryland, Virginia,
and a few of the Western States. They possess few literary or theological institutions, and are noted chiefly for
their zeal in promoting revivals and the practical aims of
religion.

METHODIST PROTESTANT CHURCH.

THIS sect arose from a secession from the Methodist
Episcopal Church, which took place about the year 1828,
and which was occasioned by the dissatisfaction of some
of the members of that denomination with the doctrine that
the entire government of the Church should be vested in
the preachers, to the total exclusion of the laity. The
Methodist Episcopal Church forbids her members to have
anything to do with ecclesiastical affairs in her deliberative
bodies, and denies that the people have any right to a
voice and a representation in the Conferences. A schism
arose in the Church about the time named, in reference to
a proposed change in this respect, which has resulted in
the organization of the Methodist Protestant Church.

The chief difference between these denominations are
two: the one being that of lay representation in the Annual and General Conferences; and the other, the parity of
the ministry, that is, the doctrine that there should be no
difference of rank or order in the ministry. Hence the
Protestant Methodists have no bishops of the sort and
jurisdiction which exist in the Methodist Episcopal
Church. At several different times about eighty preachers have seceded from the Methodist Episcopal Church,

from dissatisfaction with these tenets and usages of the Church; and all these became members of the Methodist Protestant Church. The first General Convention was held at Baltimore, in 1830. Eighty-three clerical, and an equal number of lay delegates were present from New York, Pennsylvania, Maryland, Virginia, North Carolina, Georgia, Alabama, Ohio, and New Jersey. At that period the members of the sect amounted to about five thousand. The Convention adopted a Constitution, which embodied their peculiar views, and which set forth that Christ was the true and only Head of the Church; that the Scriptures are the sufficient rule of faith and practice; and that a written constitution establishing a settled form of government, on an equal plan of representation, was necessary to secure to Christians their religious rights.

The General Conference convenes every fourth year, and consists of an equal number of preachers and laymen. One of each appears for every thousand persons in full church membership. The Annual Conferences assemble yearly, and these have power to provide the circuits with preachers, and procure means to pay their salaries. There are also Quarterly Conferences, whose duties are of a less responsible nature, being chiefly to see that the discipline of the church is properly administered towards preachers and members, and also to license persons to exhort and preach. While this denomination retain the itinerant system in theory, it is not fully carried out in practice, it being suspended in cases where the interests of the congregations may demand a more permanent relation with their ministers. Their prominent preachers have been the two Reeses, Dr. Waters of Maryland, J. R. Williams of Baltimore and T. H. Stockton. The sect numbers about fifty thousand communicants and five hundred preachers.

ADVENTISTS, OR MILLERITES.

THIS singular body of enthusiasts have been pertinaciously expecting and demanding the end of the world, and the conflagration of the universe, during some years past. Several specific dates have been named by them, as the appointed time for the occurrence of this serious and disagreeable catastrophe; and although all their predictions have hitherto failed, they still continue from time to time to repeat them, and to appoint a new era for the realization of their hopes and prophecies.

The founder of this sect was William Miller, of Low Hampton, New York, who commenced to preach in the year 1833, and to assert positively and emphatically that the end of the world was to occur in 1843. His opinions were first published in the *Vermont Telegraph.* His most earnest coadjutor was Joshua V. Himes. Other journals were commenced, advocating the same views, such as the *Advent Herald.* The Millerites based their conviction on the supposed certainty and clearness of their interpretations of the prophecies of the Bible. They computed, as they believed without any possibility of error, all the statements of the Scriptures respecting the Millennium; and their conduct was governed in accordance with their honest convictions. At the time appointed they were all prepared with ascension robes, and other fixings, to meet the expected exigences of the occasion; but their calculations were found to be erroneous. Those who still profess to belong to this sect entertain the opinion that the end of the world and the Millennial era are very near at hand. The views of Mr. Miller himself may be inferred from the following " elegant extract" from one of his published writings:

"I understand that the judgment day will be a thousand years long. The righteous are raised and judged in the commencement of that day, the wicked in the end of that day. I believe that the saints will be raised and judged about the year 1843, according to Moses' prophecy, Lev. ch. 26; Ezek. ch. 39; Daniel, ch. 2, 7, 8–12; Hos. v. 1–3; Rev. the whole book; and many other prophets have spoken of these things. Time will soon tell if I am right, and soon he that is righteous will be righteous still; and he that is filthy will be filthy still. I do most solemnly entreat mankind to make their peace with God, and be ready for these things. 'The end of all things is at hand.' I do ask my brethren in the gospel ministry to consider well what they say before they oppose these things. Say not in your hearts, 'My Lord delayeth his coming.' Let all do as they would wish they had if it does come, and none will say they have not done right if it does not come. I believe it will come; but if it should not come, then I will wait and look until it does come."

MATERIALISTS.

A short view of the distinguishing articles in this system, and a few of the arguments, which are used in defence of their sentiments, are delineated in the following summary:

I. That man is no more than what we now see of him; his being commences at the time of his conception, or perhaps at an earlier period. The corporeal and mental faculties, inhering in the same substance, grow, ripen, and decay together; and whenever the system is dissolved, it continues in a state of dissolution, till it shall please that almighty Being who called it into existence, to restore it to life again.*

---

* Dr. Priestley considers man as a being, consisting of what is called matter disposed in a certain manner. At death, the parts of this material substance are so disarranged, that the powers of perception and thought, which depend upon this arrangement, cease. At the resurrection they will be re-arranged in the same, or in a similar manner as before, and consequently the powers of perception and thought will be restored. Death, with its concomitant putrefaction and dispersion of parts, is only a decomposition. What is decomposed, may be recomposed by the Being who first composed it: so that, in the most proper

For if the mental principle was, in its own nature, immaterial and immortal, all its peculiar faculties would be so too; whereas, we see that every faculty of the mind, without exception, is liable to be impaired, and even to become wholly extinct before death. Since therefore all the faculties of the mind, separately taken, appear to be mortal, the substance, or principle, in which they exist, must be pronounced mortal too. Thus we might conclude, that the body was mortal, from observing, that all the separate senses and limbs were liable to decay and perish.

This system gives a real value to the doctrine of a resurrection from the dead; which is peculiar to revelation; on which alone the sacred writers build all our hope of future life; and it explains the uniform language of the scriptures, which speak of one day of judgment for all mankind, and represent all the rewards of virtue, and all the punishments of vice, as taking place at that awful day, and not before. In the scriptures, the heathens are represented to be without hope, and all mankind as perishing at death, if there be no resurrection of the dead.

The Apostle Paul asserts in 1 Cor. xv. 16, that, "If the dead rise not, then is not Christ raised; and if Christ be not raised, your faith is vain, ye are yet in your sins. Then they also who are fallen asleep in Christ, are perished." And again, ver. 32. "If the dead rise not, let us eat and drink, for to-morrow we die." In the whole discourse, he does not even mention the doctrine of happiness or misery without the body.

If we search the scriptures for passages expressive of the state of man at death, we find such declarations, as expressly exclude any trace of sense, thought, or enjoyment. See Psalm vi. 5. Job xiv. 7.

---

sense of the word, the same body, which dies, shall rise again; not with every thing adventitious and extraneous, as what we receive by nutrition, but with the same stamina. or those particles, which really belonged to the germ of the organical body These will be collected and revivified at the resurrection.

II. That there is some fixed law of nature respecting the will, as well as the other powers of the mind, and every thing else in the constitution of nature; and consequently, that it is never determined without some real or apparent cause, foreign to itself, *i. e.* without some motive of choice; or that motives influence us in some definite and invariable manner; so that every volition, or choice, is constantly regulated and determined by what precedes it. And this constant determination of mind, according to the motives presented to it, is what is meant by its necessary determination.* This being admitted to be fact, there will be a necessary connection between all things past, present, and to come, in the way of proper cause and effect, as much in the intellectual as in the natural world; so that according to the established laws of nature, no event could have been otherwise than it has been, is, or is to be, and therefore, all things past, present, and to come, are precisely what the Author of nature really intended them to be, and has made provision for.

To establish this conclusion, nothing is necessary, but that throughout all nature, the same consequences should invariably result from the same circumstances. For if this is admitted, it will necessarily follow, that at the commencement of any system, since the several parts of it

---

* The term *voluntary* is not opposed to necessary, but only to involuntary, and nothing can be opposed to necessary, but contingent. For a voluntary motion may be regulated by certain rules, as much as a mechanical one; and if it be regulated by any certain rules, or laws, it is as necessary as any mechanical motion whatever.

To suppose the most perfectly voluntary choice to be made without regard to the laws of nature, so that with the same inclination, and the same views of things presented to us, we might be even voluntarily disposed to choose either of two different things at the same moment of time, is just as impossible, as that an involuntary or mechanical motion should depend upon no certain laws or rule, or that any other effect, should exist without an adequate cause. If the mind is as constantly determined by the influence of motives, as a stone is determined to fall to the ground by the influence of gravity, we are constrained to conclude, that the cause in the one acts as necessarily as in the other.

and their respective situations were appointed by the Deity, the first change would take place according to a certain rule, established by himself, the result of which would be a new situation; after which, the same laws continuing, another change would succeed, according to the same rules, and so on forever ; every new situation invariably lea ling to another, and every event, from the commencement to the termination of the system, being strictly connected; so that, unless the fundamental laws of the system were changed, it would be impossible that any event should have been otherwise than it was.

In all these cases, the circumstances preceding any change, are called the causes of that change; and since a determinate event, or effect, constantly follows certain circumstances, or causes, the connection between cause and effect is concluded to be invariable and therefore necessary.

It is universally acknowledged, that there can be no effect without an adequate cause. This is even the foundation on which the only proper argument for the being of a God rests. And the Necessarian asserts, that if, in any given state of mind, with respect both to dispositions and motives, two different determinations, or violations, be possible, it can be on no other principle, than that one of them should come under the description of an effect without a cause, just as if the beam of a balance might incline either way, though loaded with equal weights. And if any thing whatever, even a thought in the mind of man, could arise without an adequate cause, any thing else; the mind itself, or the whole universe, might likewise exist without an adequate cause.

This scheme of philosophical necessity, implies a chain of causes and effects, established by infinite wisdom, and terminating in the greatest good of the whole universe. Evils of all kinds, natural and moral, being admitted, as far as they contribute to that end, or are in the nature of things inseparable from it.*

---

* Dr. Priestley says the doctrine of necessity contains all that the heart of man can wish. It leads us to consider ourselves, and every

Vice is productive not of good, but of evil to us, both here and hereafter; though good may result from it to the whole system. And according to the fixed laws of nature, our present and future happiness necessarily depend on our cultivating good dispositions.*

Our learned author distinguishes this scheme of philosophical necessity from the Calvinistic doctrine of predestination, in the following particulars:

I. No Necessarian supposes that any of the human race will suffer eternally; but that future punishments will answer the same purpose as temporal ones are found to do, all of which tend to good, and are evidently admitted for that purpose.

Upon the doctrine of necessity also, the most indifferent actions of men are equally necessary with the most important; since every volition, like any other effect, must have an adequate cause, depending upon the previous state of the mind, and the influence to which it is exposed.

II. The Necessarian believes that his own dispositions and actions are the necessary and sole means of his present and future happiness; so that, in the most proper sense of the words, it depends entirely upon himself, whether he be virtuous or vicious, happy or miserable.

III. The Calvinistic system entirely excludes the popular notion of free-will, viz., the liberty or power of doing what we please, virtuous or vicious, as belonging to every person in every situation; which is perfectly consistent

---

thing else, as at the uncontrolled disposal of the greatest and best of Beings; that, strictly speaking, nothing does, or can go wrong; and that all retrograde motions in the moral, as well as in the natural world, are only apparent, not real.

* By our being liable to punishment for our actions and accountable for them, is meant, that it is wise and good in the Supreme Being to appoint, that certain sufferings should follow certain actions, provided they be voluntary, though necessary ones. A course of voluntary actions and sufferings being calculated to promote the greatest ultimate good.

with the doctrine of philosophical necessity, and indeed results from it.

IV. The Necessarian believes nothing of the posterity of Adam's sinning in him, and of their being liable to the wrath of God on that account, or the necessity of an infinite Being making atonement for them by suffering in their stead, and thus making the Deity propitious to them. He believes nothing of all the actions of any man being necessarily sinful; but, on the contrary, thinks that the very worst of men are capable of benevolent intentions in many things that they do; and likewise, that very good men are capable of falling from virtue, and consequently, of sinking into final perdition. Upon the principles of the Necessarian, also, all late repentance, and especially after long and confirmed habits of vice, is altogether and necessarily ineffectual; there not being sufficient time left to produce a change of disposition and character, which can only be done by a change of conduct of proportionably long continuance.

In short the three doctrines of Materialism, Philosophical Necessity, and Socinianism, are considered as equally parts of one system. The scheme of necessity is the immediate result of the materiality of man; for mechanism is the undoubted consequence of materialism. And that man is wholly material, is eminently subservient to the proper, or mere humanity of Christ. For if no man has a soul distinct from his body, Christ, who in all other respects, appeared as a man, could not have a soul which had existed before his body. And the whole doctrine of the pre-existence of souls, of which the opinion of the pre-existence of Christ is a branch, will be effectually overturned.

TRACTARIANS, OR PUSEYITES.

This name has been given by their opponents to a school of theologians, members of the established Episcopal church in England, whose tenets have been set forth in a series of publications, known as the Oxford tracts, which began to appear about the year 1833-4. From one of the most able and indefatigable of the champions of the party, the Rev. Dr. Pusey, the advocates of these tenets have been also called Puseyites.

The main points, insisted on by them, according to their own accounts, are the following :

I. The doctrine of Apostolic succession as a rule of practice; that is, First, That the participation of the Body and Blood of Christ is essential to the maintenance of Christian life and hope in each individual. Second, That it is conveyed to individual Christians, *only* by the hands of the successors of the Apostles and their delegates. Third, That the successors of the Apostles are those who are descended in a direct line from them, by the imposition of hands; and that the delegates of these are the respective presbyters whom each has commissioned.

II. That it is sinful, voluntarily to allow the interference of persons or bodies not members of the church in matters spiritual.

III. That it is desirable to make the church more popular, as far as is consistent with the maintenance of its Apostolical character.

The following memorandum, drawn up by Mr. Newman, one of the most distinguished members of the school, explains more fully the original intention and peculiar doctrines of the Tractarians:

Considering, 1. That the only way of salvation is the partaking of the Body and Blood of our sacrificed Redeemer.

2. That the means, expressly authorized by him for that purpose, is the Holy Sacrament of his Supper.

3. That the security, by him no less expressly authorized, for the continuance and due application of that Sacrament, is, the Apostolical commission of the Bishops, and, under them, the Presbyters of the church.

4. That under the present circumstances of the Church of England, there is peculiar danger of these matters

being slighted and practically disavowed, and of numbers of Christians being left or tempted to precarious and unauthorized ways of communion, which must terminate often in virtual apostasy.

We desire to pledge ourselves, one to another, reserving our canonical obedience, as follows:

1. To be on the watch for all opportunities of inculcating, on all committed to our charge, a due sense of the inestimable privilege of communion with our Lord, through the successors of the Apostles; and of leading them to the resolution to transmit it, by his blessing, unimpaired to their children.

2. To provide and circulate books and tracts, which may tend to familiarize the imaginations of men to the ideal of an Apostolical commission, to represent to them the feelings and principles resulting from that doctrine, in the purest and earliest churches, and especially to point out its fruits, as exemplified in the practice of the primitive Christians; their communion with each other, however widely separated, and their resolute sufferings for the truth's sake.

3. To do what lies in us towards reviving among Churchmen, the practice of daily common prayer, and more frequent participation of the Lord's Supper. And whereas there seems great danger, at present, of attempts at unauthorized and inconsiderate innovation, as in other matters, so especially in the service of our church, we pledge ourselves,

4. To resist any attempt that may be made, to alter the liturgy on insufficient authority; *i. e.* without the exercise of the free and deliberate judgment of the church on the alterations proposed:

5. It will also be one of our objects to place, within the reach of all men, sound and true accounts of those points in our discipline and worship, which may appear, from time to time, most likely to be misunderstood or undervalued, and to suggest such measures, as may promise to be most successful in preserving them.

In regard to the charge of Romanism, so frequently brought against the Tractarians, we find in the first volume of the tracts the following statement of "irreconcilable differences" with Rome, by one of them:

Be assured of this—no party will be more opposed to our doctrine, if it ever prospers and makes a noise, than the Roman party. This has been proved before now. In the seventeenth century, the theology of the divines of the English Church was substantially the same as ours is; and it experienced the fell hostility of the Papacy. It was the true Via Media: Rome sought to block up that way, as fiercely as the puritans. History tells us this. In a few words I will state some of my irreconcilable differences with Rome, as she is; and in stating her errors, I will closely follow the order observed by Bishop Hall, in his treatise on The Old Religion, whose Protestantism is unquestionable.

I consider that it is unscriptural to say, with the Church of Rome, that we are justified by inherent righteousness.

That it is unscriptural to say that "the good works of a man justified do truly merit eternal life."

That the doctrine of transubstantiation, as not being revealed, but a theory of man's devising, is profane and impious.

That the denial of the cup to the laity, is a bold and unwarranted encroachment on their privileges as Christ's people.

That the sacrifice of masses, as it has been practised in the Roman Church, is without foundation in Scripture or antiquity, and therefore blasphemous and dangerous.

That the honor paid to images is very full of peril in the case of the uneducated, that is, of the great part of Christians.

That indulgences, as in use, are a gross and monstrous invention of later times.

That the received doctrine of purgatory is at variance

with Scripture, cruel to the better sort of Christians, and administering deceitful comfort to the irreligious.

That the practice of celebrating Divine service in an unknown tongue, is a great corruption.

That forced confession is an unauthorized and dangerous practice.

That the direct invocation of the saints is a dangerous practice, as tending to give, often actually giving, to creatures, the honor and reliance due to the Creator alone.

That there are seven sacraments.

That the Roman doctrine of Tradition is unscriptural.

That the claim of the Pope, to be universal Bishop, is against Scripture and antiquity.

I might add other points, in which also, I protest against the church of Rome, but I think it enough to make my confession in Hall's order, and so leave it.

And Mr. Newman himself says : " Whether we be right or wrong, our theory of religion has a meaning, and that really distinct from Romanism. They maintain that faith depends upon the Church ; we that the Church is built upon the faith. By Church Catholic we mean the Church Universal ; they, those branches of it which are in communion with Rome. Again, they understand by the faith, whatever the Church at any time declares to be faith ; we, what it has actually so declared from the beginning. Both they and we anathematise those who deny the faith ; but they extend the condemnation to all who question any decree of the Roman church ; we apply it to those only who deny any article of the original Apostolical creed."

Tractarians seem to insist that no vital Christianity can exist out of the pale of the Episcopal Church. " A church," says the British Critic, their principal organ in England, " is such only by virtue of that from which it obtains its *unity*—and it obtains its unity only from that in which it *centres*, viz., the Bishop. And therefore, all its teaching must be through the medium of the Episcopate, as is beautifully expressed in the act of the synod of Bethlehem, which the Eastern Church transmitted to the nonjuring Bishops.

Therefore we declare that this hath ever been the doctrine of the Eastern Church—that the Episcopal dignity is so necessary in the Church, that without a Bishop there cannot exist any Church, nor any Christian man; no, not so much as in name. For he, as successor of the Apostles, having received the grace, given to the Apostle himself of the Lord, to bind and to loose, by imposition of hands and the invocation of the Holy Ghost—by continuous succession from one to another, is a living image of God upon earth—and by the fullest communication of the virtue of that Spirit who works in all ordinances, is the source of and fountain, as it were, of all those mysteries of the Catholic Church, through which we obtain salvation. And we hold the necessity of a Bishop to be as great in the Church as the breath of life is in man, or as the sun is in the system of creation. Whence, also, some have elegantly said, in praise of Episcopal dignity, that as God himself is in the heavenly Church the first born, and as the sun in the world, so is every Bishop in the Diocesan or particular church, inasmuch as it is through him that the flock is lightened and warmed, and made into a Temple of God. But that the great mystery and dignity of the Episcopate has been continued, by succession from one Bishop to another, to our time, is clear. For the Lord promised to be with us, even unto the end of the world; and although he be indeed with us, also, by other modes of grace and divine benefit, yet does he, in a more especial manner, through the Episcopate, as the prime source of all holy ministrations, make us his own, abide with us and render himself one with us, and us with him, through the holy mysteries of which the Bishop is the chief minister and prime worker, through the Spirit.

Tractarianism has been often called a "sacramental religion," because of the extreme views of its supporters in regard to the efficacy of baptism and the administration of the Lord's Supper. It must be confessed, however, that in defence of their views they quote the earliest and most revered authorities, and adduce numerous strong passages from the writings of Cranmer and Ridley, the composers of those Thirty-nine Articles, which may be said to lie at the foundation of the Protestant Episcopal church. Thus Ridley says : " As the body is nourished by the bread and wine, at the Communion, and the soul by grace and Spirit, with the body of Christ; even so, in baptism, the body is washed with the visible water, and the soul cleansed from all filth by the invisible Holy Ghost."

And Cranmer, the martyr, is quoted in behalf of the Tractarian view regarding baptism as follows: "And when you say, that in baptism we receive the Spirit of Christ, and in the sacrament of his body, we receive his very flesh and blood, this your saying is no small derogation to baptism ; wherein we receive, not only the Spirit of Christ but also Christ himself, whole body and soul, manhood and Godhead, unto everlasting life. For St. Paul saith, as many as be baptized in Christ, put Christ upon them. Nevertheless, this is done in divers respects ; for in baptism, it is done in respect of regeneration, and in the Holy Communion, in respect of nourishment and sustentation."

" Thus it is," says Bishop Doane of New Jersey, "that the bishops, doctors, martyrs of the Reformation, teach a 'religion of sacraments.' Such and only such, is the 'sacramental religion' which the men of Oxford preach. How can they do other, when it is written, in the words of Jesus Christ himself, 'Verily, verily, I say unto thee, except a man be born of water and of the Spirit—he cannot enter the kingdom of God;' and again, 'He that eateth my flesh, and drinketh my blood, dwelleth in me, and I in him !' When it is written, in the words of St. Paul, 'According to his mercy he saved us, by the washing of regeneration, and renewing of the Holy Ghost;' and again, ' The cup of blessing which we bless, is it not the communion of the blood of Christ ? The bread which we break, is it not the communion of the body of Christ?'

When it is written in the words of St. Peter, 'Repent and be baptized every one of you, in the name of Jesus Christ, for the remission of sins, and ye shall receive the gift of the Holy Ghost;' and again, 'The figure whereunto even baptism doth now save us.' But let the whole subject be summed up in the words of Mr. Simeon : 'St. Peter says, "Repent and be baptized every one of you, for the remission of sins," and in another place, "Baptism doth now save us.' And speaking elsewhere of baptized persons, who were unfruitful in the knowledge of our Lord Jesus Christ, he says, "He hath forgotten that he was purged from his old sins." Does not this very strongly countenance the idea which our Reformers entertain, that the remission of our sins, and the regeneration of our souls, is attendant on the baptismal rite.' "

"According to our church," says Dr. Pusey, " we are, by baptism, brought into a state of salvation or justification, (for the words are thus far equivalent,) a state into which we were brought by God's free mercy alone, without works, but in which, having been placed, we are to 'work out our own salvation with fear and trembling,' through the indwelling Spirit of 'God, working in us, to will and to do of his good pleasure.' "

And the following passage from the lectures of Dr. Pusey's celebrated co-laborer, the Rev. Mr. Newman, may be regarded as sufficient in imparting an idea of the views of the Tractarians upon the subject of justification :

"In the foregoing lectures, a view has been taken, substantially the same as this, but approaching more nearly in language to the Calvinist ; namely, that Christ indwelling is our righteousness ; only what is with them a matter of words, I would wish to use in a real sense, as expressing a sacred mystery ; and therefore I have spoken of it in the language of Scripture, as 'the indwelling of Christ through the Spirit.' Stronger language cannot be desired, than that which the Calvinists use on the subject ; so much so, that it may well be believed that many who use it, as the great Hooker himself, at the time he wrote his Treatise, meant what they say. For instance, the words of a celebrated passage which occurs in it, taken literally, do most entirely express the doctrine on the subject, *which seems to me the scriptural and catholic view :* 'Christ hath merited righteousness for as many as are found in him. In him God findeth us, if we be faithful ; for by faith we are incorporated into Christ. Then, although in ourselves we be altogether sinful and unrighteous ; yet even the man which is impious in himself, full of iniquity, full of sin, him being found in Christ through faith, and having his sin remitted through repentance, him God beholdeth with a gracious eye, putteth away his sin by not imputing it, taketh quite away the punishment due thereto by pardoning it, and accepteth him in Jesus Christ, as perfectly righteous, as if he had fulfilled all that was commanded him in the Law ; shall I say more perfectly righteous than if himself had fulfilled the whole law ? I must take heed what I say ; but the Apostle saith, God made Him which knew no sin, to be sin for us ; that we might be made the righteousness of God in Him. Such we are in the sight of God the Father, as is the very Son of God Himself. Let it be counted folly, or phrensy, or fury, or whatsoever, it is our comfort and our wisdom ; we care for no knowledge in the world but this, that man hath sinned, and God hath suffered ; that God hath made Himself the sin of man, and that men are made the righteousness of God.' ''

"Justification, then," says Mr. Newman, in another place, "viewed relatively to the past, is forgiveness of sin, for nothing more can it be ; but, considered as to the present and future, it is more ; it is renewal, wrought in us by the Spirit of Him, who, withal by his death and passion, washes away its still adhering imperfections, as well as blots out what is past. And faith is said to justify in two principal ways :—first, as continually pleading before God ; and secondly, as being the first recipient of the Spirit, the root, and therefore, the earnest and anticipation, of perfect obedience."

Upon the subject of transubstantiation, Dr. Pusey says: "We believe the doctrine of our Church to be, that in the Communion there is a true, real, actual, though spiritual, (or rather the more real, because spiritual,) communication of the Body and Blood of Christ to the believer through the Holy Elements; that there is a true, real, spiritual Presence of Christ at the Holy Supper; more real than if we could, with Thomas, feel Him with our hands, or thrust our hands into His side; that this is bestowed upon faith, and received by faith, as is every other spiritual gift, but that our faith is but a receiver of God's real, mysterious, precious gift; that faith opens our eyes to see what is really there, and our hearts to receive it; but that it is there, independently of our faith. And this Real, Spiritual Presence it is, which makes it so awful a thing to approach unworthily."

In defence of these views, the authority of Cranmer, the martyr, is quoted who says: "Christ saith of the Bread, 'This is My Body;' and of the Cup He saith, 'This is My Blood.' Wherefore we ought to believe that in the Sacrament we receive truly the Body and Blood of Christ. For God is almighty, (as ye heard in the Creed.) He is able, therefore, to do all things, what He will. And, as St. Paul writeth, He called those things which be not as if they were. Wherefore, when Christ taketh Bread, and saith, 'Take, eat, this is My Body,' we ought not to doubt but we eat His very Body. And when He taketh the Cup, and saith, 'Take, drink, this is My Blood,' we ought to think assuredly that we drink His very Blood. And this we must believe, if we will be counted Christian men.

"And whereas, in this perilous time, certain deceitful persons be found, in many places, who, of very frowardness, will not grant that there is the Body and Blood of Christ, but deny the same, for none other cause but that they cannot compass, by man's blind reason, how this thing should be brought to pass; ye, good children, shall with all diligence beware of such persons, that ye suffer not yourselves to be deceived by them. For such men surely are not true Christians, neither as yet have they learned the first article of the Creed, which teacheth that God is almighty, which ye, good children, have already perfectly learned. Wherefore, eschew such erroneous opinions, and believe the words of our Lord Jesus, that you eat and drink His very Body and Blood, although man's reason cannot comprehend how and after what manner the same is there present. For the wisdom of reason must be subdued to the obedience of Christ, as the Apostle Paul teacheth."

The Tractarians are charged with inculcating the necessity of dispensing religious truth with caution, not throwing it promiscuously before minds ill-suited to receive it. What Oxford teaches may be presented, in a few words, from Dr. Pusey's Letter to the Lord Chancellor:

"In brief, then, my Lord, the meaning of our Church, (as we conceive,) in these Articles, is, that the Scripture is the sole authoritative source of the Faith, i. e. of 'things to be believed in order to salvation;' the Church is the medium, through which that knowledge is conveyed to individuals; she, under her responsibility to God, and in subjection to His Scripture, and with the guidance of His Spirit, testifies to her children, what truths are necessary to be believed in order to salvation; expounds Scripture to them; determines, when controversies arise; and this, not in the character of a judge, but as a witness, to what she herself received."

And in this view of the meaning of the Church, we are further confirmed by the Canon of the Convocation of 1571, the same Convocation which enforced subscription to the Articles.

"The preachers shall in the first place be careful never to teach any thing from the pulpit, to be religiously held and believed by the people, but what is agreeable to the doctrine of the Old or New Testament, and collected out of that very Doctrine by the Catholic Fathers and ancient Bishops.

"So have we ever wished to teach, 'what is agreeable to the Doctrine of the Old or New Testament:' and, as the test of its being thus agreeable, we would take, not our own private and individual judgments, but that of the Universal Church, as attested by the Catholic Fathers and Ancient Bishops."

Nor do we, in this, nor did they, approximate to Romanism: but rather they herein took the strongest and the only unassailable position against it. Rome and ourselves have alike appealed to the authority of "the Church;" but, in the mouth of a Romanist, the Church means so much of the Church as is in communion with herself, in other words, it means herself: with us, it means the Universal Church, to which Rome, as a particular Church, is subject, and ought to yield obedience. With Rome, it matters not whether the decision be of the Apostolic times, or of yesterday; whether against the teachers of the early Church, or with it; whether the whole Church universal throughout the world agree in it, or only a section, which holds communion with herself: she, as well as Calvin, makes much of the authority of the Fathers, when she thinks that they make for her; but she, equally with the founder of the Ultra-Protestants, sets at naught their authority, so soon as they tell against her: she unscrupulously sets aside the judgment of all the Ancient Doctors of the Church, unhesitatingly dismisses the necessity of agreement even of the whole Church at this day, and proudly taking to herself the exclusive title of Catholic, sits alone, a Queen in the midst of the earth, and dispenses her decrees from herself. No, my lord! they ill understand the character of Rome, or their own strength, who think that she would really commit herself, as Cranmer did, to Christian Antiquity, or who would not gladly bring her to that test! What need has she of Antiquity who is herself infallible, except to allure mankind to believe her so?

So much for Tractarianism by a Tractarian

REFORMED PRESBYTERIANS, OR COVENANTERS.

THIS denomination of Christians take their name from the fact that "Covenanting" has been a prominent event and characteristic of their past history. They derive their origin from the Reformed Church of Scotland; their members having united with others in signing the "National Covenant of Scotland," and subsequently the "Solemn League and Covenant," which Protestants in England, Scotland, and Ireland framed and signed in 1643, which exerted an important influence in overturning the throne of the Stuarts, and in bringing about the execution of Charles I.

During the eighteenth century a few members of this sect emigrated from time to time from Scotland to this country. At length in 1752, Rev. Mr. Cuthbertson was sent by the Reformed Presbytery of Scotland to visit these scattered members, and to ascertain their religious and social condition. He traveled and preached throughout the colonies with great zeal during twenty years; and in 1774, Messrs. Linn and Dobbin were sent to assist him. These three clergymen, and their ruling elders, organized themselves into a regular presbytery. With the progress of time the members of the sect increased, and additional ministers were sent over to supply their spiritual wants. In 1799 a constitution was adopted, and various measures were taken to give organization and solidity to the denomination. Amongst other things, they took hold of the subject of slavery at an early period, and in 1800 ordained that no person having any connection whatever with that "peculiar institution," should be allowed to have communion or membership with them, under any circumstances.

In May, 1809, at a meeting of the Presbytery which was held in Philadelphia, it was resolved to establish a Synod, in consequence of the increase of members and preachers; and the Rev. William Gibson, being the senior minister, officiated in organizing and recognizing the "Synod of the Reformed Presbyterian Church in America." Several years previous to this step, the Presbytery had issued a document termed the "Testimony of the Reformed Presbyterian Church in the United States," which set forth their doctrines and opinions at length.

The most remarkable peculiarity of this denomination is that they *refuse to support the Constitution and Government of the United States*, and condemn them as opposed to religion, as *impious and detestable*. They contend that no Christian ought to countenance any government which does not recognize the supreme authority of Jesus Christ, and acknowledge allegiance to him. They hold that the Constitution of the United States, and the Constitutions of the several States, ought directly and distinctly to introduce this topic, and to admit this principle—else in default thereof, they do not deserve the support or approval of Christians. To *our* blind and dumb vision this seems a most absurd doctrine, for this reason : Men should consider what the *intention* of such a thing as a political constitution is. If it be to proclaim *religious* truth, it is proper that due prominence should be given to that, and to the claims of Christianity and its founder. If its intention, however, be to assert and define the various *political* rights, duties, relations, and obligations of men, it has nothing whatever to do with religious principles. This sect might just as reasonably require that the declaration which the National Convention of Dentists annually puts forth, should contain a recognition of the truths of Christianity, and other religious dogmas, in order to secure the approval of Christians, as they have to require the same thing in a political document, issued by an assemblage of politicians, convened for a purely secular and political purpose.

The Covenanters, or Reformed Presbyterians, wholly condemn the Constitution and Government of the United States, on a variety of grounds. They begin by laying down a principle which is true; but they deduce from it (what we regard as) unjustifiable conclusions. That principle is that, when immorality and impiety are made *essential* to any political system, the whole system should be unconditionally condemned. Yet this premise involves an error; because, according to it, the whole Jewish system of doctrine and belief, as contained in the Old Testament, should be condemned and utterly repudiated, because that system contained some *essential* features which were wrong and censurable, and which Christ himself subsequently abrogated.

Reformed Presbyterians proceed to denounce the Federal Constitution of the United States on the following grounds: They condemn the preamble, because it does not recognize the *glory of God* as the great end in the establishment of civil governments; and because it does not propose to secure alike liberty to *all* the inhabitants of the land. They condemn the first article, because it makes a distinction between persons called "free" and "all other persons;" because, as they think, it legalizes the slave trade; because, among the qualifications required for public officers, no notice is taken of religious merits, of the piety and moral excellence of the applicants. They object to the second article, because the mode prescribed for inducting persons into office is not adapted to give glory to God, inasmuch as they swear or affirm, without any allusion to God's law and authority. They also condemn the pardoning power, as applied to murderers, allowed by this article; and the fourth article they denounce, as calculated to make them partakers of other men's sins, or at least encouraging and favoring them. They also object to restoring fugitive servants or slaves, and to making any human law the "*supreme*" law of the land. This they regard as impious in the extreme, an offence for which there is and can be no excuse.

These are the chief grounds on which the Reformed Presbyterians refuse to acknowledge the authority of the Federal Constitution, and even of the State Governments. They hold no political offices on this account, and the emotion of patriotism seems to be extinct within them. The "stars and stripes" and the most glorious reminiscences of Revolutionary days excite no enthusiasm in their breasts. Another prominent peculiarity of this denomination is, that in public worship they sing nothing but David's Psalms, translated into English. They regard it as impious and idolatrous to sing any other kind of hymns; and they condemn not only all instrumental music, such as organs and violins, but even choirs, as being abominable in the eyes of God and disgusting to Him. We never could account for the inconsistency which this opinion appears to involve, because David, in the very Psalms which these people insist so much on singing, expressly says, "Praise Him (God) with *stringed instruments and organs*," (Ps. cl. 4.) And yet there is not a "Reformed Presbyterian" Church in the United States from which, if a fiddle or organ were introduced into it, the congregation would not rush out in holy horror and detestation. Some of the peculiarities of this denomination led to a great split among them in 1830. Rev. Dr. Wylie and a few other prominent clergymen endeavored to effect a change in the existing opinions of the members and the preachers, especially with reference to the prevalent views of the government and Constitution of the United States. Their efforts were unavailing, and the result was that the innovators were suspended from the exercise of the ministry. Six preachers and five ruling elders, who were thus disciplined, then proceeded to form themselves into a new sect and a new presbytery. The seceding ministers were Drs. Wylie and McMaster, and Rev. Messrs. McLeod, Wilson, Stuart, and J. McMaster. They retained the title of Reformed Presbyterians, but entered into a separate organization. The several points on which they differ from those from whom they seceded are as follows:—They do not condemn the Constitution and Government of the United States, and they permit their members to take office, and to maintain all such relations to the civil society and institutions of the United States as are not immoral. They believe that in this government there is no apostasy from any religious covenant which had formerly been entered into; that the defects of the laws are omissions not essential to the operations of civil governments; that a constitutional way is provided by which all defects in the laws may be remedied; and that if Christians believe such defects to exist, it is their duty to mix in politics and employ all their influence in effecting a change in the objectionable features. In regard to Psalmody, or singing in public worship, this denomination, while they retain the use of David's Psalms, are not as rigid in their views about them, nor are they as strict as the old branch in their opinions respecting the terms of communion; and, while in general they practice "close communion," admitting none but their own members to the Lord's table with them, they entertain a more liberal feeling toward other Christians.

Reformed Presbyterians, in this country, have about forty ministers, fifty congregations, and eight thousand communicants. They have a theological seminary at Cincinnati, and several religious and theological magazines, such as the "Reformed Presbyterian," and the "Covenanter." Of all the various branches of the great Presbyterian family, this denomination may be regarded as one of the most conservative, the most resolutely hostile to all change, and to any departure from the "old paths."

CHURCH OF GOD, OR WINEBRENNERIANS.

THIS sect arose about the year 1825 in Dauphin county, Pennsylvania, through the agency of Rev. John Winebrenner, a German Reformed preacher, who, in 1829, settled in Harrisburg as pastor of a church of that denomination. At that period those religious excitements which are termed "revivals" were unknown among the German churches in this country; but the preaching of Mr. Winebrenner was calculated to introduce this novelty among the several congregations in town and country to whom he ministered. The consequence of this state of affairs was, that divisions and violent controversies arose in regard to the propriety of these new measures; and, ultimately, Mr. W. and his friends seceded from the Reformed Church, and formed a denomination of their own. These met together in October, 1830, at Harrisburg, and formed an association, consisting of six preachers and some elders, and this convention or assembly they called the first "Eldership." These persons set forth their belief that there is but one true Christian church; that Christians ought not to be designated by any sectarian or human name; that they should have no creed or discipline but the Bible; and that they should not be governed by any extrinsic foreign jurisdiction. John Winebrenner was elected the first president, or "speaker," as he was termed, of this gathering. Female members of the society were allowed to vote in the choice of church officers; and "feet washing" was declared to be an observance which was of perpetual obligation on all Christians until the end of time, according to the declaration of Christ, John xiii. 14, 15: "If I, then, your lord and master, have washed your feet, ye ought also to wash one another's feet; for I have given you an example, that ye should do as I have done to you." They declared, also, that the Lord's Supper should always be administered in a sitting posture, and after nightfall; because such was the posture, and that the time, which attended the first observance of this sacrament by Christ and the apostles.

Among the other peculiarities of this new sect was the use of fast days, experience meetings, anxious meetings, protracted meetings, and camp meetings. They condemn intemperance and the manufacture of ardent spirits, slavery, wars, and national conflicts. They practice baptism by immersion, and believe in the trinity, in a vicarious atonement, in man's free moral agency and his ability to repent, and that the doctrine of election and reprobation has no foundation or warrant in the Bible. They hold to the idea of Christ's personal appearance to judge the world; and that the final resurrection of the good will take place at the commencement of the millennium, and that of the wicked at the end of that period.

They call their synods "Elderships," and of these there are four in the United States: the East Pennsylvania, the West Pennsylvania, the Ohio, and the Indiana Elderships. These "Elderships" meet once a year, and the "General Eldership" assembles once in three years. A newspaper termed *The Church Advocate* is their organ, and is published at Harrisburg; its circulation is limited. This sect may now have about fifty preachers, a hundred congregations, and eight thousand members.

GERMAN SEVENTH DAY BAPTISTS.

THIS denomination of Christians is one of the most remarkable which has ever existed in the United States; and though they are not numerous, or important in point of prominence and influence, their peculiarities are such as to render them superior to many other sects in interest. Their remoter origin is to be traced to the year 1694, when a religious revival took place in Saxony, Germany, in consequence of the zealous preaching of Spener, a distinguished theologian and ecclesiastic of that period. Those who sympathized with Spener's views were persecuted by the members and dignitaries of the established religion, and the result was that about the year 1719 some of them emigrated to this country for the purpose of enjoying the blessings of religious freedom. Their leader was named Alexander Mack, and they settled at Mill Creek, in Pennsylvania. They had assumed the title of "First Day German Baptists," and among their number was one Conrad Peysel, who was destined afterward to act a prominent part in the history of the association.

Peysel conceived the idea that there was no authority in the Scriptures for the change of the Sabbath from the seventh to the first day of the week; and after some controversy with the other members of the denomination, he withdrew and retired to a solitary cell on the banks of a stream of water in the vicinity, which had once been occupied by a hermit named Elimelich. This occurred in 1724; and as soon as the place of his retreat became known, some of the members of the society at Mill Creek, who had concurred with Peysel in his opinions in reference to the Sabbath, withdrew from the old community and erected huts near his cell, in order to enjoy his society and the benefits of his religious instructions.

In the course of several years a considerable village sprang up around the habitation of the prayerful hermit; and in 1732 they resolved to change their solitary life into a monastic one, by the erection of large buildings in which they could more completely live a life of seclusion devoted to pious exercises. They enclosed a spot of ground to which they gave the title of "Euphrata," and commenced to erect a monastery. They adopted a white habit, resembling that of the Capuchins, consisting of a long gown and cowl, thrown over other garments, made of woolen web in winter and of linen in summer. A number of female members were admitted into the association who wore a similar garb, who also assumed monastic names, and employed their time, in a great measure, in monastic exercises.

In the year 1740 there were thirty-six male brethren and thirty-five sisters in the cloisters, and at one time the members of the society who resided in the neighborhood were three hundred. The latter were married people, whereas those who lived in the cloister were single. No monastic vows were required, and each one was at liberty to withdraw at any time from the association; but it is said that during the lapse of a hundred years not more than five or six of those who had once commenced the monastic life in the cloister withdrew from it and married. They maintained a community of goods, and the society was supported by the profits of the farm and the mills which they owned, and which were carried on by their own members.

The doctrinal belief of this sect was as follows: They entertained the opinion that celibacy was a higher and purer kind of life than marriage, and that the former enabled those who practiced it to attain a greater degree of holiness than the latter. In support of this opinion they quoted the express words of Paul : " He that is unmarried careth for the things that belong to the Lord—how he may please the Lord ; but he that is married careth for the things of the world—how he may please his wife. The unmarried woman careth for the things of the Lord, that she may be holy both in body and in spirit ; but she that is married careth for the things of the world—how she may please her husband. I say, therefore, to the unmarried and widows, it is good for them if they abide even as I." According to these teachings of the apostle, the followers of Peysel, who occupied the monastery at Euphrata, lived a life of rigid celibacy ; and their preachers continually dwelt in their exhortations upon the superior merit of that state, and exhorted one another to constancy in it. As soon, however, as any one expressed a desire to marry, it was allowed them, though they were compelled to withdraw from the monastery, and reside in the adjoining village.

In regard to other points of their religious belief, this sect hold to the doctrine of the Trinity and to that of "free grace," asserting that Christ died to redeem all men, and that men possessed a freedom of the will which enabled them at any time to repent and obey the demands of the gospel. They practiced baptism by immersion, and celebrated the Lord's Supper at night, washing each other's feet, according to the injunction of Christ. (John xiii. 14, 15.) They considered it essential to adhere to the time and manner, and to all the details which marked the first institution of this sacrament by Christ. The Sabbath they carefully observed on Saturday instead of the first day of the week ; and in defence of this usage they urged many plausible arguments against the unauthorized change of the day from that which was originally appointed by the author of the Sabbath. They deny the eternity of the future punishment of the wicked.

Such were the leading features of this remarkable sect. As might be supposed, their peculiarities have subjected them to a vast amount of misrepresentation; but the truth is, that a more exemplary and excellent association of persons has never existed in this country. Because they were few and feeble, and because their doctrine respecting Sunday militated against the opinions of those in greater power and place, they have been persecuted by other religious sects, which, under the guise of the law of the land, have endeavored to ruin them for not observing the prevalent Sunday as a Sabbath. Attempts have also been made to cheat them out of their property. For a long time they did not "resist evil," until at length, when their wrongs became too outrageous and infamous to be longer borne, they appealed to the Legislature of the State. The Legislature refused them any relief. Afterward they appealed to the Supreme Court, which eventually rendered a decision which shielded them in a great measure from further imposition and outrage. At the present time we believe that the monastery at Euphrata is not used for its original purpose; but many descendants of the earlier members of the Seventh Day Baptist Church still survive in the village, thus keeping alive the memory of the obscure and unobtrusive virtues of one of the most praiseworthy, though singular, of modern religious sects.

THE PROGRESSIVE FRIENDS.

THE religious community who are known by the title of "Progressive Friends," derive their origin chiefly from the Quakers. That society had been for some years disturbed by disputes and differences in regard to some important points of doctrine. Many of its members believed that a tone of domination and authority had arisen in the sect, which was at variance with the spirit of primitive Quakerism, which aimed at the suppression of free thought, and resisted all attempts at progress or development. The result of this state of things was that, in New York, Ohio, and Michigan, various secessions took place from the Quaker community, and the persons who thus withdrew formed themselves into a new association, under the title of Congregational Friends.

In May, 1853, a similar movement took place in Pennsylvania, which was produced by similar causes. On the 22d of that month an assemblage was held at Old Kennett, in Chester county, composed of those members of the Society of Friends who were in favor of progress, and of separating religion from technical and dead theology. These persons, however, did not exclude from their association any who had been members of other sects, or who were members of no sect, who agreed with them in their opinions; and all were welcome who, being moral in their lives, sympathized with the professed aims and purposes of the convocation.

In answer to the published call, a very large number of persons convened at the time and place appointed. The meeting was organized and officers selected. There were delegates present from a number of the Eastern and Western States. Testimonies or reports were read in reference to the most prominent evils and social crimes of the day. Thus a distinctive form was given to the views entertained by those present, and those whom they represented; and the Pennsylvania yearly meeting of Progressive Friends was, after a session of several days, duly organized and concluded. From that period till the present, yearly meetings have been regularly held in May of each year, and an increase of numbers and of interest would seem to indicate that a marked progress has thus far characterized the existence of this religious community.

The various orthodox sects have regarded and still regard the Progressive Friends with great apprehension and some horror; stigmatizing them as persons who, under the disguise of religion, and as seekers after truth, are engaged in diffusing the most rank and ravenous infidelity.

That the reader may judge for himself how true or how false this accusation is, we will set forth the prominent opinions entertained by this sect, as avowed in their published testimonies and other authorized documents.

I. And first, of their views of Physical Reforms. At their meetings, from time to time, some of their testimonies refer to the "Deleterious Effects of Tobacco." They condemn the use of this popular weed on the ground that it occasions a great waste of money, and produces the most injurious effects on health, and leads to a want of cleanliness of person. Instances were adduced where children, who had been induced to taste tobacco, expired in convulsions. The various results which follow the use of this article were cited — the gradual decay of health, the gradual enervation of the mind, stupor, headache, tremors, prostration, coma. They assert that in the United States alone twenty thousand persons die annually of diseases directly produced by the use of tobacco. They also condemn it because it tends to the use of alcoholic drinks, and in various ways deteriorates and degrades humanity.

II. Another important question with the Progressive Friends is the treatment which the Indians of our country have received from the nation. These unfortunate people are regarded as the victims of a selfish and cruel spirit, which has for several generations promoted national and personal aggrandizement at the expense of the rights of the weak and the defenceless. They hold that in all those cases where the Indians have been treated with humanity, they have reciprocated with a friendly feeling, but that one of the blackest pages in the history of our country is the long array of persecutions and wrongs which these people have suffered. Every humane heart must approve of the sentiments expressed by the Progressive Friends on this subject, for it would be difficult to excuse, on any ground of religion or human justice, the innumerable outrages which the white man has inflicted upon the aborigines of this country and their descendants.

III. But the most vehement and earnest testimony of Progressive Friends is against Southern Slavery. This they regard as the great social and political evil of the day. They contend that the holding of a human being as property is a crime against God and against humanity; that every bondman in the land is entitled to full and unrestricted liberty; and they demand that these inalienable, but plundered rights, shall be immediately and universally restored. They denounce the Supreme Court of the United States, because they have proclaimed the doctrine that persons of African descent, or whose descent is even *partly* African, cannot enjoy or claim the rights of citizenship under any circumstances. They assert that neither of the great political parties which now exist in this country is entitled to their support, because the one (the Democratic) is the avowed protector and partisan of the institutions of the Southern States, while the other (the Republican) merely compounds with the felony, takes half-way ground, and endeavors to "carry water on both shoulders." They also condemn the popular and more prevalent churches of the country, because they are in fact the bulwarks of the sin, defending it on the ground of religion and the Scriptures. They stigmatize the American Tract Society, because, while it rebukes with great outcry and clamor such harmless indulgences as sleeping in church, dancing, and attending theatres, refuses to say a word in regard to a colossal crime which outrages the most valued rights of three millions of human beings. The same objection they make to the American Bible Society, which refuses to distribute the Bible among the slaves, and uses its influence to discountenance agitation on the subject of slavery. In all its bearings the Progressive Friends condemn the "peculiar institution" as an unmitigated sin and curse.

IV. The question of Women's Rights is an important one with this sect. They contend that women are entitled to an equal voice with men in making and administering the laws; that they are entitled to equal rights in regard to the use and possession of property; and that the doctrine of the mental inferiority of women to men is erroneous and absurd. They denounce the tyranny of husbands over wives, and condemn the outrages which the existing laws enable the former to inflict upon the latter with impunity. In order to prepare women to exercise their rights with prudence and success, they contend that such an education should be given to women as will fit them for that end and duty.

Under the head of women's rights comes the important question of marriage and divorce. The Progressive Friends hold that marriage is simply a civil contract, and nothing more. Hence they believe that divorces are justifiable whenever any of the essential ingredients or elements of the marriage contract are violated by either party. Thus they think that divorces are justifiable for desertion, for abusive treatment, for habitual neglect, and for all the other causes which the law of the land—the protector of civil rights and the punisher of civil wrongs—may permit and allow. This opinion is at variance with the Orthodox Church doctrine, which generally (though not always) inculcates that Christ intended to restrict divorces to cases of adultery alone. Progressive Friends condemn the idea that marriage is a sacramental rite invested with a priestly sanctity, or deriving any virtue whatever from priestly benediction. In a word, they leave the question of marriage and divorce entirely with the law of the land; yet they do not countenance the careless or unnecessary dissolution of the marriage tie, because *that* extreme leads to pernicious social and domestic evils. To justify divorces for desertion they quote Paul, in 1 Corinthians vii. 12–15.

V. Another point concerning which Progressive Friends have sent forth their testimony, and have taken decided ground, is *war*, both offensive and defensive. They deny that human liberty has ever been really promoted by conflicts; and while they do not approve of submitting to the burdens and exactions of tyranny with a servile and cowardly spirit, they think it is still worse to resist them by bloody means. Rather submit with the spirit of meekness, and while protesting against tyranny in the cause of humanity, refrain from all retaliation and violence. That is the highest display of courage, the noblest exhibition of heroism of character. They commend the teachings of the New Testament: "Overcome evil with good; recompense no man evil for evil; love your enemies; bless them that curse you, do good to them that hate you, and pray for them that despitefully use you and persecute you."

VI. The opinions of Progressive Friends are decided on the subject of Temperance. They are in favor of total abstinence from the use of intoxicating drinks as a beverage, as the only effectual safeguard against the evils of drunkenness. They also hold, that the adoption of penal laws against the sale of liquors is not as effectual in suppressing this vice as the use of moral suasion; and that the drunkard himself is much more effectually reached and reformed by those means than by the terrors of the penalties of the law.

VII. The Progressives also condemn capital punishment for crime as a relic of a barbarous age, as originating in a spirit of revenge, and as tending to increase the evils it professes to remedy. They hold that the chief intention of all punishment should be to reform and elevate the offender; and that the death penalty accomplishes neither of these results. They also condemn the recent revival which has taken place throughout a portion of the country, on the ground that it is a revival of the prevalent and popular religion, which they believe to be full of errors and perversions; the revival of that religion which sanctions war, slavery, sectarian exclusiveness, priestcraft, superstition, and hypocrisy.

The Progressive Friends, in establishing their new society, appointed no forms or ceremonies as the peculiar badges of their association. Nor did they adopt any particular creed as containing a system of dogmas to which those who associated with them were compelled to adhere.

Though they set forth, as we have stated, those chief points on which the majority of them seemed to agree, yet all were allowed the most complete liberty in the sentiments which they espoused. Creed-making was not among the purposes of the association. Pure Christianity, without any human alloy, was the boon after which they professed to search. The terms of membership were confined to morality of life and general sympathy in behalf of intellectual freedom on the part of those who join them. The most prominent persons who have identified themselves with this movement are Oliver Johnson, Charles C. Burleigh, S. P. Curtis, J. A. Dugdale, Joshua R. Giddings, William Lloyd Garrison, James F. Clarke, and Theodore Parker.

As might be anticipated, the Progressives reject the doctrines of the Trinity, a vicarious atonement, the necessity of forms, ordinances, and ceremonies, the efficacy of a priesthood, and the eternity of the future torments of the wicked. They believe in the entire spirituality of Christianity, and in the idea that virtue and vice, religion and sin, constitute their own reward, and confer happiness or inflict misery of themselves, both in this world and in that which is to come. They admit the truth of no dogma, the inherent nature of which outrages reason or contradicts reason, and which must be accepted and entertained by a constant process of ignoring and stultifying that standard of human knowledge and consciousness which is the admitted and indispensable organ and medium of mental and moral apprehension in all other things—common sense. Guided by this standard, they reject the popular idea of the nature of the Supreme Being, by which He is made, as they think, a cruel, revengeful, changeable, and short-sighted being, imperfect in his power, in his wisdom, in his justice, and in all the other attributes of his character.

APPENDIX,—BIOGRAPHICAL NOTICES.

REV. CHARLES WADSWORTH.

THE pulpit is the most favorable arena for the cultivation and display of eloquence which the usages and institutions of modern times present. Whatever other disagreeable incidents may attend the clerical office, the moment a preacher ascends the pulpit, he occupies for the time being a vantage ground and an eminence above the rest of the community. The inherent dignity and importance of the subjects which he is called upon to discuss; the direct personal interest which every hearer possesses in the truth or falsehood of the doctrines which he inculcates, and the positions which he assumes; the immense influence exerted by Christianity upon the laws, literature, social life, and political relations of the community; the long array of impressive historical associations which are connected with the past fortunes and vicissitudes of this most ancient and potent of all existing institutions; the fact that the preacher is supposed to be a man of spotless character, and of competent intellectual training; and also, the circumstance that his utterances, whatever they may be, remain uncontradicted and uncontroverted except by the secret and inaudible dissent of the hearer; —all these reasons often render the Pulpit the throne of eloquence.

The Rev. Charles Wadsworth is the pastor of the Arch Street Presbyterian Church, in Philadelphia. He is regarded by a large portion of the community as standing at the head of the pulpit orators of that city; and this estimate, taking all things into consideration, is probably a just one. Those who are attracted to his church by his widely-spread fame will be disappointed if they expect to see a polished, graceful and ornate speaker, who modulates his voice, who moulds his gestures, and who arranges the details of his attire, with all the scrupulous and childish care of a boarding-school miss. He despises these insignificant matters as being beneath his notice. He deals in weightier affairs. The visitor will see in the pulpit a man of small stature, about forty-three years of age, with thin black hair, wearing gold spectacles, of singular and significant physiognomy, exhibiting the care-worn marks of thought, the dilapidating physical effects of protracted and intense study. His gestures are usually made in violation of all the rules which teachers of elocution enjoin and commend as being most appropriate and effective: they are wholly impulsive, seeming to be merely the spasmodic effects of the electrical impetus of the powerful thinking-machine which works within him; and they are generally awkward, but always suggestive, and sometimes impressive. As the hearer watches and listens, he discovers, while the speaker is advancing in the discussion of his subject, that he is an original and a profound thinker, whose eloquence is solely the unadorned eloquence of thought; that the deep and overwhelming effect produced on the hearer's mind is the result of the boldness, the freshness, the gorgeous richness, the quaint, lurid, meteoric quality and splendor of those conceptions which the speaker has gathered in his intellectual rambles in realms unfamiliar and unknown to the generality of mortals, and has reproduced in his pulpit. Some of Mr. Wadsworth's thoughts are like thunderbolts, gleaming, glittering, far-flashing to and fro through the intellectual heavens; and no beholder can witness one of these in their full extent and power without remembering the impression produced by it for a long time afterward. It is chiefly this quality which lies at the foundation of Mr. Wadsworth's fame as a pulpit orator. He is also original in his use of words, and is very felicitous sometimes in reproducing such as are either unused and unfamiliar, or are perhaps entirely unknown; and this peculiarity gives that freshness to his sermons which always renders them a treat when compared with the tame, arid and uninteresting effusions which frequently characterize the pulpit.

We may illustrate a portion of this remark by an example. What could be more refreshing than a paragraph like the following, taken from his published sermon on "Development and Discipline:"

"Here is a man—it may be truly a Christian—whose earthly life is full of gladness and glory: his dwelling-place is a palace; his name is a power in the land's language; fair and fond children love him; honorable men honor him; no corroding sorrow tortures his heart; no insatiate ambition embitters his life-spring; a happy and joyous man he is on earth. Now, though this man may be a Christian, he is not ready to die. So rich and fair in its coloring falls round him this massive curtain of things temporal, that even the revealed lustres of eternity shine but faintly through; and if the fire-car which came for Enoch and Elijah should descend visibly to his portal, Oh! it would be almost with the recoil of a breaking heart that he looked the last on his princely possessions, and said 'farewell' to his beloved household, and flung the reins loose on the winged coursers, turning his face forever from the earthly, and rushing up to the skies."

Truly, if such a magnificent passage as this—and Mr. Wadsworth's sermons abound with them—were declaimed by an accomplished elocutionist, the effect produced would be overwhelming. But it must be admitted that Mr. Wadsworth's peculiar and pointless delivery often weakens the power with which such majestic thoughts are always pregnant. If some modern Whitefield, or some living Bascom, were to deliver a few of his sermons as they should be delivered, it would be an intellectual luxury which is enjoyed but once in a cycle of ages, and would revive the palmy era of a Chalmers and a Robert Hall.

What, then, are Mr. Wadsworth's defects? We answer, a monotonous and tiresome tone of voice; a mumbling of his words, by which he fails to expel their articulation beyond his teeth—a peculiarity which frequently deprives his original and expressive nomenclature of half its effect; and as his words are the vehicles which convey his thoughts, this peculiarity deadens and weakens the impression which his conceptions would otherwise constantly make upon the hearer.

The construction of Mr. Wadsworth's sermons is somewhat peculiar. It has both its merits and its defects. The affluence of his ideas leads him to despise all the established rules, according to which the homiletical writers of the elder schools divided and subdivided, framed and fabricated, their sermons. There is not the least resemblance between his productions and those sermons which harmonize with the rules of Simeon, or the examples of Dwight, in which the various formal heads and sub-heads amount to some fifteen or twenty. But he seizes three or four of the chief thoughts contained in, or suggested by, the text, and expounds and illustrates them after his own fashion, in utter indifference to all that Porter or Gresley may have enjoined in their manuals on Homiletics. This plan of sermonizing may do very well for men of such superior talent as Mr. Wadsworth; but it would be very injudicious for the great majority of preachers, whose intellects are barren, and whose thoughts are commonplace. To such men as the latter the various subdivisions of a discourse are indispensable helps, and enable them to fill out the requisite amount of matter, of which they would otherwise be incapable.

REV. J. B. DALES.

The Rev. Dr. Dales is pastor of the Associate Reformed Church, in Race street, in Philadelphia. He is a native of Pennsylvania, and is about forty-eight years of age. The denomination to which he belongs is one of that cluster of minor Presbyterian Churches which have separated from time to time in Scotland from the great Presbyterian National Church; some of which have afterward divided and subdivided again among themselves, until the magnitude of the fragments has become very inconsiderable, and the doctrinal differences whereon they disagree are almost imperceptible. They are all extreme Calvinists. A portion of them, such as the Seceders, and the Associate Reformed, use no hymns in public or private worship, except the Psalms of David, as originally translated into horrific verse by Rouse, and modified from time to time by subsequent ameliorations. Quite recently a union has been effected, by the Synods at Pittsburg, between the Associate Reformed Church to which Dr. Dales belongs, and the body known as the Seceder, or Associate Church; and this new denomination is now and henceforth to be known by the title of the United Presbyterian Church. Their doctrines remain unchanged. These are in substance the same as those of the Old School Presbyterian denomination; but they differ from these in matters of public worship. Some of them go so far as to insist that the use of Watts' hymns, or any other uninspired composition, in the public or private worship of God, is idolatry or blasphemy. None of these churches permit the use of choirs. A precentor, whose performances rarely rival the artistic skill of Mario or Brignoli, leads the singing, and he is usually well supported by the congregation.

Dr. Dales has been pastor of his present church for some eighteen or twenty years. His congregetion is a portion of the same to whom Mr. Chambers originally officiated in Thirteenth street, above Market, previous to the secession which led to the erection of the present church of that gentleman on Broad street. It was originally known as the Ninth Presbyterian Church, and was built in 1814. An old lady named Margaret Duncan, who for many years had been a shop keeper in this city, left a sum of money by her last will, together with the lot in Thirteenth, above Market, for the purpose of erecting a church. Mrs. Duncan was herself a member of the Seceder denomination, and her intention doubtless was that the building constructed by her bounty should be connected with the same body. It is said that, whilst upon her passage to this country, she encountered at sea a storm of fearful violence, and the vessel was threatened with certain destruction; but that she made a vow that, should she escape a watery grave, she would testify her gratitude for her preservation by erecting a church for the worship of God, should she ever possess the means so to do. The vessel outrode the tempest; Mrs. Duncan was saved; and after many years she fulfilled her promise as aforesaid. Recently, the congregation of Dr. Dales have sold their former property, and erected the church in which he now preaches, in Race street, below Sixteenth. The official connection of the congregation and pastor is with the United Presbyterian Church.

This new edifice is a large, commodious, and, in many respects, a handsome one. Simplicity and plainness are generally regarded by the denomination to which Dr. Dales belongs as proper and essential qualities in the construction of houses of worship. They regard all unnecessary ornament as unbecoming; and look upon the Gothic and other antique styles of architecture as inappropriate to places used for the service of God, and as approximations to the horrid abominations of Rome. But in this instance the congregation seem to have made an innovation, and have introduced a degree of ornament into their new edifice, which is an anomaly among the other Associate Reformed Churches in this country. Stained windows are even used in the building, which, could old Margaret Duncan arise from her sunken grave and see, we fear she would condemn in no very equivocal terms. The whole arrangement of this church is convenient and pleasing, with one solitary exception. This is the singular and shapeless top-knot or frontispiece which surmounts the roof in front, and is in itself a most detestable deformity. What it resembles, what it is intended to represent, or what use it is supposed to accomplish, we cannot divine; but certain it is, that it is an injury to the appearance and beauty of the otherwise chaste and elegant building.

One very commendable peculiarity of the large congregation who worship here is the fact that they generally join heartily and devoutly in the singing. It is bad enough when the whole musical part of the divine worship

is executed by three or four operatic singers, who are paid
so much per day for their performances; in whose singing
there is not a particle of devotion; and who are, themselves,
as is sometimes the case, persons of notoriously immoral
lives. In such instances it is bad enough when no person
in the congregation praises God except these musical hire-
lings—for such music and such singing must be as great
an abomination to the Deity as is the wicked prayer of a
wicked man. But the case is still worse when there is but
a single singer or precentor, who "does" the hymn while
the whole congregation listen aloof, curiously or negligently, and take no part whatever in the exercise, which
thus becomes a feeble and preposterous *solo*. Dr. Dales'
congregation neither use an operatic choir, nor permit
a solo performance. They all join heartily and solemnly,
after the good old Scotch fashion in the exercise of singing.

As an orator Dr. Dales is peculiar. He is an excellent
sermonizer. His discourses are systematic in their struc-
ture; they exhibit clear evidence of the possession of much
more than ordinary learning; and they are rendered valuable
and instructive by the frequent introduction of appropriate
proof-texts. His language is choice and appropriate; and
this is the more remarkable, as he usually extemporises
from well prepared memoranda or skeletons. Nor is the
subject matter of his sermon dry and tasteless, as is too
often the case with preachers of his denomination. He
possesses a considerable share of imagination. He uses
tropes and figures; he even employs them appropriately
and effectively; and his manner of delivery is such as to
increase the impression which they produce. He commences his discourse slowly and almost inaudibly; but as
he progresses, he increases in fervor and in excitement.
He gesticulates with singular appropriateness and propriety; and when he arrives at the argumentative part of
his sermon, he reasons with clearness and power. His
sermons exhibit unusual symmetry of construction, and
they generally go regularly through the formal yet judicious routine of introduction, division, narration, argument,

illustration and conclusion. Nor does this formality seem tedious, for he possesses the ability to render each part interesting and instructive.

Nevertheless, these superior merits are rendered almost useless by one defect, which is radical and ruinous, but over which, unfortunately, he has no control. He has the worst *voice* of any public speaker to whom we have ever listened. We believe he has suffered from bronchial disease, and the result is, that his vocal organ is one which would condemn even Demosthenes himself. It is difficult to describe it, for there is scarcely anything of it to describe. When sparingly used by him, it is both weak and screechy; and when he endeavors to speak loudly, it almost resembles the echo of a frantic scream.

REV. ALBERT BARNES.

The Rev. Albert Barnes is the pastor of the First Presbyterian Church, located on Washington Square, Philadelphia. He has occupied, for many years, a prominent position among the clergymen of Philadelphia; and, in consequence of his labors as an author, his name has extended throughout many distant countries, where even the existence of the majority of his associates is unknown.

Mr. Barnes was born, we believe, at Rome, in the State of New York, and is now about sixty years of age. His youth was passed in manual labor; and he was apprenticed in his boyhood to learn the art and mystery of a miller. He had scarcely reached his majority, when certain infidel notions which he had previously imbibed were exploded; he became pious, and determined to prepare himself for the ministry. This purpose he carried into effect at Princeton. His collegiate and theological course having been completed, he was ordained as a clergyman by the Presbytery under whose care he had placed himself and had been studying. His first pastoral charge was at Morristown, New Jersey. About the year 1830 he was invited to become pastor of the church with which

he is now connected, and to which he has laboriously ministered ever since. He has on several occasions been invited to remove to other posts of responsibility and honor,
but he has uniformly declined. Some years since he was
elected President of the Auburn Theological Seminary;
but he preferred to retain his pastoral position, greatly to
the gratification of the members of his congregation.

Shortly after his removal to Philadelphia, Mr. Barnes
became the unintentional cause of bitter theological disputes, and eventually of a great ecclesiastical schism, in
the Presbyterian Church. This event took place in 1835.
Until that period, that numerous and powerful body of
American Christians had remained undivided and harmonious, at least so far as outward seeming and union were
concerned. But there had been, during many years, a
difference of opinion gradually growing among their members and divines in reference to certain theological dogmas,
especially with regard to those points which are distinct-
ively termed Calvinistic. The nature of the divine decrees, the doctrines of election, reprobation, free-grace,
infant damnation, perseverance of the saints, and similar
theories, which form the central points of the Calvinistic
or Augustinian system, were those respecting which this
difference of sentiment among Presbyterians was silently
and slowly progressing. How long that diversity might
have existed in the church without producing open conflict
and a public schism, it would be difficult to say; but Mr.
Barnes was unconsciously destined to become the apple of
discord among his brethren. He prepared and published
a commentary, or practical and exegetical notes, on the
Gospels, in which he set forth his peculiar views on the
points just mentioned. These views were what might be
termed liberal, in comparison with the old fossilized theories which had been held by that denomination ever since
the days of John Knox; and the great exponent of which
in this country was Jonathan Edwards. Mr. Barnes, in
interpreting certain passages of the Gospels, gave utterance to opinions which were at once stigmatized by some

of his brethren as new school, as innovations, as uncalvin-istic or Pelagian, as heterodox and unchristian. An awful hue and cry was raised against him. The whole country resounded with the yells of an indignant, outraged, impla-cable orthodoxy. Calvin himself, when burning the un-happy Servetus at Geneva for teaching sentiments which such men as Milton, Priestley, and Channing have since entertained, could not have been more ravenously intent on wreck and ruin, than were some of the persecutors of Mr. Barnes for inculcating doctrines which, before and since, have been believed and taught by myriads of the most excellent of men, the salt of the earth.

The publication of Mr. Barnes' Notes concentrated around his own head the storms which had been brewing for some years in the Presbyterian body. Already had he excited censure and suspicion by publishing a sermon, in February, 1829, while yet residing at Morristown, en-titled "The Way of Salvation," which dimly foreshadowed the views which were more fully expressed in his Commen-tary. When, therefore, he was about to remove to Phila-delphia, as the successor of Dr. Wilson, a portion of the congregation objected to his settlement and entered their protest. When that protest was overruled against the dis-affected party, and after Mr. Barnes had been duly in-stalled by the Philadelphia Presbytery, a formal complaint was made to that tribunal against him as a teacher of heresy. The charges were not prosecuted for some time, as the assailants of Mr. Barnes were fearful lest they might be discomfited in their assault upon him, by a greater and wider prevalence of his views among his clerical breth-ren than they anticipated. At length, however, when Mr. Barnes published his "Notes of Romans," the sup-posed bulwark of intensified Calvinism, wherein his inter-pretations were more bold, free and clear than they had previously been, his opponents became frantic; a hue and cry, louder, fiercer, hoarser, than before, was raised, and they proceeded to impeach him in form, as being guilty of "damnable heresies."

The controversy which ensued occupied the attention of the church during the progress of several years. A great deal of learning, eloquence, and acrimony were elicited on both sides, which furnished another and a memorable evidence that of all hatreds the *odium theologicum* is the most intense and unchristian. The Presbytery voted on the question of heresy in July, 1835, and Mr. Barnes was acquitted. The Inquisitor General, Mr. Junkin, appealed from this decision to the Synod of Philadelphia, which convened at York, in May, 1836. By that body Mr. Barnes was condemned, and suspended from all the functions of the ministry until he should furnish evidence of repentance. But, instead of repenting, he appealed from the Synod to the General Assembly, which subsequently convened at Pittsburg. By that body, after a full hearing and protracted argument, his appeal was sustained by a vote of 134 to 94. He was thus reinstated in the ministry and in his church, having suffered suspension during a year. But the defeated side were not satisfied; and the trial of Mr. Barnes resulted finally in the entire splitting of the Presbyterian denomination into two distinct and hostile bodies, then and since known as the Old and New School churches.

This controversy, in which Mr. Barnes was the central figure, extended his fame widely and familiarly throughout the country. He was justly regarded by all as the standard-bearer of the New School, and by many as the martyr of a persecuting party. Others, who were not Presbyterian, either Old or New, admired him for the courage with which he asserted the principle of rational progress and Christian freedom in the study and interpretation of the Scriptures. Not a few hated him as the teacher of false, pernicious, and detestable heresies; nor have their prejudices yet passed entirely away.

Unconcerned either with the praise or the censure of men, Mr. Barnes continued, after the formal settlement of this great dispute, to devote himself to the performance of his pastoral duties and to the completion of Exegetical Notes on the Scriptures. The church of which he was and still is pastor, is a very large one, and the congregation are numerous and intelligent. As a preacher, Mr. Barnes is peculiar in his style. He makes no pretentions to oratory or eloquence. He rarely or never gesticulates, and he usually stands bolt upright, and perfectly still, in the delivery of his discourses. This was more especially the case when he preached from his notes; for since the failure of his eyesight, and his inability to make much use of his pen, his extemporaneous efforts are more genial, less formal, and, it may be added, more acceptable to the majority of his hearers. His sermons possess in an unusual degree the quality of thorough, exhaustive thinking. Many of them are doctrinal discussions, which evince a mind trained to logical reflection, and fully competent to follow out all the details and sequences of an investigation. When he preaches practical sermons, expressly as such, he exhibits deep feeling and pious earnestness. His volume of Practical Sermons, already published, are characterized by great evangelical fervor. In the pulpit, Mr. Barnes is well adapted to edify, instruct, and benefit the hearer; he never charms him by the attractions of eloquence, nor by the arts of the rhetorician; but he often enlightens by more than ordinary freshness, depth, and thoroughness of discussion.

Mr. Barnes is more remarkable as a writer of commentaries than in any other intellectual respect. He is the most voluminous author in Philadelphia. He has written notes on all the books of the New Testament, and on Job, Daniel and Isaiah in the Old. As a Biblical critic he has considerable merit; his expositions being generally sound and safe. In point of critical and philological learning, however, he will not compare with Moses Stuart, or Professor Robinson, in this country; or with Tholuck, Kuinoel, or De Wette, in Germany. His acquaintance with the Oriental languages is evidently only such as it became necessary for him to acquire, in order to read and appreciate the works of the great critics who have already commented on the Scriptures, and to make use of their labors in compiling his own writings. But for practical purposes, this acquaintance was sufficient, as is evinced by the popularity which his comments have obtained throughout the religious public, both in this country and in England. People talk everlastingly about "the learned and judicious Hooker." They might say with equal propriety and frequency, "the laborious and useful Barnes."

Yet it should not be inferred, from the fact that Mr. Barnes has written so much, that he is not capable of compact and logical thinking. In his controversy with the deposed, dram-drinking Bishop Onderdonk, on Episcopacy, he reasoned with great force, clearness, and conclusiveness. In his Introduction to his edition of Butler's Analogy, he produced an essay not unworthy to stand by the side of that colossal monument of logic; and it admirably supplies the deficiencies which till then marred its completeness. Had Mr. Barnes written only one-third of what he has accomplished, his fame as an author (but not perhaps his usefulness) would stand much higher than it does, because mankind are always disposed to infer that when a writer produces so much, a large proportion of it must be of inferior quality. In general, this dictum or judgment is true; but Mr. Barnes is an exception, for the most part, to the rule.

The personal incidents of the life of this distinguished clergyman are few. His life has been chiefly passed in his study. His devotion to his literary labors has been rarely equalled. For many years he commenced his studies at four o'clock in the morning, in his library in the church in which he preaches, and he generally continued them till late at night. On one occasion, it is said that a new watchman, who met him long before the dawn of day, on his way to his study, carrying a bundle of kindling wood in his hands, regarded him as a suspicious person, arrested him, and retained him until enlightened as to the true nature of the case and the real character of his victim. A real thief would most probably have not been arrested at all, or would have been compelled merely to divide the plunder! The constant devotion of Mr. Barnes to study during so many years, resulted in the serious injury of his eye-sight. Some time since he was compelled to suspend his labors entirely. He embraced the opportunity to visit Europe, and employ the most competent medical aid there accessible. It is not likely that he will ever be able to resume the same prodigious habits of application which he practiced during so many years; yet he can console himself with the reflection that, though he cannot claim to stand beside Robert Hall or Edward Irving as a preacher, or beside Gesenius and the younger Rosenmüller as a critic, he will always rank honorably and eminently as the Matthew Henry of his country.

REV. W. H. FURNESS.

The Rev. Dr. Furness is the most distinguished representative in Philadelphia of that class of divines to whom the term "Liberal" is applied, both by themselves and by the general custom of the religious public. He preaches in the Unitarian Church, at the corner of Locust and Tenth Streets; and has during many years been regarded as one of the most intellectual and cultivated of the Philadelphia clergy. Notwithstanding the large amount of prejudice which the "Orthodox" churches have always entertained, and do still entertain, against what they term heterodox denominations, all have concurred in rendering a just tribute of esteem and respect for this clergyman personally.

Dr. Furness was born at Boston, Massachusetts, in 1802, and was educated at Cambridge University. Having terminated his course of studies, he visited Philadelphia in the summer of 1824, and preached a series of trial sermons to those few Unitarians who then constituted the society in that city. At the conclusion of the series, he was invited to become the regular pastor of the church;

he accepted the invitation, and was ordained in June, 1825, to the office which he still retains. Thus thirty-three years have elapsed since the connection of Dr. Furness with his present church began; and it is probable that he is one of the oldest settled ministers in Philadelphia. This church is the most ancient professedly Unitarian society in the United States; and as such it possesses more than ordinary historical interest. It was commenced sixty-two years ago, in 1796; and was composed at first of fourteen members, most of whom were natives of England, and men of wealth, who, finding themselves in the new world where all the existing denominations differed fundamentally in their views from themselves, resolved to organize a church, and conduct religious services in accordance with their own convictions.

A short time previous to the adoption of this resolution, Dr. Joseph Priestley, the celebrated English philosopher and theologian, had removed to this country; having been driven from his home at Birmingham, and his residence destroyed, by the insane violence of a popular tumult. Having located himself at Northumberland in this State, he occasionally visited Philadelphia. Great and enlightened as he was, he was still the object of universal prejudice even here. His co-religionists in Philadelphia alone regarded him with the respectful consideration which he deserved; and by his advice, and under his direction, the fourteen Unitarians already alluded to combined together in the organization of a church. It is said that Dr. Priestley's autograph appears among the signatures of the first members of the society, and he no doubt assisted in the public services of the congregation whenever he visited Philadelphia. These exercises were carried on during some years by the members of the society, it being impossible for them at that time to procure the services of a Unitarian minister. So great was the prejudice then prevalent in the community against those who believed in the unity of the Supreme Being, that it was with great difficulty that the infant church could even procure a place for public worship. At length, in 1813, they purchased the lot upon which the present edifice stands, and erected an octagonal building upon it, capable of accommodating several hundred people. In 1822 the congregation succeeded in obtaining the occasional ministrations of students of divinity from the theological department of the University of Cambridge. This arrangement continued until the arrival, the preaching, and the permanent settlement of Dr. Furness, at the period already referred to. From that date until the present, during a long lapse of tranquil years, he has devoted himself to the quiet, regular and unobtrusive performance of his pastoral and pulpit duties.

For twenty years after the formation of the Unitarian Church in Philadelphia, there was no similar organization throughout the United States. Even at Boston, which has since become, and now is, the head-quarters of Liberal Christianity in the United States, there was no open avowal of Unitarianism, and no professedly Unitarian Church until 1810. At this period the church known as King's Chapel, in Boston, was ministered to by two clergymen, Dr. Freeman and Mr. Carey, men of learning and piety, who had become convinced of the absolute unity of the object of divine worship, had boldly taught that doctrine from the pulpit, and had brought over the majority of their members to a harmony of opinion with themselves. Gradually the number of converts increased; this new or old doctrine, this heretical or divinely taught opinion, just as you choose to consider it, spread more and more through the churches of Boston, through Massachusetts, through New England, and through other States of the Union, until it now comprises among its members a large portion of the most intelligent and cultivated part of the community; sending forth from year to year, from Cambridge, the chief University in the land, men of science, men of eloquence, men of piety, to promulgate the doctrines which they have there imbibed and adopted.

At the period of the arrival of Dr. Furness in Philadelphia, his position, as one of the few Unitarian pastors in this country, was a very difficult one. The religious public even at that time, regarded a Unitarian with about that same sort of indefinable horror and nameless dread with which the most extreme and radical infidels are now esteemed by the majority of them. Shortly before that period a controversy had taken place in Boston in reference to this new doctrine, and its apprehended ravages in that neighborhood, in which Dr. Channing had greatly distinguished himself; and although he defended the Unitarian views with superior learning, with rare amiability, and with unrivaled eloquence, the Orthodox community far and near united in condemning, excommunicating, and repudiating the persons and the opinions of those who chose to interpret strictly that saying of Scripture : " Hear, O Israel, the Lord our God is one Lord." Mr. Furness incurred his full share of this prejudice. He was then but in his twenty-second year, and his position required great circumspection and prudence. He proved himself fully equal to the task which he had assumed. Avoiding the noisy clamors of controversy and all uncharitable assaults upon the opinions and prejudices of others, he devoted himself to his duties, and preached what he believed to be the truth, whether men would hear or forbear. This course he has pursued during many years with signal success. His congregation has flourished; his views have gradually become more and more disseminated ; and while other churches have been torn and distracted by innumerable feuds and implacable divisions, his society has ever been strangers to the distractions of party and the miseries and animosities of schism.

As a preacher, the style of Dr. Furness is peculiar. At one period he was one of the most *popular* clergymen in this city. We may say that he occupied this position *in spite of* himself; for no man would seem to take less pains to secure the notoriety which "fame's obstreperous trump" bestows, than he. His manner of preaching is quiet, reflective, subdued, but none the less on that account impressive. He rarely gesticulates; yet his manner seems instinct with earnest feeling, which, by some mysterious process, he communicates to the hearer. His most striking quality as a preacher is his *intellectuality*. His sermons are calm embodiments of pure thought. Frequently, from first to last, they are continued utterances of unbroken, instructive, attractive ratiocinations on religious themes. One of the most remarkable peculiarities of his ministrations, is his intense and never ceasing opposition to American Slavery; and he embraces every opportunity afforded, even by the ordinary services of the pulpit, to express his abhorrence of this prominent and anomalous element in American society and government.

The denomination to which Dr. Furness belongs entertain three cardinal principles as the foundation of their faith. The first is, that the Scriptures are the proper source of religious truth and knowledge. The second is, the full and unrestricted right of private judgment, and the perfect freedom of the human mind, in the interpretation of the contents of the Scriptures. The third is, the undeniable truthfulness of the doctrine of the Divine Unity. On minor points American Unitarians not only differ, but they expect to differ, as a necessary and natural result of the full operation of the second of the preceding canons of belief. This right of private judgment in religious matters, was the great *principium cognoscendi* of the Protestant Reformation in the sixteenth century; yet, as Unitarians say, the reformers and their followers do not carry it out to its legitimate results, but annul it by the fabrication of creeds and confessions, and other theological straitjackets, which as effectually interfere with the exercise of private judgment, and with the spirit of progress and development, as did the decrees and persecutions of the Roman Catholic Church, during the Dark Ages. Doubtless, arguments of great weight may be urged on both sides of this question; and it is undeniable, that, if the unrestricted freedom of private judgment favors the discovery and development of truth, it has on the other hand a tendency to destroy that unity and harmony of sentiment which *some* Christians regard as essential elements or characteristics of the true Church.

REV. JOHN WESLEY.

JOHN WESLEY, the founder of the sect of the Methodists, was born June 17, 1703, at Epworth. He was educated at the Charterhouse, and Christchurch, Oxford, and was ordained in 1725. Naturally of a devout disposition, he was rendered still more so by the perusal of devotional treatises ; and, in conjunction with his brother Charles and some friends, he formed a religious society, to the members of which his gay fellow collegians applied the name of Methodists. In 1735, with Charles Wesley and other missionaries, he visited Georgia to convert the Indians ; but after a residence of less than two years in the colony, during which he became extremely unpopular, he returned to England. In 1738 he began those public labors which ultimately produced such prodigious effects, and in 1739 the first meeting-house was built at Bristol. For some time he acted in conjunction with Whitefield, but the radical difference in their opinions at length produced a separation. Over the sect which he had founded, Wesley obtained an unbounded influence ; and it must be owned that he deserved it by his unwearied zeal and his astonishing exertions. Two sermons he usually preached every day, and often four or five. In the course of his peregrinations he is said to have preached more than forty thousand discourses, and to have travelled three hundred thousand miles, or nearly fifteen times the circumference of the globe. On the 17th of February 1791, he took cold, after preaching at Lambeth. For some days he struggled against an increasing fever, and continued to preach until the Wednesday following when he delivered his last sermon. From that time he became daily weaker, and died on the second of March, 1791, being in the eighty-eighth year of his age, and the sixty fifth of his memorable ministry.

Featured Titles from Westphalia Press

Issues in Maritime Cyber Security Edited by Nicole K. Drumhiller, Fred S. Roberts, Joseph DiRenzo III and Fred S. Roberts

While there is literature about the maritime transportation system, and about cyber security, to date there is very little literature on this converging area. This pioneering book is beneficial to a variety of audiences looking at risk analysis, national security, cyber threats, or maritime policy.

The Rise of the Book Plate: An Exemplative of the Art by W. G. Bowdoin, Introduction by Henry Blackwel

Bookplates were made to denote ownership and hopefully steer the volume back to the rightful shelf if borrowed. They often contained highly stylized writing, drawings, coat of arms, badges or other images of interest to the owner.

The Great Indian Religions by G. T. Bettany

G. T. (George Thomas) Bettany (1850-1891) was born and educated in England, attending Gonville and Caius College in Cambridge University, studying medicine and the natural sciences. This book is his account of Brahmanism, Hinduism, Buddhism, and Zoroastrianism

Unworkable Conservatism: Small Government, Freemarkets, and Impracticality by Max J. Skidmore

Unworkable Conservatism looks at what passes these days for "conservative" principles—small government, low taxes, minimal regulation—and demonstrates that they are not feasible under modern conditions.

A Place in the Lodge: Dr. Rob Morris, Freemasonry and the Order of the Eastern Star by Nancy Stearns Theiss PhD

Ridiculed as "petticoat masonry," critics of the Order of the Eastern Star did not deter Rob Morris' goal to establish a Masonic organization that included women as members. As Rob Morris (1818-1888) came "into the light," he donned his Masonic apron and carried the ideals of Freemasonry through a despairing time of American history.

Demand the Impossible: Essays in History as Activism
Edited by Nathan Wuertenberg and William Horne

Demand the Impossible asks scholars what they can do to help solve present-day crises. The twelve essays in this volume draw inspiration from present-day activists. They examine the role of history in shaping ongoing debates over monuments, racism, clean energy, health care, poverty, and the Democratic Party.

International or Local Ownership?: Security Sector Development in Post-Independent Kosovo
by Dr. Florian Qehaja

International or Local Ownership? contributes to the debate on the concept of local ownership in post-conflict settings, and discussions on international relations, peacebuilding, security and development studies.

The Bahai Movement: A Series of Nineteen Papers
by Charles Mason Remey

Charles Mason Remey (1874-1974) was the son of Admiral George Collier Remey and grew up in Washington DC. He studied to be an architect at Cornell (1893-1896) and the Ecole des Beaux Arts in Paris (1896-1903), where he learned about the Baha'i faith, and quickly adopted it.

Ongoing Issues in Georgian Policy and Public Administration
Edited by Bonnie Stabile and Nino Ghonghadze

Thriving democracy and representative government depend upon a well functioning civil service, rich civic life and economic success. Georgia has been considered a top performer among countries in South Eastern Europe seeking to establish themselves in the post-Soviet era.

Poverty in America: Urban and Rural Inequality and Deprivation in the 21st Century
Edited by Max J. Skidmore

Poverty in America too often goes unnoticed, and disregarded. This perhaps results from America's general level of prosperity along with a fairly widespread notion that conditions inevitably are better in the USA than elsewhere. Political rhetoric frequently enforces such an erroneous notion.

---

westphaliapress.org